Cybersecurity Governance

Kok Boon Oh · Giang Hoang · John Sturdy ·
Sarah Shuaiqi Guo

Cybersecurity Governance

An Enterprise Risk Management Strategy for Cyber Risk Control

Springer

Kok Boon Oh
eGalaxy Solutions Pty Ltd
Melbourne, VIC, Australia

Giang Hoang
Monash University
Melbourne, VIC, Australia

John Sturdy
Texila College Australia
Melbourne, VIC, Australia

Sarah Shuaiqi Guo
SERVTAC Chartered Accountant, Melbourne
Melbourne, VIC, Australia

ISBN 978-981-95-3864-5 ISBN 978-981-95-3865-2 (eBook)
https://doi.org/10.1007/978-981-95-3865-2

This Springer imprint is published by the registered company Springer Nature Singapore Pte Ltd.
The registered company address is: 152 Beach Road, #21-01/04 Gateway East, Singapore 189721, Singapore

Preface

In an era marked by rapid digital transformation, cybersecurity has become a cornerstone of organizational resilience and strategic management. The increasing frequency, sophistication, and impact of cyber threats have made it imperative for enterprises to adopt a strategic, structured and proactive approach to cybersecurity governance. This book addresses that critical need, providing leaders, executives, and cybersecurity professionals with a comprehensive framework to navigate the complexities of cyber risk in today's volatile digital landscape.

The significance of cybersecurity governance cannot be overstated. As businesses and institutions become more interconnected, their exposure to cyber risks grows exponentially. Traditional reactive measures are no longer sufficient; organizations must integrate cybersecurity into their strategic decision-making processes to ensure long-term stability and continuity. It must be emphasized that while strong individual security components (standards, policy, technology, people, and resources) are necessary, governance is the glue that binds them into a seamless, resilient security ecosystem. This book bridges the gap between governance and cybersecurity, presenting a systematic and holistic methodology for managing threats while aligning security initiatives with broader business objectives.

One of the key contributions of this work is its emphasis on reducing risk exposure through structured governance. By implementing the principles and frameworks discussed herein, enterprises can achieve greater certainty in their operations, safeguard critical assets, and maintain stakeholder trust in an environment where cyber threats are a constant concern. The strategies outlined are designed not only to mitigate risks but also to enhance organizational agility, enabling businesses to adapt to evolving threats without compromising innovation or growth.

Whether you are a board member, a C-suite executive, a cybersecurity practitioner, an academic, or a policymaker, this book provides actionable insights to strengthen an organization's cyber resilience. It combines theoretical rigor with practical applications, ensuring that readers gain both the knowledge and the tools needed to build a robust cybersecurity governance framework.

In a world where digital volatility is the new norm, proactive and strategic cybersecurity governance is no longer optional—it is a necessity. This book serves as a guide to achieving that imperative, empowering organizations to thrive with confidence in the digital age.

Melbourne, VIC, Australia
November 2025

Kok Boon Oh
Giang Hoang
John Sturdy
Sarah Shuaiqi Guo

Acknowledgements Writing this book on cybersecurity governance has been a challenging yet enriching journey, and we are deeply grateful to the many individuals and organizations who supported us along the way.

First and foremost, we extend our heartfelt thanks to our families for their unwavering patience, understanding, and encouragement. Your support during the long hours, late nights, and weekends spent researching and writing was invaluable. This book would not have been possible without your love and sacrifice.

We are also profoundly grateful to our colleagues and peers, whose insights, feedback, and constructive discussions enriched the content of this book. Your expertise and willingness to engage in thoughtful debates helped shape our perspectives and strengthen the final work.

A special thanks goes to our friends who offered encouragement, motivation, and occasional distractions to keep us balanced throughout this process. Your belief in this project kept us going even when the task seemed daunting.

We also acknowledge and appreciate the organizations we work for, which provided us with the time, resources, and flexibility needed to focus on this endeavor. Your support in allowing us to pursue this project demonstrates a genuine commitment to advancing knowledge in cybersecurity governance.

Finally, we thank the broader cybersecurity community for its collective wisdom and dedication to improving governance practices. We hope this book makes a meaningful contribution to the ongoing dialogue in this critical field.

We also wish to thank the editorial and production teams at Springer Nature for their unwavering support and attention.

To everyone who played a role in this journey, thank you. Your support made all the difference.

—*The Authors*

Competing Interests The authors have no competing interests to declare that are relevant to the content of this manuscript.

Contents

About the Authors

Dr. Kok Boon (KB) Oh is the director of eGalaxy Proprietary Limited in Melbourne, Australia. He is a chartered accountant and an academic who has taught finance, strategic management, cybersecurity, and risk management in undergraduate and postgraduate programs at Australian universities. He developed and taught the cybersecurity governance subjects for the Bachelor of Cybersecurity and Master of Cybersecurity courses at La Trobe University, Melbourne. He has extensive experience in risk management and cybersecurity, both through his work as an adviser, corporate executive, and academic. He has co-published over 70 peer-reviewed papers and 12 reference books in the areas of corporate governance, finance, cybersecurity, risk management, and strategic management. He completed Harvard's VPAL Cybersecurity: Managing Risk in the Information Age program in 2018.

Dr. Giang Hoang is an Assistant Lecturer at the Department of Banking and Finance and Research Associate at the Centre for Development Economics and Sustainability, Monash Business School, Monash University. She holds a bachelor's degree from Foreign Trade University (Vietnam), an MBA from the Asian Institute of Technology (Thailand), a Master of Science in International Finance from SKEMA Business School (France), and a Ph.D. focusing on Finance and Governance from La Trobe University (Australia). She has worked extensively in Vietnam's investment banking and higher education sectors. She has over 18 years of experience in financial education, research, and advisory services in various areas of finance and governance. Her previous roles have also included being an Equity Analyst at a securities company and a Finance Specialist for World Bank-financed projects.

John Sturdy is a Professor and CEO at Texila College, which is based in Melbourne, Australia. John is highly regarded as a thought leader in executive business practice. He has consulted in several countries, including China, Vietnam, Mongolia, Taiwan, Hong Kong, Malaysia, Singapore, and New Zealand. John has delivered papers and seminars locally and internationally on a range of subjects associated with the growth and development of businesses in these markets. His expertise has been acknowledged in the areas of the Talent lifecycle (i.e., Attraction, Retention, Development, and Engagement of staff), cybersecurity awareness and training, and business and strategic management.

Sarah Shuaiqi Guo is a chartered accountant and principal partner of SERVTAC, a Melbourne-based public accounting practice. Shuaiqi has practiced as a chartered accountant for over 25 years and has worked with clients on enterprise cybersecurity in her role as a corporate adviser both in Australia and overseas. Her special interests are in enterprise risk management, digital accounting, fintech and the financial aspects of cybersecurity.

Abbreviations

AI & GenAI	Artificial Intelligence & Generative Artificial Intelligence
ALE	Annual Loss Expectancy
APT	Advanced Persistent Threat
AUP	Acceptable Use Policy
B&SM	Board of Directors and Senior Management
BCP	Business Continuity Plan
BoD	Board of Directors
BYOD	Bring-Your-Own-Device
CASB	Cloud Access Security Broker
CCM	Cloud Controls Matrix
CG	Corporate Governance
CGP	Cybersecurity Governance Plan
CIA	Confidentiality, Integrity, and Confidentiality of information Triad
CIS	Center for Internet Security
CISO	Chief Information Security Officer
COBIT	Control Objectives for Information and Related Technology Framework
COSO	The Committee of Sponsoring Organizations of the Treadway Commission
CSA	Cloud Security Alliance
CSRM	Cybersecurity Risk Management
CTM	Cybersecurity Technology Management
CyG	Cybersecurity Governance
DA	Data Analytics
DLP	Data Loss Prevention
DNS	Domain Name System
DRM	Digital Rights Management
DRP	Disaster Recovery Plan
E-CyG	ERM embedded cybersecurity governance framework

ECyG-M	Enterprise Cybersecurity Governance Model (Proposed)
EDR	Endpoint Detection and Response
EISP	Enterprise Information Security Policy
ERM	Enterprise Risk Management
FAIR	Factor Analysis of Information Risk
FIN/CyG	Finance Cybersecurity Governance
GDPR	General Data Protection Regulation
GVC	Governance Value Chain
HR/CyG	Human Resource Cybersecurity Governance
IAM	Identity Access Management
IDP/IDS or IDPS	Intrusion Detection and Prevention Systems
IP	Intellectual Property
IR	Incident Response
IRP	Incident Response Plan
ISO	International Organisation for Standardization
IT	Information Technology
IT/CyG	Information Technology Systems Cybersecurity Governance
KPI	Key Performance Indicator
KRI	Key Risk Indicator
MFA	Multi-Factor Authentication
MRR	Monitor, Report, and Review
MSR	Minimum Standard Requirements
MSSPs	Managed Security Service Providers
NGFW	Next-Generation Firewalls
NIST CSF	National Institute of Standards and Technology—Cybersecurity Framework
O&M	Operations and Maintenance
OT	Operational Technology
PAM	Privileged Access Management
PCI DSS	Payment Card Industry Data Security Standard
PII	Personally Identifiable Information
Privacy Act 1988	Australian Privacy Act 1988
RBAC	Role-Based Access Controls
ROI	Return on Investment
SaaS	Software-as-a-Service
SbD	Security by Design
SCRG	Strategic Cybersecurity Risk Governance
SDLC	Secure Development Lifecycle or Software Development Lifecycle
SIEM	Security Information and Event Management Systems
SOAR	Security Orchestration, Automation, and Response
SOC 2	Security Organisation Control 2
SOPs	Standard Operating Procedures
SOX	Sarbanes-Oxley Act
TCRG	Tactical Cybersecurity Risk Governance

TM	Technology Management
TM/CyG	Technology Management Cybersecurity Governance
TPM	Trusted Platform Module
UBA	User Behaviour Analytics
VAR	Value-at-Risk
ZTA	Zero Trust Architecture

Chapter 1
Cybersecurity and Governance in the Digital Age

Abstract Organizations must understand the role governance plays in cybersecurity management and familiarize themselves with the relevant mechanisms for operationalizing governance programs in the digital landscape. Corporate governance describes the methods used to govern businesses and their goals. It indicates who is in charge, who is responsible, and who makes choices. It also serves as an essential toolkit for the Board and management to deal with business difficulties more skillfully. This chapter introduces cybersecurity governance and the essentials for developing a holistic and practical governance framework that optimizes cyber risk control. The essential ingredients for creating a solid cybersecurity governance posture in the firm include leadership, strategic and tactical planning, structure, tools and techniques, policies, and procedures. For instance, leadership is crucial in managing and aligning people within a company by incorporating and interconnecting the corporate vision, strategies, policies, and procedures in all cybersecurity activities. This chapter previews how governance is essential in framing the policies, systems, and procedures for managing cyber threats and maintaining compliance.

1.1 Introduction

Adopting technology in business significantly affects enterprises' cyber threat environments due to their global prevalence, rapid spread, and evolving nature. Cyber risk refers to the potential for an organization to be exposed to or suffer damage from a cyberattack on its digital infrastructure. The World Economic Forum has ranked cybersecurity among the top five global risks in the short term (World Economic Forum, 2025). This exposure has governance implications for sustainability, investment, technology, resource management, efficiency, human behavior, and corporate strategies. Consequently, it gives rise to new concerns (Katos et al., 2018) that require programs for updated cybersecurity governance strategies, tactics, structures, and policies aimed at strengthening the principles of risk control, responsibility, accountability, and transparency. Organizations must recognize the role that governance plays in cybersecurity management and be familiar with the relevant mechanisms to

K. B. Oh et al., *Cybersecurity Governance*,
https://doi.org/10.1007/978-981-95-3865-2_1

implement governance programs in the digital landscape. This understanding necessitates broad government and organizational efforts to establish national and international frameworks that foster cooperation and address the challenges associated with emerging technologies.

Corporate Governance (CG) refers to the methods used to govern companies and achieve their goals (Chartered Governance Institute). It involves exercising authority to conduct and regulate business functions in specific areas, such as cybersecurity. Governance within an organization means ensuring compliance with laws, regulations, and established corporate policies and procedures. It clarifies who is in charge, who is responsible, and who makes decisions. Additionally, it serves as a vital toolkit for the Board of Directors and management to address business challenges more effectively. Corporate governance ensures that organizations implement proper controls and decision-making processes to balance the interests of all stakeholders, including shareholders, regulators, employees, suppliers, customers, and the community. Therefore, sound corporate governance is a means through which stakeholders' expectations can be met (Shleifer & Vishny, 1997). In this book, we address the current framing of cybersecurity issues to demonstrate a preference for a multistakeholder governance model (Eggenschwiler, 2018) rather than a sovereign model. This approach aims to collaboratively meet the critical expectations of stakeholders by discussing and implementing governance solutions for shared challenges.

The gist of this chapter is a preview of how governance plays a pivotal role in shaping the strategy, goals, objectives, policies, systems, and procedures for managing cyber threats and ensuring compliance. We connect the concepts of enterprise risk management, governance, structures, hierarchies, policies, systems, and methods to technology, people, and finance, which together make up the organization's digital space, to provide a governance framework for effectively managing and mitigating cyber-related threats.

1.2 Information Security and Cybersecurity

This book focuses on the strategy, goals, and objectives of enterprise cybersecurity, aiming to develop a governance framework for addressing the cyber threats that organizations face in the digital age. Cybersecurity and information security are closely related areas that share many similarities but have distinct focuses. Information security is a broader field that safeguards all types of data. Cybersecurity is a subset of information security that protects digital networks, systems, and data against various cyber threats, including hacking, malware, ransomware, and phishing. Both aim to secure data from unauthorized access and adhere to security best practices. The main conceptual difference between cybersecurity and information security is that the former protects additional assets, while the latter pertains specifically to information security. Cybersecurity is passive when it comes to identifying and mitigating threats and reactive in incident response when dealing with vulnerabilities and breaches.

1.3 Methodology

The book draws its content from academic research and the authors' professional experience in governance and cybersecurity management. Its central theme is cybersecurity governance at both the strategic and tactical levels in policymaking, and how this trickles down through the organization via strategic initiatives, operational systems, and procedures aimed at efficiency. Our study relies on secondary research sources to compile existing data from various avenues, including internal research, academic literature, leading industry institutions, government bodies, statistics, regulators, and international standards organizations. We summarize, collate, and synthesize the research data to explain, support, and justify our propositions regarding the best practices and processes for establishing an optimal cybersecurity governance program.

An enterprise is a company where the top of the hierarchy has specific responsibilities for risk management. Understanding the main risks a company faces, determining the best ways to mitigate those risks, and ensuring that the necessary steps are followed are all components of enterprise risk management (Stine et al., 2020). Since the success of a corporate strategy depends on optimizing all interdependent functions, we embrace the concept that the "whole is greater than the sum of its parts" in our approach to cybersecurity governance. The scope is to identify, investigate, analyze, and emphasize the success factors, connections, interdependencies, and complementarities among the organization's broader risk-based corporate governance standards, policies, processes, practices, and strategic management. The goal is to consolidate these attributes to create and propose a strategic and holistic enterprise "Cybersecurity Governance" (CyG) framework embedded within the organization's enterprise risk management (ERM) function, also known as the "Enterprise Cybersecurity Governance Model" (ECyG-M)—Fig. 1.1.

The essentials of cybersecurity governance are identified through our secondary research analysis and integrated into our hypothesis to develop a practical cybersecurity governance framework that optimizes and mitigates cyber risk. Swinton and Hedges (2019) highlight five fundamental challenges to cybersecurity governance faced by many organizations: (1) developing a cybersecurity strategy, (2) implementing standardized processes, (3) enforcing and ensuring accountability, (4) obtaining senior leadership oversight, and (5) allocating sufficient resources. Leadership, structure, policies, and procedures are essential for establishing a robust cybersecurity governance framework within the firm. Since leadership plays a crucial role in managing and aligning personnel within a company by incorporating and interlinking the corporate vision, objectives, strategies, policies, and procedures in all operational activities, we emphasize the essentials of cybersecurity and their importance in constructing a comprehensive enterprise governance structure within an ERM framework.

ERM and corporate governance are closely connected, as ERM is a crucial tool for protecting the enterprise against risk exposure and ensuring long-term success. Cybersecurity management, a key aspect of both Enterprise Risk Management

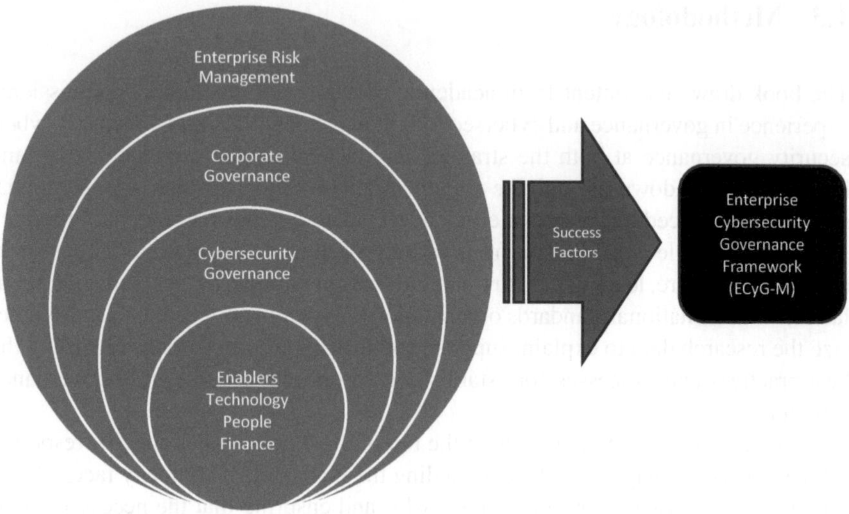

Fig. 1.1 Cybersecurity governance investigation framework

(ERM) and corporate governance, provides a framework for defining and formalizing governance practices that enable enterprises to implement effective cyber risk control activities. Therefore, this book's chapters are based on existing literature, identifying the cybersecurity governance success factors related to ERM, corporate governance, technology, people, and finance to elucidate and include the "what, why, where, who, when and how" elements in the ECyG-M for effective cyber risk control (Fig. 1.1).

This book investigates and proposes a strategic cybersecurity governance framework that captures the key elements of enterprise risk control, corporate governance, technology (including systems and management), people, and finance, all operating within the broader context of the enterprise risk management program. The proposed ECyG-M framework reflects the strategic aspects, structures, risk control, standards, policies, procedures, and best practices crucial for optimal enterprise cybersecurity risk management. The framework aims to inform businesses about relevant cybersecurity governance principles and practices by demonstrating how to apply them to mitigate and optimize their cyber risks.

1.4 Cybersecurity Governance

Many organizations, in both the public and private sectors, have prioritized improving digital information management practices. This initiative is driven by several considerations, including the need to enhance business process efficiency, comply with regulations, and provide new services. Information security is a crucial component of information management, essential for achieving these goals. It must be incorporated into every organization's strategic plan. However, information security management extends beyond mere technological solutions; it often involves implementing robust governance measures as well.

The primary objective of cybersecurity governance is to protect the organization from cyber threats by establishing goals through strategies, policies, and procedures. Consequently, cybersecurity governance necessitates knowledge from various fields, including technology, human resource management, law, sociology, finance, psychology, and management science. Thus, responses to cybersecurity threats must consider the complexity of cybersecurity risk.

As cybersecurity is a component of information security, cybersecurity governance is also a part of corporate governance that strategically addresses cyber threats. Generally, cybersecurity governance is achieved through the concept of "Governance, Risk Management, and Compliance" (GRC) (Mitchell, 2007a, 2007b). The central theme of this book, which explores the practice of cybersecurity governance within the context of an enterprise risk management framework, is to provide a foundation for building a strategic and practical organizational cybersecurity governance regime that is holistic, strategic, systematic, and effective. Cybersecurity is "protecting systems, networks, and programs from digital attacks" (CISCO, 2023; Scala et al., 2019). Its objective is to maintain the confidentiality, integrity, and availability—the "CIA triad" (Anderson, 1972)—of a firm's networks, business systems, and data. As a management tool, cybersecurity governance collectively refers to strategies, hierarchies, policies, guidelines, technologies, organizational structures, processes, risk management techniques, communication, compliance, best practices, and security concepts and protections that safeguard a company's digital assets and cyber environment. These governance structures and components are organized to "formalize the relationships across all levels and operating units" (Stine et al., 2020) for cyber risk control within the organization.

This chapter introduces the focus of this book and the strategic cybersecurity factors deemed essential for cybersecurity governance (see Fig. 1.2), which assist managers in mitigating cyber risks and enhancing performance. We posit that the key components of a cybersecurity strategy include effective governance, technology, people, and finance, which form dynamic links connecting planning to policy evaluation (Fig. 1.2). These components act as cybersecurity enablers, serving as strategic and operational management (i.e., qualitative) tools for developing cybersecurity strategies that maximize traction and impact in reinforcing enterprise cybersecurity.

Technology encompasses the deployment of technological applications and the adoption of technology management to plan, stage, and implement technological solutions (Pullin, 2018) for cybersecurity. In other words, information security management involves utilizing technology, hardware, software applications, and technology management processes (Madnick et al., 2017). These two different components of technology will be discussed separately in the later chapters of this book. The contributions of individuals are vital for securing the digital environment by actively engaging in cybersecurity safeguards, such as awareness and training, adhering to cybersecurity regulations, and reporting incidents (Li et al., 2019; Pullin,

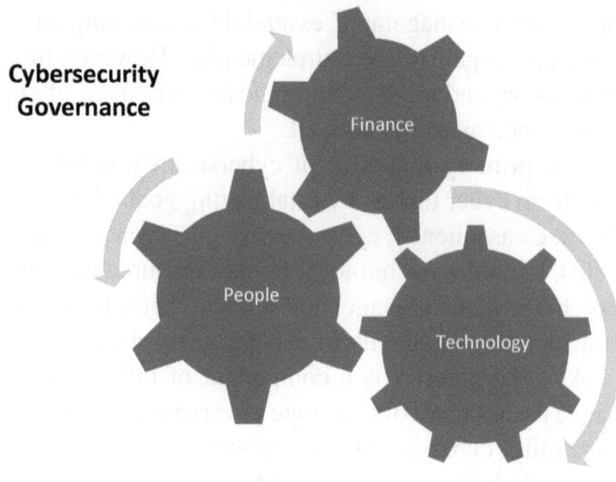

Fig. 1.2 Governance, technology, people, and finance nexus

2018). In our cybersecurity model, finance refers to how financial disciplines, such as budgeting (Madnick et al., 2017), valuation, and risk assessment, enhance the cybersecurity governance function.

1.5 Prioritizing Cybersecurity Governance

Cybersecurity has become the primary challenge for governments and industries alike. Organizations must prioritize cybersecurity governance from the perspectives of strategic management, technology, personnel, and finance. They can achieve this by adopting an objective and holistic approach that includes the following steps:

- Risk assessment and control: The first step in identifying potential cybersecurity threats and vulnerabilities involves conducting a comprehensive risk assessment to evaluate the risk of cyberattacks and their probable impacts. The firm must assess its networks, systems, data, procedures, and personnel, along with the strategies and risk control objectives designed to mitigate cyber threats and vulnerabilities.
- Create a strategic cybersecurity plan: The business must develop a Cybersecurity Governance Plan (CGP) that aligns with its goals. The plan should outline the strategies, policies, procedures, and standards for the cybersecurity process designed to achieve the firm's cybersecurity objectives. It should also be based on a risk assessment that identifies the policies, procedures, and technologies needed to mitigate risks.
- Cybersecurity governance framework: At the highest level, a practical cybersecurity governance framework is necessary to shape the corporate vision, goals, and objectives for safeguarding the company's information assets. The framework will reference relevant standards and comply with applicable legal regulations.

- Budgeting and allocating resources: After designing its cybersecurity plan, the company must allocate the resources necessary for its implementation. These resources encompass technological investments, hiring staff, and providing training. The amount will be determined based on the risk assessment, prioritization, and the overall importance of cybersecurity to the organization's operations.
- Establishing policies, procedures, and accountability: A governance framework that defines how cybersecurity functions is essential for establishing governance policies, rules, and processes. This includes defining decision-making hierarchies, roles, and responsibilities to guide decisions regarding security measures, risk monitoring, incident reporting and response, and periodic reviews of emerging threats.
- Review and update the cybersecurity plan regularly: Given that cybersecurity threats are constantly evolving, businesses should periodically assess and revise their cybersecurity strategy.
- Management oversight: Traditionally, managing end-to-end information systems and cybersecurity issues has fallen under the jurisdiction of the technical and IT departments. However, more recently, non-technical employees and members of the C-suite have been included in security teams responsible for cybersecurity and cyber risk. Senior management must be involved and committed to ensuring the company's cybersecurity efforts receive the necessary time and attention.
- Regulation compliance: Businesses must ensure that their cybersecurity initiatives comply with all applicable laws and regulations, including data privacy laws and industry-specific rules.

By taking these actions, businesses can prioritize cybersecurity from a risk control, technology, personnel, and financial perspective, ensuring they have the tools and plans to protect their assets and maintain their reputation. Collectively, these elements provide a seamless and integrated approach to an organization's overall operations, ensuring that cybersecurity measures align with its business objectives and activities.

In Chapter 10, we will propose a cybersecurity governance framework, a crucial tool for managing and mitigating cyber risks within organizations. This framework is based on the nexus of Enterprise Risk Management (ERM), corporate governance, technology, people, and finance (Fig. 1.2). It employs a strategic and structured approach to outline objectives, benchmarking, policies, and procedures that guide risk governance and decision-making for information security.

1.6 Importance of the Nexus

In today's corporate world, when business organizations rely on technology to execute their operations for optimum returns, it is crucial to proactively and effectively manage critical cybersecurity governance factors. A solid cybersecurity posture is necessary for leveraging technology for risk control and the efficient management of technology,[1] people, and finance to guard against online risks and attacks.

Here are some examples of the relationship among cybersecurity governance, technology, people, and finance:

Technology Management and Systems Technology: Cybersecurity hazards pose significant threats to operations that rely on technology. Therefore, implementing proper security controls, conducting regular risk assessments, and monitoring systems for potential threats are essential for effective risk management in cybersecurity. To successfully identify and manage cybersecurity risks, complementary technology management and systems technology must be in place to provide an optimal cybersecurity program.

People and Human Factors: Individuals play a vital role in the cybersecurity value chain by providing leadership, authority, decision-making, clarity, and direction, as well as promoting compliance and ethics, and fostering employee engagement and culture. This includes human elements, such as being targets of cyberattacks (Von Solms & Van Niekerk, 2013), responsibilities for establishing strategy and policies, and overseeing the entire cybersecurity value chain.

Financial Impact: Cybersecurity incidents can result in substantial economic losses for organizations (Roskot et al., 2020; Smith et al., 2019). For instance, a data breach may result in the loss of sensitive information, regulatory penalties, legal fees, and customer trust, which can diminish a company's value and lead to a decline in sales. Teams responsible for technology management and finance must collaborate closely with cybersecurity experts to identify, assess, and mitigate potential financial risks associated with cybersecurity incidents. Additionally, these teams need to discuss budgets for investments in cybersecurity technology.

Compliance: The General Data Protection Regulation (GDPR), Health Insurance Portability and Accountability Act of 1996 (HIPAA), and the Payment Card Industry Data Security Standard (PCI DSS) are cybersecurity laws and regulations governing technology, healthcare, and financial operations. Adhering to these regulations is crucial for minimizing legal risks and reputational damage. Cybersecurity experts must collaborate closely with the technology management and finance departments to ensure their operations comply with these rules.

Due Diligence: To better understand the risks associated with investing in companies, investors and analysts are increasingly conducting due diligence on their cybersecurity practices. This due diligence involves evaluating the company's governance, technology management, financial management, and cybersecurity posture. Senior management, technology, human resources, and finance departments must

---

[1] Leveraging technology for risk control and the efficient management of technology are collectively referred to as "technology" in this book. The individual methods of technology applications are only referred to, and they need to be distinguished separately. Chapter 5 covers the governance essentials of the decision-making process for leveraging technology, encompassing both hardware and software applications, as a tactical tool for mitigating cyber risk. Chapter 6 addresses the various aspects of management governance related to technological investment and operational management for cybersecurity.

work closely with cybersecurity experts to ensure their operations meet the highest cybersecurity standards.

In conclusion, the interaction between cybersecurity, technology, people, and finance is crucial in today's business climate. Effective governance of technology, personnel, and financial operations related to cybersecurity is essential for establishing a robust cybersecurity posture that protects against cyber threats and risks, complies with regulations and standards, and mitigates potential financial risks associated with cybersecurity incidents. To effectively manage cybersecurity risks, organizations must prioritize cybersecurity and ensure that their technology, human resources, finance departments, and cybersecurity teams work together closely.

1.7 Cybersecurity Governance as a Management Discipline

Despite global variations in data governance and law, citizens can now be monitored more efficiently, providing governments, technology corporations, and threat actors greater access to people's personal information (WEF, 2025). Data mining, user profiling, and other forms of exploitation without users' consent pose the most significant threats of the digital revolution. Cybersecurity is shifting from being purely an information technology (IT) concern to becoming a crucial management discipline (Kshetri, 2019). As businesses increasingly rely on technology, cybersecurity concerns have grown more complex. An effective cybersecurity management strategy requires a multifaceted approach that involves governance, people, and procedures in both finance and technology. The study of the tripartite nexus provides insights into how firms can prioritize cybersecurity from technological, personnel, and financial perspectives, as well as the potential impact of cybersecurity risks on firm performance and market value.

Some critical components of cybersecurity as a management discipline include:

- *Governance:* Effective cybersecurity governance entails establishing strategies, policies, and procedures to manage cybersecurity risks throughout the organization effectively. This includes fostering a corporate cybersecurity risk tolerance and culture, defining and documenting roles, responsibilities, and accountability, and ensuring that cybersecurity policies and procedures align with corporate objectives.
- *Risk-based approach:* Risk management involves implementing a process to identify, evaluate, mitigate, monitor, detect, and report cybersecurity risks. This enables the enterprise to develop plans to mitigate those risks and establish controls to reduce the likelihood and impact of cybersecurity incidents, all of which are essential components of effective risk management.
- *Technology:* Technology systems enhance cybersecurity capabilities by leveraging automation and efficiency with tools such as software, hardware, artificial intelligence, and machine learning.

- *Technology management:* It is responsible for the decision-making and oversight of the tools and instruments used to implement and maintain cybersecurity policies.
- People: Cybersecurity management depends on both human and non-human factors, including hardware and software, because cyberattacks are designed to create confusion and information overload that influence human behavior (Cayirci & Ghergherehchi, 2011). Human factors are crucial in the cyber risk environment as they not only provide leadership and human resources in risk management processes but also represent a vulnerable aspect that can expose the company to cyber risk.
- *Training and awareness:* Human error poses the most significant cybersecurity risk. An awareness and training plan must be developed to inform employees about these risks and equip them with the knowledge and skills needed to mitigate them.
- *Budgeting and financial management:* Cybersecurity financial governance helps evaluate and prioritize cyber threats that could impact corporate operations. It is also responsible for distributing funds for cybersecurity investments.
- *Compliance:* Organizations must adhere to numerous cybersecurity laws, regulations, and standards. An organization managing cybersecurity must ensure that its procedures are up to date and regularly reviewed to account for changes in legal, regulatory, and industry requirements.
- *Incident response and recovery management:* Cybersecurity events can lead to reputational damage and financial losses for businesses. Effective cybersecurity management requires the development of incident response plans, regular training sessions and simulations, as well as ongoing evaluation and updates to incident response processes.

Addressing cybersecurity risks across the organization requires a comprehensive strategy, which is what cybersecurity as a management discipline entails. Collaboration between various levels of the organization's hierarchy and both technical and non-technical stakeholders is essential, as is a commitment to continuous improvement and an emphasis on aligning cybersecurity procedures with corporate goals. The following sections highlight the fundamental structures and components of cybersecurity governance as a risk control discipline.

1.7.1 Cybersecurity Governance Structures

Cybersecurity governance is a comprehensive strategy that integrates and regulates activities in the digital space at the state, industry, and organizational levels to protect against operational disruptions caused by cyber threats or attacks. Effective cybersecurity governance requires adaptable frameworks to manage the complexity, pervasiveness, ethics, and human and financial dynamics of the digital threat landscape. Thus, cybersecurity governance entails designing frameworks that incorporate decision-making processes, accountability, identification and prioritization of business risks, strategies and measures for mitigating risks, and procedures for monitoring threats and responding to cyber incidents. There must be a shared responsibility that assigns ownership of specific risks to various organizational stakeholders (i.e., the Board of Directors, C-suite, CISO, and security teams) to ensure all areas are addressed by those best positioned to do so. This creates an effective risk management and governance mechanism for addressing cybersecurity vulnerabilities and incidents.

For cybersecurity governance, the relevant models reflect those that govern cyberspace. Generally, the two basic models are the sovereign model (Leiter, 2020; Schneier, 2015) and the multistakeholder model, which represent the most prominent ideological conflict dividing cyberspace (Rosenbach & Chong, 2019). China and Russia's cybersecurity governance adopts the sovereign model or state governance, under which governments control Internet sections within their borders. Through state governance, the government creates and implements rules on cybersecurity. Most liberal democracies, on the other hand, adopt the multistakeholder model, which encourages the participation of various entities and individuals in developing consensus policies. The model emphasizes collaboration across social, political, and economic divides to achieve efficient and effective consensual solutions.

1.7.2 Risk-Based Cybersecurity Governance

With risk-based cybersecurity governance, cybersecurity becomes a strategic, business-focused activity rather than a task driven by compliance. It creates a strong, flexible security posture that adapts to evolving threats and commercial goals by concentrating on what matters most to the company. Risk-based cybersecurity governance is a strategic framework that ensures alignment with business objectives, regulatory requirements, and risk tolerance by prioritizing and managing cybersecurity initiatives based on an organization's identified risks. It strongly emphasizes making proactive decisions to allocate resources and effectively mitigate the most significant hazards. It includes a risk management process that evaluates, ranks, monitors, and systematically adjusts to risks.

1.7.3 Technology

The two dimensions of cybersecurity technology are technology management and systems technology. Technology management oversees the tools and instruments used for implementing and maintaining cybersecurity policies (Choong, et al., 2019). Additionally, it ensures secure coding techniques by integrating cybersecurity into the software development lifecycle. Since governance involves decision-making frameworks, technology management plays a role in governance by shaping cybersecurity strategy, planning, investments, and deployment decisions. They provide the technological expertise necessary to support those choices. On the other hand, systems technology has a significant influence on cybersecurity governance. Systems technology enhances cybersecurity capabilities through automation and efficiency, utilizing tools such as artificial intelligence and machine learning for monitoring, threat detection, incident response, and reducing human error. In summary, systems technology empowers cybersecurity governance with resilience, efficiency, and compliance, enabling effective navigation of cybersecurity's complexity, rapidly evolving threats, ethics, and human dynamics.

Technology management focuses on effectively and efficiently utilizing technology within organizations to drive productivity and efficiency. It encompasses the planning, execution, and control of technology resources to achieve business goals. This field includes the strategic and tactical decisions related to the purchasing, development, deployment, and maintenance of technology within an organization. To establish a strong defense against cyberattacks, the governance role of technology management in business cybersecurity involves monitoring and coordinating technological strategies with organizational security objectives. It requires strategic alignment with risk tolerance and business goals, identifying vulnerabilities in IT infrastructure, setting hardware and software security standards, planning and implementing technologies to comply with standards and regulations such as ISO 27001, NIST CSF, GDPR, or HIPAA,[2] and maximizing investments in cutting-edge technologies. Monitoring KPIs (such as mean time to detect and respond) and providing leadership with security posture reports are also advantageous. By bridging the gap between technical execution and strategic oversight, technology management enables proactive, adaptable, and resilient cybersecurity governance in response to evolving threats.

Systems technology refers to the knowledge, tools, techniques, and systems humans use to create, modify, or interact with their environment to meet their needs and desires. It includes a wide range of practical and scientific skills, methods, processes, and devices that have been developed and applied to solve problems, enhance productivity, and improve the quality of life. It also includes software and hardware applications.

This book defines information technology as processes, hardware, software, and information employed in a business. Cybersecurity technology comprises protective and management technologies (Fig. 1.3). From a governance perspective, technology management encompasses the policies governing the use of protective technologies. Technological solutions are tools and applications implemented for protective purposes against cyberattacks.

[2] ISO 27001- International Standard on Requirements for Information Security Management; NIST CSF- The National Institute of Standards and Technology (NIST) Cybersecurity Framework (CSF); GDPR- The General Data Protection Regulation (EU); and HIPAA- Health Insurance Portability and Accountability Act (US).

Fig. 1.3 Information technology and cybersecurity governance

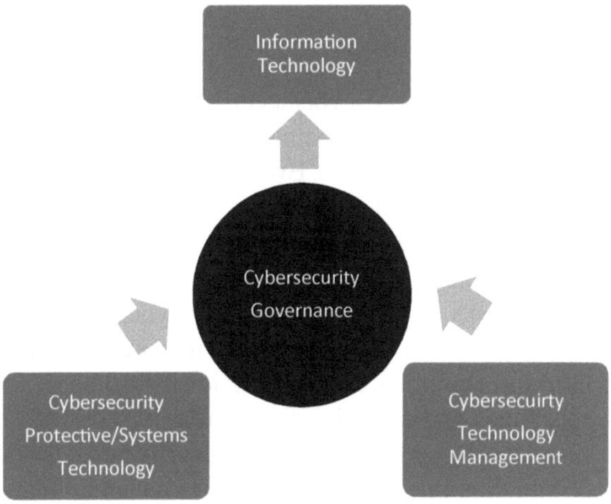

A thorough understanding of the latest technology and trends is crucial for staying current with cybersecurity developments (Mahmud et al., 2019). As the threat landscape continues to evolve, new technologies and strategies are likely to emerge, helping businesses and organizations protect their networks and data from cyberattacks (Mohammadi et al., 2020). Companies must integrate advanced technologies into their cybersecurity strategy to fend off threats and better safeguard their critical information. Since cybersecurity is an ongoing process, it's crucial to stay informed about the latest advancements to ensure data protection.

1.7.4 People and Human Factors

Roles in cybersecurity governance are established to ensure effective operational risk management, policy development, compliance, and strategic oversight. In governance, the Board of Directors allocates resources and approves policies. It holds executive management accountable, reviews risk management frameworks, ensures cybersecurity is prioritized, and provides strategic oversight.

Strategic decision-making and resource allocation are key governance priorities for senior executive management (CEO, CISO, CFO, and CIO). The CEO sets the "tone at the top" for security culture. It allocates funds, establishes organizational priorities, and integrates cybersecurity into corporate strategy. By developing and implementing cybersecurity plans, managing incident responses, and reporting risks to the Board of Directors, the CISO governance function plays a vital role in oversight, executing policies, and communicating risks effectively (NACD, 2023). Other staff members support operational responsibilities by implementing policies and overseeing cybersecurity controls to ensure successful governance.

1.7.5 Finance

Finance is critical to cybersecurity governance because it ensures cost-effective protection, regulatory compliance, and financial resilience against cyberattacks (Ponemon Institute, 2018). Even the strongest technical security solutions may fail if they are underfunded or misaligned with the commercial threats they are intended to address. Finance plays various roles in company cybersecurity governance, ensuring that cybersecurity plans are feasible, aligned with corporate goals, and effective in reducing risks. Finance is crucial to cybersecurity governance because it ensures that organizations spend adequate resources to protect against cyber risks while preserving compliance and operational resilience. Its primary duties include allocating funds and assessing financial risk to prioritize resources, planning strategic investments by coordinating cybersecurity budgets with evolving business needs and risks, funding incident response, and managing financial reporting and disclosures. It also quantifies cyber risks in financial terms, determines the need for cyber insurance policies to offset financial losses from breaches, keeps breach response reserves, measures the effectiveness of cybersecurity spending, and evaluates financial risks from third-party vendors.

1.8 Significance and Contribution

The strategic significance and contribution of technology, human resources (HR), and finance to cybersecurity governance and Enterprise Risk Management (ERM) are critical in ensuring organizational resilience, compliance, and competitive advantage. The synergy across technology, HR, and finance for cybersecurity involves a holistic governance and integrated risk management approach, where technology detects threats, human resources (HR) mitigate human risks, and finance assesses the impact of risk and allocates resources for defense. Therefore, by aligning IT security, workforce policies, and budgeting, organizations ensure a resilient cybersecurity posture. Aligning cybersecurity governance with an ERM-coordinated approach ensures that cyber risks are managed in conjunction with operational, financial, and reputational risks.

The primary objective of this book, in terms of contribution to knowledge, is to present a comprehensive framework for governance that promulgates the attributes and values of these relationships to optimize cybersecurity within the industry. To achieve this, the authors will analyze relevant governance frameworks, theoretical models, and industry practices, focusing on the roles of enablers, strategy, policy, and risk management, to develop a peak cybersecurity governance model for the sector. The focus of cybersecurity will be on safeguarding confidentiality (preventing unauthorized access), integrity (ensuring that information is accurate and trustworthy), and availability (guaranteeing that only those who are authorized to access it may do so), which is known as the CIA triad, of networks, systems, and data. This protection is even more urgent given recent technological advancements in the field of digitalization, which connect information technology (IT) and operational technology (OT) in commerce and Internet of Things (IoT) connectivity, thereby increasing the attack surface and posing a greater risk of contagion. In this context, firms should view cyber resilience as a priority governance issue for top management and employees.

1.9 Overview of the Chapters

Cybersecurity continues to pose a systemic and revolutionary challenge for many countries, industries, and organizations. Due to debates surrounding sovereign versus multistakeholder considerations, there are no universal (global) or cohesive rules governing international cyberspace or cybersecurity governance. A coherent global governance framework for cyberspace, particularly in the context of cybersecurity, is essential in the spirit of interconnectivity and shared responsibility for the Internet. The primary challenge for organizations is to establish a relevant cybersecurity regime that is systematic, comprehensive, and effective. This necessitates understanding how they are affected by cyber risks and what measures can be implemented to mitigate these risks.

This book attempts to meet these challenges through its ten chapters, which are synopsized in this section. This chapter discusses the role governance plays in cybersecurity management and is intended to provide the reader with an overview of cybersecurity governance, detailing the relevant mechanisms required for and the operation of a governance program in today's digital landscape. It introduces cybersecurity governance and the essentials for developing a holistic and practical governance framework that optimizes cyber risk control. Chapter Two highlights the central theme of the relationships between cybersecurity governance, theoretical models, standards, and the key factors crucial for designing an effective cybersecurity governance architecture. Chapter Three explains how governance underpins an organization's strategic and tactical cybersecurity management and why it is essential to embed it within the organization's broader Enterprise Risk Management (ERM) framework. It covers the design and implementation of various forms and processes of cyber risk governance within a holistic and integrated ERM framework. In Chapter Four, we introduce an integrated cybersecurity governance and Enterprise Risk Management (ERM) framework along with its strategic and tactical components (i.e., E-CyG). Chapter Five discusses the various aspects of technology that have implications for cybersecurity and systems technology used for automating cyber risk control in organizational information security management. In Chapter Six, we explain the concept of cybersecurity technology management, its significance, and its application to cybersecurity governance. Chapter Seven focuses on people as a source of cyber threats, as well as utilizing human resources governance to mitigate cyber threats and optimize cyber risk control. Chapter Eight addresses the role of finance and its significance, contributions, and benefits to cybersecurity governance.

Chapter Nine outlines the cybersecurity value chain, a crucial dimension in cybersecurity governance, as it enables organizations to visualize, comprehend, and optimize the various processes involved in mitigating cyber threats. The value chain approach enables organizations to determine strategic options at multiple levels and stages of the process. By understanding where value is added, companies can concentrate on enhancing those areas to improve their cybersecurity posture. Chapter Ten consolidates all the relevant literature, guidelines, concepts, standards, best practices, and materials covered in the preceding chapters to recommend a comprehensive and practical strategic framework for an enterprise cybersecurity governance model (i.e., ECyG-M). The model, which incorporates significant strategies, policies, systems, procedures, and preventative and corrective measures, is one that firms can adopt to safeguard the CIA triad attributes of their information system assets.

References

Anderson, J. P. (1972). Information security in a multi-user computer environment. *Advances in Computers, 12*, 1–36.

Cayirci, E., & Ghergherehchi, R. (2011). *Modelling cyber-attacks and their effects on decision process*. In Proceedings of the 2011 Winter Simulation Conference. In S. Jain, R. R. Creasey, J. Himmelspach, K. P. White, & M. Fu (Eds.). IEEE Publications.

Choong, Y.-Y., Chou, C. W., & Lin, P.-H. (2019). The Nexus of cybersecurity and new technology: A review of the literature. *Journal of Information Privacy and Security, 15*(1), 1–23.

CISCO. (2023). *What is cybersecurity?* https://www.cisco.com/site/au/en/learn/topics/security/what-is-cybersecurity.html#tabs-ca6b81272f-item-baa4a3100a-tab

Eggenschwiler, J. (2018). A typology of cybersecurity governance models. *St Antony's International Review, 13*(2), 64–78.

Katos, V., Sgaras, C., & Stavrinides, E. (2018). The nexus of cybersecurity and mobile devices: A review of the literature. *Journal of Cybersecurity, 4*(1), tyy002.

Kshetri, N. (2019). Managing the nexus between cybersecurity and information technology governance: A conceptual framework. *Journal of Information Systems Applied Research, 12*(2), 3–18.

Leiter, A. (2020). Cyber sovereignty: A snapshot from a field in motion. *Harvard International Law Journal Frontiers, 61*, 2020.

Li, L., He, W., Xu, L., Ash, I., Anwar, M., & Yuan, X. (2019). Investigating the impact of cybersecurity policy awareness on employees' cybersecurity behavior. *International Journal of Information Management, 45*, 13–24.

Madnick, S., Jalali, M., Siegel, M., Lee, Y., Strong D., Wang, R., Ang, W., Deng, V., & Mistree, D. (2017, January). Measuring stakeholders' perceptions of cybersecurity for renewable energy systems. *Lecture Notes in Computer Science*, 2017.

Mahmud, M., Ali, A., & Muzaffar, A. W. (2019). The nexus of cybersecurity and cloud computing: A systematic literature review. *Journal of Cybersecurity, 5*(1), tyz005.

Mamani, H., & Otondo, R. M. (2015). Information security investment and performance: Evidence from the retail industry. *Journal of Business Research, 68*(7), 1575–1583.

Mitchell, S. L. (2007a). GRC360: A framework to help organisations drive principled performance. *International Journal of Disclosure and Governance, 4*(4), 279–296.

Mitchell, S. L. (2007b). GRC360: A framework to help organizations drive principled performance. *International Journal of Disclosure and Governance, 4*(4), 279–296.

Mohammadi, S., Beheshti-Kashi, S., & Hosseini-Khayat, A. (2020). The nexus of cybersecurity and artificial intelligence: A systematic literature review. *Journal of Cybersecurity, 6*(1), tyaa001.

NACD (National Association of Corporate Directors). (2023). *Managing cybersecurity risk: A governance framework for boards of directors.* https://www.nacdonline.org/all-governance/governance-resources/governance-research/director-handbooks/nacd-directors-handbook-on-cyber-risk-oversight/

Ponemon Institute. (2018). *The Financial Impact of Cyber Risk*, 2018 Edition.

Pullin, D. (2018). Cybersecurity: Positive changes through processes and team culture. *Frontiers of Health Services Management, 35*(1), 3–12.

Rosenbach, E., & Chong, S. M. (2019). *Governing cyberspace: State control vs. the multistakeholder model.* Belfer Center for Science and International Affairs, Harvard Kennedy School.

Roskot, M., Wanasika, I., & Kroupova, Z. (2020). Cybercrime in Europe: Surprising results of an expensive lapse. *Journal of Business Strategy, 42*(2), 91–98.

Scala, N., Reilly, A., Goethals, P., & Cukier, M. (2019). Risk and the five hard problems of cybersecurity. *Risk Analysis, 39*(10), 2119–2126. https://doi.org/10.1111/risa.13309

Schneier, B. (2015). *Data and Goliath: The hidden battles to collect your data and control your world.* W. W. Norton & Company.

Shleifer, A., & Vishny, R. (1997). A survey of corporate governance. *Journal of Finance, 52*(2), 737–783.

Smith, K., Jones, A., Johnson, L., & Smith, L. (2019). Examination of cybercrime and its effects on corporate stock value. *Journal of Information, Communication and Ethics in Society, 17*(1), 42–60.

Stine, K., Witte, G., Quinn, S., & Gardner, R. K. (2020). *NISTIR 8286—Integrating cybersecurity and enterprise risk management (ERM).* National Institute of Standards and Technology.

Swinton, S., & Hedges, S. (2019). *Cybersecurity governance, Part 1: 5 Fundamental Challenges.* Carnegie Mellon University, Software Engineering Institute's Insights (blog). Accessed September 27, 2024. https://insights.sei.cmu.edu/blog/cybersecurity-governance-part-1-5-fundamental-challenges/

Von Solms, R., & Van Niekerk, J. (2013). From information security to cybersecurity. *Computers & Security, 38*, 97–102.

World Economic Forum (WEF). (2025). *The Global risks report 2025—20th Edition: Insight Report*, Switzerland. https://www.weforum.org/publications/global-risks-report-2025/in-full/global-risks-2025-a-world-of-growing-divisions-c943fe3ba0/

Chapter 2
Cybersecurity and Governance

Abstract Many organizations, in both the public and private sectors, have made improving digital information management practices a top priority. They are motivated by several considerations, such as the need to increase business process efficiency, the requirements of compliance rules, and the desire to offer new services. Information security is a critical aspect of information management that ensures the achievement of these objectives. However, information security management is much more than just new technical solutions. It has frequently involved implementing robust governance measures, too. This chapter's central theme is the relationships between the cybersecurity governance function and its design, manifestation, and embedding in a digital organization. We introduce the role of governance for information security by providing an overview of the relevant governance key factors such as strategies, policies, procedures, oversight, decision-making hierarchies, risk management, due diligence, compliance, accountability frameworks, security concepts, safeguards, standards and guidelines, activities, training, best practices, assurance, economic considerations, and technology in the organization's digital environment. The scope of this chapter is to enable the reader to explain how governance underpins an organization's strategic and tactical cybersecurity management and the roles of the Board, senior management, technology management and investment, people and financial management in facilitating cyber risk management for better performance.

2.1 Introduction

Cybersecurity protects systems, networks, and programs from digital attacks (Cisco). Many organizations, in both the public and private sectors, have prioritized improving digital information governance and management practices. They are motivated by several factors, including increased business process efficiency, compliance requirements, and the desire to offer new services. Information security, also known as cybersecurity, is essential for managing information effectively to achieve these business objectives. However, information security management involves much more than

K. B. Oh et al., *Cybersecurity Governance*,
https://doi.org/10.1007/978-981-95-3865-2_2

just new technological solutions. It also frequently includes implementing robust governance measures. The need to focus on governance is becoming increasingly urgent and compelling as cyber threats grow more sophisticated, marking a paradigm shift in the business sector characterized by greater instability and disruptions. The current governance frameworks seem unprepared to address known and emerging global threats or to combat the fragility that those risks create (WEF, 2025); therefore, it is vital to research and develop appropriate governance frameworks to tackle this situation.

The central theme of this book is the relationships between the cybersecurity governance function and its design, manifestation, and embedding within a digital organization. As part of the corporate governance architecture, we examine the value chain of enterprise cybersecurity governance by analyzing its strategic and tactical activities, such as goal alignment, policy implementation, service delivery, risk control, resource management, compliance, performance measurement, and continuous improvement. The purpose is to understand their roles and identify the key factors that contribute to developing an effective and practical cybersecurity governance (CyG) framework.

This chapter introduces governance for information security by first discussing corporate governance, its concepts, characteristics, and key constructs. These characteristics form the foundation for establishing the corporate governance function as a management discipline. They encompass strategies, policies, structures, tactics, decision-making processes, risk management, due diligence, compliance, responsibility, accountability, security concepts, safeguards, standards, best practices, assurance, and economic considerations. This book will extrapolate and discuss these factors in the context of the organization's cyber risk control function.

This chapter aims to help readers understand how cybersecurity governance and its relevant factors support an organization's strategic and operational management, including technology, personnel, and financial management. These factors enable the firm to manage cyber risk effectively and achieve improved performance. In cybersecurity management, technology, personnel, and finance serve as enablers, acting as tools and resources that enhance and complement organizational information security through strategic and operational management.

We address international and industrial standards and regulations concerning cybersecurity governance, discussing their key features to explain how they can be integrated into an organizational enterprise governance framework (E-CyG). This chapter examines our studies on corporate governance in relation to cybersecurity governance. We suggest that incorporating essential cyber governance constructs, features, and strengths into a corporate governance framework can establish a practical E-CyG framework that aligns with the organizational expectations and needs of various stakeholder groups, thereby maximizing shareholder value. The goal is to establish an enterprise cybersecurity governance framework (ECyG-M). The sequence of our discussion on cybersecurity governance from theory to the proposed ECyG-M is illustrated in Fig. 2.1. Thus, without assuming the completeness of our analysis, we examined the environmental, economic, institutional, regulatory, and

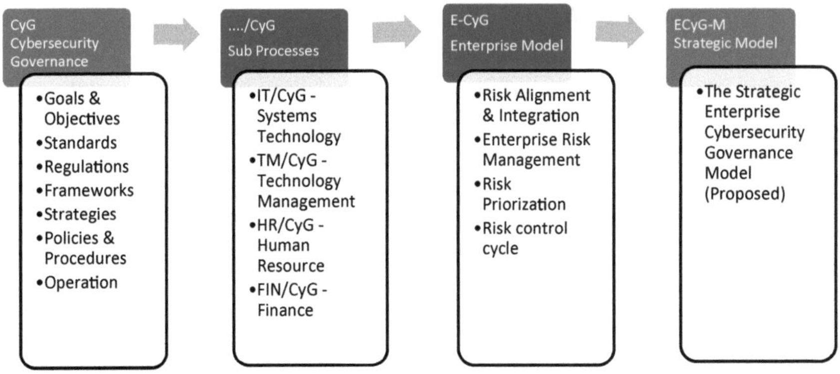

Fig. 2.1 Sequence for developing the ECyG-M

cultural factors that could influence the decision to select a particular governance system within the complex debate on cybersecurity governance.

2.2 Corporate Governance

Corporate governance refers to how companies are governed and the purposes for which they are governed. The Chartered Governance Institute defines it as "a toolkit that enables management and the Board of Directors to deal more effectively with the company's challenges. Corporate governance ensures that businesses have appropriate decision-making processes and controls in place so that the interests of all stakeholders are balanced."[1] Therefore, corporate governance refers to the methods used to govern businesses and their objectives. It indicates who is in charge, who is responsible, and who makes choices. It is also an essential toolkit for management and the Board of Directors to address business challenges more effectively. Corporate governance ensures that organizations have the proper controls and decision-making processes to balance the interests of all parties involved (shareholders, employees, suppliers, customers, and the community). Therefore, good corporate governance ensures that stakeholders' expectations can be attained (Shleifer & Vishny, 1997).

Corporate governance includes the processes for achieving and implementing a company's objectives within the digital, social, regulatory, and market environments. It aids in establishing managerial policies and priorities in a technological context (Starbucks, 2014). In terms of cybersecurity, it emphasizes strategy, policies, procedures, and practices to ensure that the firm's digital operations align with its goals and that stakeholders can trust the business.

[1] https://www.cgi.org.uk/about-us/policy/what-is-corporate-governance.

2.2.1 *Governance Theory*

Corporate governance refers to the objectives, strategies, policies, rules, and processes that guide the management of an enterprise. Agency theory and the stakeholder approach serve as the primary conceptual frameworks for corporate governance (Allen & Gale, 2002). Agency theory addresses the issues that arise from the separation of ownership and control, while the stakeholder approach focuses on managing relationships with stakeholders. Agency theory enhances our understanding of cybersecurity governance by examining the interactions and conflicts between principals (i.e., shareholders) and agents (i.e., managers). This understanding is crucial for grasping accountability and decision-making in cybersecurity governance.

The shareholder model is the traditional Anglo-American system of corporate governance, focusing on maximizing shareholder wealth. Agency theory, commonly referred to as Principal-Agent (P-A) theory, aims to clarify the problems that arise when cooperating parties, namely the principal and the agent, have conflicting agendas. One of the biggest challenges in this scenario is that employers struggle to identify and monitor an employee's behavior and performance. This issue has been extensively researched in economics utilizing P-A theory. According to the theory, an agent is more likely to act in the principal's best interests if the principal (i.e., employer) and the agent (i.e., employee) have the same information or if the agent's activities are verifiable. In contrast, the agent may not act in the manner the principal intended (i.e., moral hazard; Eisenhardt, 1989) if the dispersion of information is not symmetric between them, meaning the principal cannot check the agent's activity.

The German corporate governance system is viewed as a model of the stakeholder approach, which prioritizes addressing the needs and expectations of a broader range of stakeholder groups. It highlights the necessity for businesses to consider the interests of their stakeholders and expand management's focus beyond the traditional shareholder group (Ayuso et al., 2014). Tirole (2001) defined the stakeholder approach as a "design of institutions that induce or force management to internalize the welfare of stakeholders."

2.2.2 *Corporate Governance in the Digital Age*

The digital era presents distinct opportunities and challenges for corporate governance, driven by the rapid growth of technology. What are the differences between practicing corporate governance in the digital era and a digital environment? Agency theory focuses on the interactions and tensions between principals (e.g., shareholders) and agents (e.g., board members and managers), which is crucial for understanding decision-making and responsibility in cybersecurity governance. We highlight several governance differences that firms must consider between traditional business and the digital era. They are:

Shareholders (Principals): Cybersecurity governance has a direct impact on an organization's long-term viability, reputation, and financial health, raising significant concerns among shareholders. These concerns encompass economic costs such as ransomware payments, legal fees, penalties, loss of market value, and incident response expenses. Shareholders expect the Board of Directors and management to prioritize cybersecurity and establish robust governance frameworks to ensure the protection of shareholder interests. They demand transparent communication regarding cybersecurity incidents, threats, and mitigation strategies. The company's capacity to build long-term resilience against evolving cyber threats is important to shareholders, who will hold the BoD accountable for this.

Governance, Leadership, and Oversight: Governance issues include a lack of board-level awareness regarding technology and cybersecurity, leading to poor risk prioritization. This may also create a siloed and fragmented approach to cybersecurity operations, hindering IT, security, and business teams and reducing the effectiveness of incident response. Additionally, cybersecurity funding may be perceived as having a low return on investment (ROI) and lagging behind evolving threat levels. Traditional Boards of Directors should include digitally literate members to manage technology issues effectively. BoDs need to stay informed about new technologies impacting corporate operations, such as blockchain, artificial intelligence, machine learning, quantum computing, and the Internet of Things. Proactively evaluating the firm's digital environments to identify and mitigate risks is essential. Leadership with a strong understanding of digital technology is vital for making informed decisions in a rapidly evolving landscape. A digitally literate Board of Directors is likely to provide better leadership and oversight, facilitating proactive evaluation and mitigation of cyber risks through the adoption of technology.

Decision-Making: Due to their operational architecture, stakeholder dynamics, and technical effects, traditional and digital organizations have distinctly different governance and decision-making processes. Decision-making in the digital age is more decentralized, data-centric, utilizing analytics, machine learning, and user behavior tracking, as well as compliance-driven, agile methodologies, and real-time data. Additionally, key stakeholders are internal and include board members, committees, senior management, and major investors. New management tools and processes have emerged due to the introduction of advanced technology. Modern digital applications, such as data analytics, machine learning (ML), and artificial intelligence (AI), are just some of the digital tools that have transformed the decision-making process by providing enhanced monitoring capabilities for more effective real-time threat detection, comprehensive analysis, and timely results for policy enforcement.

Responsibility and Accountability: The operational models, stakeholder expectations, and regulatory frameworks of traditional and digital enterprises all contribute to significant differences in governance responsibility and accountability. Data, compliance, algorithms, and user trust create a broader responsibility in digital business. Accountability is more public and immediate in digital firms due to user scrutiny and regulatory pressure. Governance is evolving from top-down control to decentralized, participatory models as digital applications permeate organizations vertically and horizontally. Businesses can leverage technology to enhance responsible governance and accountability by tracking practices, ensuring compliance, promoting ethical behavior, and evaluating performance metrics.

Transparency: Digitalization enables the collection, sharing, and reporting of real-time data, enhancing transparency and analytics. This makes managing cybersecurity and data privacy issues increasingly important. The need for transparency in governance differs significantly between traditional businesses and digital businesses, primarily due to their distinct operational models, varying stakeholder expectations, and different regulatory environments. There is a higher demand for transparency expected due to digital visibility and concerns about user trust (e.g., data privacy). Firms face stricter regulations, such as GDPR, HIPAA, SOX, and the Privacy Act 1988, and must disclose their data collection practices, algorithmic biases, and content moderation policies. Customers demand greater transparency and real-time accountability. Regulators expect real-time compliance due to the rapid pace of technological changes. However, it is essential to strike a balance between openness and privacy.

Stakeholders: Digital platforms enable businesses to interact more directly with clients, vendors, investors, regulators, and employees. Cybersecurity governance promotes open and honest communication with stakeholders regarding cybersecurity threats and effective countermeasures. Therefore, the impact of technology on methods for engaging and communicating with stakeholders requires greater consideration. This supports informed decision-making and fosters trust. Involving stakeholders in discussions about cybersecurity risk management ensures their expectations and concerns are reflected in governance plans.

Cyber Threats: The digital era presents new hazards, including cyberattacks that lead to data breaches, technological downtime, financial losses, and a negative impact on corporate reputation. Strong enterprise risk management, which includes cybersecurity governance frameworks, is crucial for effectively managing risks and mitigating these threats. Boards of Directors must actively assess and minimize risks related to technology. Evolving cyber threats encompass sophisticated attacks, where cybercriminals deploy advanced techniques such as AI-driven malware, zero-day exploits, and ransomware. Additionally, supply chain vulnerabilities stemming from attacks on third-party vendors expose organizations to indirect risks. Furthermore, state-sponsored actors are involved in espionage, sabotage, and disinformation campaigns.

Corporate Culture: Technology has a significant influence on organizational culture and ethical behavior; therefore, firms are responsible for creating a digitally oriented culture, such as a cybersecurity risk culture and awareness, that ensures operational efficiency while upholding moral principles. Addressing ethical issues related to automation and data usage is crucial.

Complex Regulatory Compliance: The complexity of regulatory compliance arises from fragmented rules and regulations across different regions and countries, each with its own set of privacy laws (for example, the Australian Privacy Act 1988, GDPR). This fragmentation makes compliance challenging for multinational organizations. It also requires staying current with evolving regulatory and industry standards, such as HIPAA and jurisdictional bank cybersecurity regulations, which include strengthened bank cyber regulations (Crisanto et al., 2023). This process is time-consuming and costly.

Effective corporate governance in the digital age demands technical knowledge, expertise, and a proactive, adaptable approach to business and risk management. It requires a forward-thinking, flexible approach that integrates technology, people, finance, processes, and global collaboration. Ensuring sound governance in an ever-evolving environment necessitates blending traditional concepts with digital insights.

2.3 Cybersecurity Governance and Its Benefits

Enterprise cybersecurity governance (E-CyG) refers to the process of making and implementing decisions to enhance an organization's cybersecurity posture. E-CyG is a dynamic concept that addresses the risks associated with rapidly changing digital landscapes. It is a leadership, oversight, participatory, representative, accountable, responsive, transparent, and consensus-oriented mechanism that is effective, efficient, and compliant with generally accepted standards and practices.

As a component of the E-CyG, the cybersecurity strategy is integral to every business plan. While meeting business demands and goals, an effective cybersecurity plan enhances digital operations, protects data, and deters hackers. Cybersecurity governance ensures that the business operates efficiently with effective cyber risk management, maximizing performance by utilizing industry-approved standards and best practices. Nowadays, enterprises prioritize cybersecurity to remain safe and effective while staying ahead of the latest cyber threats.

According to the ISO/IEC 27001 standard, cybersecurity governance is a component of overall corporate governance that focuses on an organization's reliance on cyberspace and its vulnerability to cyber threats. Thus, cybersecurity governance involves a clearly defined strategy, accountability, structure, oversight responsibility, and monitoring to ensure effective risk reduction.

Cybersecurity governance protects by managing and maintaining the confidentiality, integrity, and availability (CIA triad) of data and information. It involves establishing a comprehensive approach to managing and mitigating the organization's exposure to cyber risk. Calls for more extensive governance have increased as the number of cybersecurity risks has grown. The precise definition of what cybersecurity governance entails requires clarification. However, drawing from the definition of corporate governance by the Chartered Institute of Governance, cybersecurity governance is fundamentally a "toolkit that enables management" to mitigate the threats of cyberspace, ensuring that the "appropriate decision-making processes and controls are in place so that the interests of all stakeholders are balanced." Despite the increasing importance of this topic, corporate governance in cybersecurity remains a dynamic and evolving aspect of cybersecurity management. To clarify and address the practical aspects of this area, this chapter first explores the concepts, characteristics, and issues of corporate governance by discussing the development of the theory and various approaches to corporate governance. The aim is to comprehend the function and purpose of corporate governance within an organization and how cybersecurity governance, as a process, integrates into the company's digital environment.

An organization's well-developed cybersecurity regime, comprehensive strategy, and detailed plans yield better, more measurable results. When a company effectively protects its business operations from cyber threats, it can operate more seamlessly and efficiently without interruptions. Even if a digital breach or cybersecurity incident occurs, a well-defined governance plan will help reduce disruption and swiftly restore normal business operations. To anticipate risks, a cybersecurity governance process provides access to all relevant information, including details of any potential hazards. It also accelerates decision-making, which builds confidence and strengthens collaboration among employees and stakeholders.

A governance program enables ideas to be quickly transformed into action by providing a formal structure for their consideration and deliberation. It offers individuals appropriate guidelines, tools, and resources to simplify and manage the enterprise cybersecurity process. Therefore, an effective governance structure is crucial for ensuring cybersecurity readiness, mitigating risks, and responding to incidents. A multidimensional approach is necessary for effective cybersecurity governance, encompassing strategic and operational governance, risk management, and the establishment of measurable targets. In summary, cybersecurity governance is a comprehensive strategy that integrates with organizational operations to safeguard against disruptions caused by cyberattacks or threats. From a firm's perspective, enterprise risk management, accountability, and decision-making structures are fundamental characteristics of cybersecurity governance.

A governance structure or framework facilitates the implementation, management, and monitoring of cybersecurity processes, providing detailed specifications for regulations, personnel, budgets, tools, and instruments. Such a framework enables a business to closely monitor all activities in cyberspace, manage risks, resources, and performance, ultimately enhancing outcomes. This chapter first examines traditional governance models and seeks to adapt them to a cybersecurity context by analyzing the key characteristics and components relevant to effective cybersecurity governance.

2.4 Cybersecurity Governance Models

The literature outlines various governance approaches to mitigate cybersecurity risks. Our proposition, along with many modern frameworks, prioritizes dynamic responses to evolving digital threats and technologies, alongside a strategic management of a structured and systematic approach. Developing an effective cybersecurity governance model requires relying on numerous theoretical underpinnings and constructs that address multiple aspects of organizational security, culture, risk management, and governance structures. Organizations should consider integrating elements from these theoretical methods to create a framework tailored to their specific objectives, industry requirements, and risk profile when establishing a cybersecurity governance model. The best models take into account technological, human, and organizational factors such as finance, rather than viewing cybersecurity merely as a technical issue. The theoretical models discussed below offer practical propositions and constructs that can address complex cybersecurity governance challenges, spanning strategic planning to policy review.

At the corporate level, we envision a nexus of the Hierarchy Model, the Rational Goal Model, the Risk-based Model, the Maturity Model, the Learning Organization, and Hofstede's cultural dimensions as pertinent to cybersecurity governance. The concepts and constructs underlying these models can guide the development of governance frameworks, strategies, objectives, policies, and procedures related to cybersecurity. The most effective models strike a balance between strategic direction, constructs, and operational reality, while remaining adaptable to changing cyber threat scenarios. Based on our research and industry practices, we highlight the most important theoretical models and their significance in building our ERM-based cybersecurity governance framework below.

2.4.1 Sovereign Model Versus Multistakeholder Model

There are two fundamentally opposing views on how cyber governance, and therefore cybersecurity, should be approached: the sovereign model and the multistakeholder model. The sovereign model, advocated by China, emphasizes the authority of a sovereign state to independently formulate cybersecurity-related policies and regulate the flow of information within its borders. In the West, the framing of current cybersecurity issues indicates a preference for a multistakeholder governance model (Eggenschwiler, 2018). The goal is to gather key stakeholders to discuss and collaborate on solutions to shared problems. However, a country's sovereign right to control the information conveyed by its domestic information infrastructure must always be respected (United Nations Group of Governmental Experts).[2] Accepting the sovereign model does not mean dismissing the multistakeholder model; thus, Eggenschwiler (2018) argues that "cybersecurity governance entails multiple types of governance, including hierarchical, multistakeholder-based, and market-based types." The relevant cybersecurity governance regime can exist at any point along the sovereign-multistakeholder continuum (Fig. 2.2).[3]

[2] Report of the Group of Governmental Experts on Advancing Responsible State Behaviour in Cyberspace in the context of international security, 28 May 2021. https://front.un-arm.org/wp-content/uploads/2021/06/final-report-2019-2021-gge-1-advance-copy.pdf.

[3] Sovereign model, depending on its architectural design, contrasts and differs from the "multilateral" governance model in areas and layers of cyberspace.

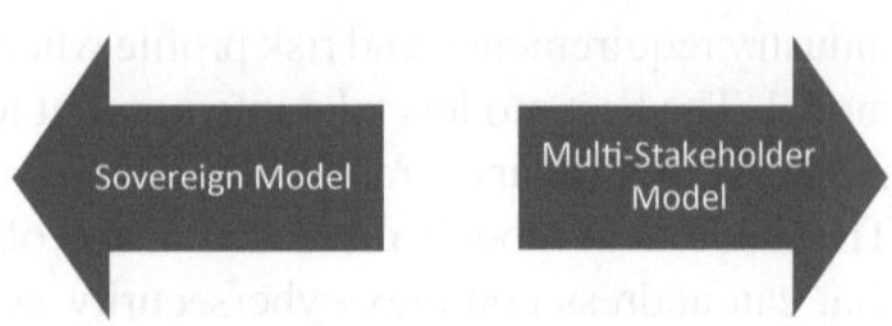

Fig. 2.2 Sovereign-multistakeholder governance continuum

2.4.2 *The Hierarchy Model*

The hierarchical model involves assigning responsibilities from the top tier of a hierarchy to the lower tiers. Predictability, control, and responsibility are the three central tenets of the hierarchy model (Simon, 1962). It is characterized by vertical patterns of interaction that flow up and down the hierarchies and traditional bureaucratic power. The strategy, policy formulation, and implementation of this model are formalized and functionally differentiated. Change can occur gradually and is often prompted by adjustments to policies, procedures, or guidelines, or by adhering to new standards. These changes cascade down the vertical hierarchies of the governance system. Individuals in charge of various tasks are held to a high standard of responsibility within this paradigm, which is often process oriented and more focused on maintaining continuity than introducing change.

Organizations that use "search" or "the generation of alternatives" to solve problems often face challenges because senior management may struggle to develop optimal task solutions independently. Choosing which alternative is better presents a "satisficing" issue in a decision-making strategy that seeks adequate rather than perfect results (Simon, 1982). Instead, they need to assign tasks, make decisions, provide incentives, and coordinate communication among the various members of the organization (Mihm et al., 2010). Therefore, a collaborative approach is necessary that involves participants and experts from diverse areas and disciplines. Mihm et al. (2010) studied organizations that required "decisions with many parameters to be taken quickly." In today's digital age, managing cybersecurity challenges is no different. Prior research has shown that a hierarchy enhances the organization's capacity to adapt to changes in the environment (Siggelkow & Rivkin, 2005), while centralized decision-making at the top better regulates search, reduces failure risk, and results in quicker decisions by enhancing "search dynamics" decision-making and the quality of the solution (Mihm et al., 2010; Rivkin & Siggelkow, 2003).

2.4.3 *The Rational Goal Model*

The Rational Goal Model (Taylor, 1911), known as scientific management, aims to produce results as quickly as possible. According to this paradigm, power is distributed across several specialized groups. Although authority and accountability are delegated, this style exhibits a centralized approach. It is most effective in results-oriented environments where clear objectives (which assist in setting policies and procedures), efficiency (e.g., timely incident response to contain an attack), and rapid results (e.g., incident recovery situations) are crucial. Top management establishes the goals and targets, and performance is closely monitored, examined, and audited. A fundamental characteristic of this model is change, which is achieved by adjusting incentives and is linked to accomplishing objectives and policy goals. Its primary traits include a systematic, pragmatic, and instrumental approach that emphasizes efficiency, economic rationality, external influence, and management authority. The model particularly highlights the importance of external management control within the firm. Compliance with cybersecurity standards (NIST CSF, ISO 27001) and legal and regulatory requirements (GDPR, HIPAA) serves as a typical external influence. External influencers are the primary source for establishing the necessity of a policy and providing the scope for control objectives, and they are often mandatory.

Taylor's Rational Goal Model emphasizes clear objectives, rational planning, scientific analysis, efficiency, control and measurement, specialization, and organizational control (top-down management) to maximize productivity and efficiency. Table 2.1 summarizes the action items related to cybersecurity that can be derived from this theory.

The cybersecurity governance function is essentially a centralized approach with B&SM oversight, where tasks are distributed across various areas or specializations, each managed by specific personnel and assigned a dedicated portion of responsibility. Large projects should not be assigned to a single individual to ensure transparency in the production process. Consequently, management can break down more complex jobs into smaller, manageable tasks. The cybersecurity governance process can be segmented into smaller components based on task-oriented functions, embracing Hofstede's high-power distance and high uncertainty cultural traits for improved oversight and control in an evolving and unpredictable cybersecurity environment. Meanwhile, matrix workflows that reflect Hofstede's individualism and low power distance serve as effective cultural values for fostering broad consensus, expertise-oriented tasks, individual responsibility, and accountability, thereby promoting specialization and familiarity.

According to the Rational Goal Model, efficiency is paramount, and B&SM ensures that employees perform as intended through regular performance reviews and audits. B&SM and other supervisors identify the most effective approach to completing a task and assign it to employees with the necessary skills. Employees receive additional training to enhance their performance, and when new processes are introduced or more efficient methods are discovered, management ensures that employees are retrained accordingly.

Table 2.1 Rational goal model for cybersecurity governance

Rational Goal Dimension	Cybersecurity Application
Clear Objectives	• Alignment of cybersecurity objectives with business goals
Rational Planning	• A comprehensive strategic cybersecurity plan; • Establish strategies that help to achieve cybersecurity objectives, and • An effective Incident Response Plan
Scientific Analysis	• Tools & techniques for assessing threats, and • Technology to monitor, detect, and respond to risks
Efficiency	• Compliance with standards and regulations; • Clear and effective policies and procedures to identify and mitigate current and emerging threats; • Timely incident response and recovery, and • Assign tasks to employees with the necessary skills and abilities
Control and Measurement	• Board of Directors and management oversight; • Regular reviews, evaluation (KPIs & KRIs), and audits (for compliance) ensure performance is measured and tightly controlled to meet standards, legal, and regulatory requirements, and • Continuous efficiency improvement
Specialization	• Strategic and tactical role specialization and accountability; • Training and war drills to improve performance, and • Tasks for managing processes are allocated according to expertise (CISO, IT, HR, Finance) and departments
Top-Down Organizational Control	• Organizational structure and functions are highly hierarchical, while adaptable to cross-functional processes

2.4.4 Maturity Model

A cybersecurity maturity model demonstrates an organization's capability to achieve continuous improvement in its efforts to meet cyber risk control objectives. Continuous improvement entails investing in technology, talent, and knowledge to mitigate cyber risks through the organization's risk control mechanisms, such as Enterprise Risk Management (ERM).

According to McKinsey (2019), a maturity-based approach is essential for developing a risk-based strategy. The traditional method for managing cyber risk is the maturity-based approach, in which companies employ specific risk management capabilities and controls to achieve a desired level of maturity. Hillson (1997) proposes a risk maturity model that enables organizations to enhance their risk management strategy by assessing their current level of maturity, setting achievable improvement targets, and developing action plans to improve their risk capabilities. The model is divided into four stages, each labeled "naive," "novice," "normalized," and "natural" in progressive order. The naive risk organization is unaware of the importance of risk management and lacks a well-defined plan for addressing uncertainty. The novice risk organization understands the potential advantages of risk management but is still experimenting with it, typically through a small group of selected individuals, without a formal or organized approach. The normalized risk organization acknowledges the benefits of risk management and integrates it into daily business operations. The natural risk company fosters a risk-aware culture and proactively implements risk management standards and best practices.

The Framework Tiers (FT) approach in the NIST CSF functions like a maturity model, allowing organizations to contextualize their approach to cybersecurity risk management. The Tiers align with Hillson's Risk Maturity Model, which includes "naive," "novice," "normalized," and "natural." Similar to the Risk Maturity Model, an organization can utilize the NIST CSF's Tiers system to monitor and assess the effectiveness of its enterprise risk management strategies for improvement. The NIST CSF Tiers categorize businesses based on the implementation of risk management practices. The Tiers consist of principles that guide organizations in determining the appropriate level of rigor for their cybersecurity programs. Below is a list explaining the four Tiers:

Tier 1—Firms' risk management strategies are ineffective. Their risk management programs and methods are fragmented, unreliable, and unsystematic, with limited management involvement; this corresponds to the "Naive" stage, as described by Hillson (1997).

Tier 2—Firms employ ineffective ad hoc risk management strategies based on poorly designed and implemented policies and procedures, i.e., the "Novice" stage, as described by Hillson (1997).

Tier 3—Firms have a structured risk management program with effective systems and ongoing management oversight and participation, i.e., the "Normalized" stage per Hillson (1997).

Tier 4—Firms employ dynamic and sophisticated proactive risk management systems, with regular communication regarding strategic goals, culture, risk appetite, and funding, i.e., the "Natural" stage per Hillson (1997).

The NIST CSF Tiers approach determines an organization's "Current Tier" by identifying the category that best describes the organization's current risk management processes. The next step is to select the "Target Tier" that most accurately reflects the risk management strategies the organization plans to employ.

ISO 31000 outlines a Risk Management Maturity Model that features five maturity levels (ERMA ISO 31000 RM3): "Initial," "Repeatable," "Defined," "Managed," and "Optimized."

Initial: Risk management is often reactive and ad hoc, relying on individual initiative and concentrating on managing specific hazards.

Repeatable: Risk management begins with a systematic implementation but lacks alignment with organizational governance and management. Additionally, there is an uneven distribution of competencies, leadership, and risk management commitments.

Defined: The ISO 31000 Risk Management Guideline or Standard is being followed to ensure systematic and consistent risk management practices. It is part of organizational governance and management. However, positive risk management behavior remains limited. Leadership, competency, and commitment are evenly distributed among team members.

Managed: The ISO 31000 Risk Management Guideline or Standard has been utilized to incorporate risk management into organizational governance and management practices. The culture emphasizes leadership, competency, and risk management. The organization is proactive and supports risk management through reviews and ongoing development.

Optimized: The ISO 31000 Risk Management Guideline or Standard emphasizes the importance of risk management as a part of organizational governance and management. The corporate risk culture values leadership, competence, and prudence in risk management. This creates a solid foundation for business resilience and sustainability.

2.4.5 Risk-Based Model

A risk-based cybersecurity governance model systematically prioritizes security operations based on risk assessment and management for an organization's digital assets. This methodology ensures that cybersecurity is more than just an IT concern; it is a strategic business requirement driven by risk considerations. Management should focus on identifying and assessing the gaps and vulnerabilities that pose significant risks to the business through a risk-based approach. A risk-based model is a mathematical approach used to evaluate risk and predict potential outcomes. It aids companies in their strategic and operational decision-making. Cybersecurity operational and compliance risks are prioritized in a risk-based strategy, which focuses on eliminating or mitigating them to acceptable levels.

The primary objectives of a risk-based model are to identify, evaluate, and mitigate the organization's most significant cybersecurity threats. It continuously assesses risks to analyze threats, weaknesses, and commercial repercussions. It monitors key performance indicators (KPIs) and key risk indicators (KRIs) to evaluate performance and efficacy, as well as to support informed investment decisions. Risk-based models facilitate the development of plans for continuous improvement, incident response readiness, and business continuity, thereby prioritizing cyber resilience.

Risk management, or RM, identifies, evaluates, prioritizes, mitigates, monitors, detects, reports, and responds to risks that could negatively impact an organization's goals. To ensure strategic alignment and resilience, Enterprise Risk Management (ERM) is a risk-based approach that offers a comprehensive framework, integrating risk management across all business functions, including IT, HR, finance, operations, compliance, and more. Cybersecurity is a crucial component of enterprise risk management, providing a structured method for addressing uncertainties. Consequently, organizational survival and success hinge on ongoing adaptation and integration with Enterprise Risk Management (ERM) as cyber threats become increasingly complex. By employing frameworks such as COSO, ISO 31000, COBIT, and

NIST CSF, organizations can effectively protect themselves from cyber threats and align their risk management strategies and tactics with their objectives.

2.4.6 Learning Organization

Senge (2006) defines a learning organization as one in which individuals continuously deploy their talents, achieve their goals, support new ways of thinking, and deliver shared aspirations. It is also a place where people learn to learn together. Vision is a crucial ingredient of a learning organization, motivating a business to perform tasks (e.g., establishing cyber risk control governance) that facilitate growth. To achieve growth, businesses must strategize and learn from their own experiences and those of others to guide them and manage or optimize risks. In terms of cybersecurity governance, a learning organization has a risk management plan that integrates visions, strategies, goals, benchmarking, policies, and learning processes.

A good learning organization can adapt to changing environmental conditions and new perceptions. In the rapidly shifting digital environment, organizations must quickly adapt and mitigate the bane of cyber threats through continuous learning and revision. A cybersecurity strategy necessitates a comprehensive approach that encompasses the various levels and functions of an organization. This can be achieved through systems thinking (Senge, 2006), where the organization combines different disciplines and functions into a cohesive practice through comprehensive strategy and policy designs.

A learning organization strives for continual vigilance and development by enhancing its ability to adapt, innovate, and shape its future in a rapidly changing digital world. In cybersecurity, a learning organization's governance mechanisms encourage employees to engage in thoughtful discussions regularly and collaboratively reflect on their roles, responsibilities, and actions, translating those insights into tangible results.

2.4.7 Five Lines Accountability

The Three Lines of Defense Model was first popularized as a governance framework for risk management and internal controls in various industries by the Institute of Internal Auditors (IIA) in 2013. In 2020, the IIA developed it into the "Three Lines Model" to emphasize teamwork and clear roles. Since then, academics and practitioners have utilized it as the principal governance framework for risk management or have studied it in-depth across different fields (Valkenburg & Bongiovanni, 2024). The Three Lines of Defense Model established a layered management approach: the first line consists of the frontline IT function responsible for implementing security controls; the second line is in charge of risk management policies, monitoring the first line's controls, and ensuring compliance both internally and externally; lastly, the third line involves the internal audit role that provides independent assurance and guidance on the overall quality of cyber risk governance.

One criticism directed at the classic Three Lines of Defense Model was its focus on the defensive aspect of cyber risk management. It fails to acknowledge the role of executive management or the Board of Directors in cybersecurity governance. In response to this critique, a revised model effectively incorporates two additional lines of accountability: executive management as the fourth line, responsible for managing the organization and allocating resources to cyber risk management (following enterprise risk management-ERM), and the Board of Directors as the fifth line, accountable for approving cybersecurity strategy, policies, resource allocation, and oversight. The Five Lines of Accountability (5 LoA) model serves as a foundation for identifying the structures, roles, and accountability needed for cybersecurity governance (Slapnicar et al., 2023). The model remains a popular benchmark for governance best practices, engaging all levels of the organizational hierarchy.

2.4.8 Hofstede's Cultural Dimensions

Hofstede (1980) and Hofstede et al. (2010) developed Hofstede's Cultural Dimensions Theory to understand how cultural values influence communication and behavior across different countries. The theory identifies six aspects that help gauge how culture impacts individuals and organizations:

Power Distance (PD): The degree to which less powerful individuals in a society defer to more powerful members. High-PD cultures (e.g., Russia, Malaysia, Mongolia, Philippines) typically employ top-down cybersecurity governance, characterized by centralized decision-making. Employees are less likely to challenge authority, leading to strict adherence to security policies without dispute. This can lead to more effective enforcement but may restrict bottom-up reporting of security vulnerabilities. Low-PD cultures (e.g., the USA, UK, New Zealand, Germany) favor decentralized cybersecurity strategies that involve participatory risk management. Employees expect to contribute to security rules, resulting in collaborative threat reporting but potentially slower response times due to the need for consensus-building.

Collectivism vs. Individualism: The extent to which a person integrates into a group. Collectivist cultures (e.g., China) prioritize group-oriented security measures such as team-based responsibility, monitoring, and response scenarios. Individualistic cultures value personal accountability in cybersecurity, with governance centered on individual responsibility, training, and explicit personal repercussions for breaches. Onumo et al. (2017) found that individualism has a significant correlation with cybersecurity development.

Masculinity vs. Femininity: How roles are assigned to the sexes and the significance placed on competition versus caring. Masculine-oriented cultures emphasize winning and defeating attackers when implementing cybersecurity governance, prioritizing competitive performance metrics. Feminine-oriented cultures prioritize thorough risk assessment, collaborative security strategies, and enhancing individual employee security awareness and proficiency.

Uncertainty Avoidance (UA): UA refers to the extent to which individuals in a culture feel threatened by ambiguous situations. Cultures with high UA rely on highly structured cybersecurity frameworks that include specific protocols for all potential scenarios. They invest heavily in compliance certifications (such as ISO 27001) and prefer established technologies over innovative but unproven options. In contrast, low UA cultures adopt more flexible governance, enabling adaptive responses to emerging threats. They are more open to taking risks when experimenting with new security technologies, such as AI-driven or machine learning threat detection.

Long-Term vs. Short-Term Orientation: Emphasizing future benefits rather than adherence to customs and the past. Long-term-oriented businesses invest in core cybersecurity infrastructure and employee training programs, showing a willingness to implement risk control measures for long-term resilience. Onumo et al. (2017) found that long-term orientation strongly correlates with cybersecurity development. Short-term-oriented organizations prioritize immediate ROI, favoring quick fixes over long-term transformation; therefore, incident response takes precedence over preventive measures.

2.5 Essential Governance Factors

A cybersecurity maturity assessment of the firm's current security control gaps and risks is essential to determine its state of information security exposure. This assessment will facilitate the design of an effective governance architecture to efficiently manage cybersecurity. The five core principles of awareness, accountability, transparency, fairness, and responsibility underpin the corporate governance framework of policies and guidelines.

The generic cybersecurity governance process outlined in Sect. 2.6 below provides a framework for developing strategies, policies, procedures, and controls that enable informed decision-making and the realization of value. The key factors that must be incorporated into the process to ensure its efficiency and help an organization enhance and refine its cybersecurity governance program are:

2.5.1 Leadership—Board of Directors

According to Coase (1937), leadership is crucial in a world with transaction costs, as its purpose is to guide the organization toward optimizing those costs through collective decision-making. The scope of leadership varies based on the nature of the role. In an organizational context, distributed leadership emphasizes group accountability, dynamic interactions between leaders and their subordinates, and cooperative decision-making (Harris et al., 2007; Spillane, 2005). A management strategy known as "distributed leadership" empowers every member of an organization to share decision-making authority and take on leadership roles. Effective cybersecurity leadership requires a strategic vision, flexibility, and strong communication skills to navigate technological risks and human challenges (Gilbert & Gilbert, 2024). Integrating cybersecurity strategies into overall enterprise governance demands effective communication, operational efficiency, and business sustainability, all of which can be accomplished through leadership approaches that manage the interaction between organizational dynamics and technological vulnerabilities (Alston et al., 2021; Gilbert & Gilbert, 2024; Kshetri, 2021). Thus, strong leadership ensures that cybersecurity acts as a business enabler, protecting the organization while fostering trust, innovation, and resilience.

The strategic role of leadership in cybersecurity governance is crucial for safeguarding an organization's digital assets, infrastructure, and data against emerging threats. Leadership in cybersecurity governance encompasses more than just technology; it also includes strategy, culture, and risk management. Effective leadership nurtures a robust security culture, integrates cybersecurity into corporate objectives, and ensures regulatory compliance. Leaders articulate the cybersecurity vision and embed it into the overall business plan. They establish and implement structured governance frameworks to systematically manage cybersecurity risks, including policies and processes that define roles, responsibilities, and accountability across the organization. They prioritize cybersecurity spending based on risk assessments and business implications. Leaders leverage innovative and emerging technologies (machine learning, AI, blockchain, threat intelligence) to stay ahead of attackers and enhance cyber resilience, ensuring business continuity even after an incident.

The Board of Directors' responsibilities extend beyond approving frameworks and strategies; they also encompass leadership, oversight, and the supervision of efficient implementation and execution. The BoD must be committed to fostering a culture of risk awareness, adopting a risk-based approach, and implementing consistent best practices for cyber risk controls throughout the organization. The BoD needs to adhere to and follow corporate governance rules and best practices to effectively fulfill its leadership and oversight duties in cyber risk governance. BoDs are responsible for creating and implementing specific structures, policies, and principles that serve as the foundation for these rules and best practices. Therefore, the BoD oversees and ensures that an organization's operational risk management objectives, strategies, policies, and procedures are authorized, regularly reviewed, and effectively executed. To achieve this, the BoD should optimize the cybersecurity function by allocating resources, delegating responsibilities, and balancing the relative priority of cybersecurity investments with other types of investments.

The Board of Directors should also expect everyone to engage in cybersecurity monitoring and accountability within the broader framework of enterprise risk management. The firm achieves this by overseeing cyber risk through the entire board or by delegating this oversight to a board committee, typically the Risk Committee or a committee led by a director with expertise in technology or cybersecurity, who will provide the BoD with regular and comprehensive updates.

2.5.2 Leadership—Senior Management

The senior manager, typically the C-suite executives and the Chief Executive Officer, should proactively participate in establishing and explicitly endorsing the cybersecurity framework, policies, and procedures. Senior management must take a leadership role in cybersecurity that extends beyond merely approving new cybersecurity processes, making IT investments, and adhering to security regulations. Instead, senior management, particularly the Chief Information Security Officer (CISO), needs to view cybersecurity from an organizational perspective, comprehend its impact on the entire organization, and consistently develop innovative ideas for improvement. CISOs must collaborate with other executives, including IT, HR, and finance, to instill a security mindset in corporate culture and values. Cybersecurity governance necessitates agility, adaptability, and a profound understanding of the continually evolving threat landscape. The Board of Directors and senior management teams must actively oversee and collaborate with other stakeholders to protect their organizations from cyber risks.

2.5.3 Budget and Resources

The justification for budgeting in cybersecurity governance is the need to effectively allocate resources to protect an organization's digital assets, ensure regulatory compliance, and mitigate risks. In cybersecurity governance, budgeting is an essential strategy. Insufficient resource allocation can lead to risks affecting an organization's finances, operations, reputation, and legal standing. Budgeting supports compliance, as laws such as GDPR and HIPAA require security measures, and adequate resource allocation helps to avoid legal penalties. A well-planned cybersecurity budget fosters long-term resilience against cyber threats by aligning security investments with business objectives. The Board of Directors must secure sufficient funding for cybersecurity initiatives and tools. Resources should be prioritized and allocated to meet the most critical cybersecurity needs.

2.5.4 Establishing the Framework

In a world increasingly digital and prone to threats, firms must implement effective compliance and cybersecurity frameworks to protect their networks, systems, and data, reduce risks, and ensure operational continuity. A cybersecurity governance framework provides a structured approach to managing the cyber risks associated with critical assets, ensuring that an organization's security strategies align with its business objectives, regulatory requirements, and risk management practices. Beyond being a legal requirement, a robust cybersecurity and compliance framework also acts as a strategic business enabler. It safeguards resources, fosters trust, and ensures long-term viability in a landscape that is increasingly digitalized. Establishing a cybersecurity governance framework involves selecting the relevant frameworks (such as NIST CSF, COBIT 5, or ISO 27001) that best meet the company's needs.

The key components of a framework are policies and standards that formalize rules for security controls (e.g., access control, SIEM, IDS/IPS, encryption), alignment with industry standards (NIST CSF, ISO 27001, COBIT), risk management process (risk identification, assessment, mitigation, monitoring, and reporting), regular audits and penetration testing, clear roles and responsibilities and accountability (e.g., Board of Directors oversight, CISO, security/IT teams), compliance and legal requirements (e.g., GDPR, HIPAA, PCI DSS), regular compliance audits, security awareness, training and simulations on threats, and incident response and recovery plans, and regular reporting to executives and stakeholders.

Having a solid Cybersecurity Governance Framework in place ensures security is deeply ingrained in an organization's culture and operations. By taking a structured approach—from assessing risks to ongoing monitoring—businesses can proactively protect against cyber threats while meeting compliance and operational resilience requirements.

2.5.5 Risk-Based Approach and Enterprise Risk Management

A risk assessment of the firm's digital inventory of systems and assets is conducted to provide a snapshot of its current security posture, aligning with its objectives. Alternatively, gaps are identified by comparing existing controls to framework requirements. A thorough cyber risk assessment is essential for establishing the current state, identifying gaps, and developing a plan to address them. Such assessments help a company evaluate the status of its security controls and, if necessary, provide strategic planning guidance to establish an effective security plan. The cybersecurity plan adopts a risk-based approach consistent with enterprise risk management. Demonstrating an organization's ability to recognize external and internal threats, align its cybersecurity functions with business objectives, and prevent, detect, and respond to cyber threats necessitates a comprehensive assessment of its cybersecurity maturity. The maturity assessment process entails creating, reviewing, and updating all cybersecurity standards, policies, and procedures.

Cyber risk analytics and modeling are crucial for evaluating and contextualizing cyber threats to inform effective mitigation and control strategies. An organization's risk exposures must be considered to enhance its cybersecurity posture, involving effective monitoring, measurement, mitigation, detection, reporting, and response to risks. Analytics and modeling are ongoing processes. B&SM must determine what is essential to measure, establish regular assessment intervals, analyze the data, and develop a strategy for improvement and risk modeling.

After assessing the current state, the firm must establish the structure and expectations of cybersecurity governance. Furthermore, the organization must regularly identify, evaluate, and prioritize cybersecurity risks to mitigate them effectively. Identified risks are managed, and their controls are routinely monitored for effectiveness.

2.5.6 *Policies and Procedures*

At the core of a cybersecurity governance framework are policies and procedures. These provide clear, enforceable guidelines that outline how an organization handles cyber risks, meets regulatory requirements, and safeguards its assets. Policies address the security mechanisms that protect an organization's network and infrastructure from unauthorized access, attacks, and various security risks. A comprehensive, clear, and well-maintained set of cybersecurity policies that align with business objectives and regulatory requirements is a critical foundation for managing corporate security. Standard Operating Procedures (SOPs) are essential for clarifying the implementation and enforcement processes of these policies.

The key steps to establish cybersecurity policies and procedures start with defining the governance structure and objectives, followed by conducting a risk assessment to identify, evaluate, and prioritize threats, then selecting a compliance framework as a foundation, and develop core security policies (e.g., data protection, access control, AUP, IRP, remote work/BYOD, third-party management). It is necessary to obtain leadership approval for the policies and procedures to ensure their formal adoption, and these must be communicated to employees through workshops, training, and simulations. Policies and procedures require regular assessments and updates to ensure policy effectiveness and adaptability to emerging threats. Having solid policies and procedures in place is crucial for a secure, compliant, and resilient organization. By taking a structured approach, from assessing risks to continually improving, businesses can build a strong foundation for their cybersecurity governance.

2.5.7 *Implementation Plan*

A well-structured implementation plan is essential to the success of any Cybersecurity Governance Framework (e.g., NIST CSF, ISO 27001, COBIT). Even the strongest regulations and controls are ineffective if not properly executed. Cybersecurity is a dynamic element, and its implementation plans must include key components and adaptability to accommodate updates for new threats. Therefore, a comprehensive implementation strategy is essential, detailing the deadlines, resources, and specific actions needed to deploy the governance framework across the organization. A well-thought-out and structured implementation plan ensures cybersecurity measures support business goals by establishing roles and accountability (i.e., B&SM, CISO, security and IT teams, employees) to avoid gaps in security enforcement, helps allocate budget, tools, and personnel based on risk assessments, establishes KPIs, KRIs, and milestones to track performance, and provides a structured plan that includes disaster recovery protocols, minimizing downtime. This strategy integrates the framework's policies, procedures, tools, and regulations into the organization's IT and broader enterprise risk management environments.

2.5.8 *Monitor, Report, and Review*

Having a solid monitoring, reporting, and review (MRR) process is the backbone of effective cybersecurity governance. The Board of Directors, risk committee, and management team stay informed through regular updates on the effectiveness of cybersecurity measures. This is done through ongoing oversight, periodic audits, providing feedback, and adjusting the framework to ensure it aligns with the company's goals and responds to shifting risks. Even the best-designed security frameworks can't keep up with changing threats if they're not constantly monitored. By implementing a continuous monitoring, reporting, and review cycle, cybersecurity becomes a dynamic, adaptive defense system that prevents breaches through real-time tracking, demonstrates compliance to regulators and customers, optimizes security spending with risk-based and ROI-driven insights, and builds resilience by learning from incidents.

2.5.9 *Technology*

Technology provides the tools to transform governance frameworks (like NIST, ISO 27001, or COBIT) into actions. It is the foundation of effective cybersecurity governance, enabling firms to enforce policies, detect threats, and respond to incidents promptly. Technology gives the means to put governance frameworks (such as NIST, ISO 27001, and COBIT) into effect. A robust security infrastructure requires planned management (i.e., technology management) and investment in appropriate cybersecurity technologies, including firewalls, intrusion detection systems, and encryption. Technology management serves as a tool for systematic oversight in planning, implementing, and maintaining security systems technology within cybersecurity governance. Regular updates are crucial to ensure that all software and systems are properly patched and equipped with the latest security patches to protect against vulnerabilities. Thus, technology enhances cybersecurity governance by automating real-time threat detection, enforcing policies, accelerating incident response, and providing an audit trail as proof of compliance.

2.5.10 *Corporate Culture, Risk Awareness, and Training*

The organization should cultivate a culture of security awareness and accountability, promoting behaviors that support cybersecurity. B&SM must develop policies and allocate resources to foster a culture of cyber risk awareness and training, thereby strengthening cybersecurity. Employees should receive regular training to enhance their understanding of cybersecurity best practices and potential security threats. A strong corporate culture, a risk-aware mindset, and effective training are fundamental to cybersecurity governance, as they ensure that cybersecurity is prioritized at all levels, reduce human error risks, and prepare staff to become active defenders against cyberattacks.

2.5.11 *Communication and Information Sharing*

Communication should be regular and comprehensive, facilitated through reporting mechanisms to the Board of Directors and senior management to report cybersecurity incidents and track performance metrics. This enables the firm to assess and evaluate its cyber maturity and its impact on the organization's cyber risk posture. Sharing information breaks down silos and aligns stakeholders, as cybersecurity is not just an IT issue, but rather a requirement that necessitates coordination across the entire organization, including committees, executives, HR, finance, operations, legal, and employees. Sharing information and collaborating with industry peers, cybersecurity organizations, and government authorities helps businesses stay informed about the latest cybersecurity trends and best practices. They also serve as an essential source of threat intelligence, allowing organizations to remain informed about emerging risks and best practices.

Effective communication and information sharing are key components of cybersecurity governance, as they ensure executive buy-in for critical investments, facilitate policy understanding, promote collaborative threat mitigation, and expedite incident resolution. Communication and sharing transform cybersecurity governance from a static policy to a dynamic, organization-wide defense system by preventing breaches through awareness and collaboration, responding quickly to incidents with clear escalation pathways, and ensuring compliance and trust through transparency.

2.5.12 *Legal and Compliance Management*

Legal and compliance requirements ensure that firms fulfill their regulatory obligations, mitigate legal risks, and maintain stakeholder trust, as cybersecurity laws, such as GDPR and HIPAA, mandate specific protections for data privacy and reporting breaches. The cybersecurity governance framework, including its policies and regulations, should ensure the firm's compliance with relevant laws, industry regulations, contractual obligations, and other applicable requirements. The firm conducts regular assessments and audits to verify compliance and identify areas for improvement.

2.5.13 *Incident Response Management*

The Incident Response Plan (IRP) outlines the procedures for responding to cybersecurity incidents promptly and effectively. Incident response rules detail the necessary actions for security teams when addressing security issues, including detection, reporting, and containment procedures. Regular staff training and drills are crucial to ensure readiness for potential crises. The IRP should incorporate disaster recovery plans (DRPs) and business continuity plans (BCPs) to enhance resilience against cyberattacks. Regular updates and testing of the IRP are essential to maintain its effectiveness.

2.5.14 *Performance Measurement*

Key KPIs and metrics are essential for assessing the effectiveness of cybersecurity governance. These measurements can be used to enhance cybersecurity processes and governance continually. The reduction in high-risk vulnerabilities and breaches, along with improvements in detection and incident response times, training completion rates, phishing test results, compliance audit pass rates, and third-party compliance percentages, represents several critical performance indicators.

Measuring performance is a key part of governing cybersecurity, making sure security controls work, risks are handled, and business goals are met. It informs decision-making by showing how well security measures work, evaluating whether cybersecurity investments lower risks, providing proof of compliance with regulations, and pinpointing gaps in security controls that need to improve. It also boosts accountability by tracking whether security teams and employees follow policies, identifying bottlenecks in security operations, driving ongoing improvement, and allowing for benchmarking against industry standards.

2.5.15 *Supply Chain*

The company needs to manage the entire cybersecurity governance process. This includes assessing and mitigating risks posed by third-party vendors and partners. Supply chain management is a crucial aspect of cybersecurity governance, as modern businesses increasingly rely on third-party vendors, software providers, and cloud services, all of which can pose risks. A single weak link in the supply chain can result in massive breaches, compliance failures, and operational disruptions. Supply chain management is critical in cybersecurity governance, as 60% of breaches originate from third parties (Ponemon, 2025), with attackers targeting suppliers with vulnerable security to gain access to larger organizations. Evaluating cybersecurity requirements in contracts and service agreements is necessary from a regulatory perspective.

2.6 The Cybersecurity Governance Process

The cybersecurity governance framework is a strategic requirement for safeguarding a company's digital assets and advancing its business objectives. It offers a structured and systematic approach to establishing a strategy for managing and mitigating enterprise cyber risks. It is not merely a technical issue. A cybersecurity strategy equips businesses with a comprehensive defense against constantly evolving cyber threats, enabling them to plan for the future, develop a successful strategy, and implement it effectively. A well-thought-out governance strategy helps prevent tactical cybersecurity problems or misunderstandings by providing clarity and purpose during cyber protection activities. A cybersecurity governance program outlines and reflects the organization's strategy and operations for a comprehensive defense process against cyber threats. It encompasses policies, procedures, protocols, and practices designed to protect digital assets and ensure compliance with legal and regulatory requirements.

A suitable cybersecurity assessment framework is essential for evaluating the company's security posture and developing a robust cybersecurity strategy. This framework identifies and prioritizes the networks, business systems, and data critical to corporate operations, enabling targeted action. With a solid cybersecurity framework, the business can pinpoint the threats and vulnerabilities of its digital assets, subsequently crafting a strong cybersecurity strategy to leverage cybersecurity solutions fully.

The sequence of activities that constitute cybersecurity governance is illustrated in Fig. 2.3 and discussed in the sections below.

2.6.1 Strategic Alignment and Governance (I)

The initial step in this process is to establish the connection between business objectives and cybersecurity goals. Companies must conduct a comprehensive cybersecurity risk assessment to align their cyber risk control objectives with their operations. This alignment is essential, as organizations can only create an effective cybersecurity plan if they comprehend the potential risks, information security vulnerabilities, and data privacy challenges they face. The hardware, software, databases, networks,

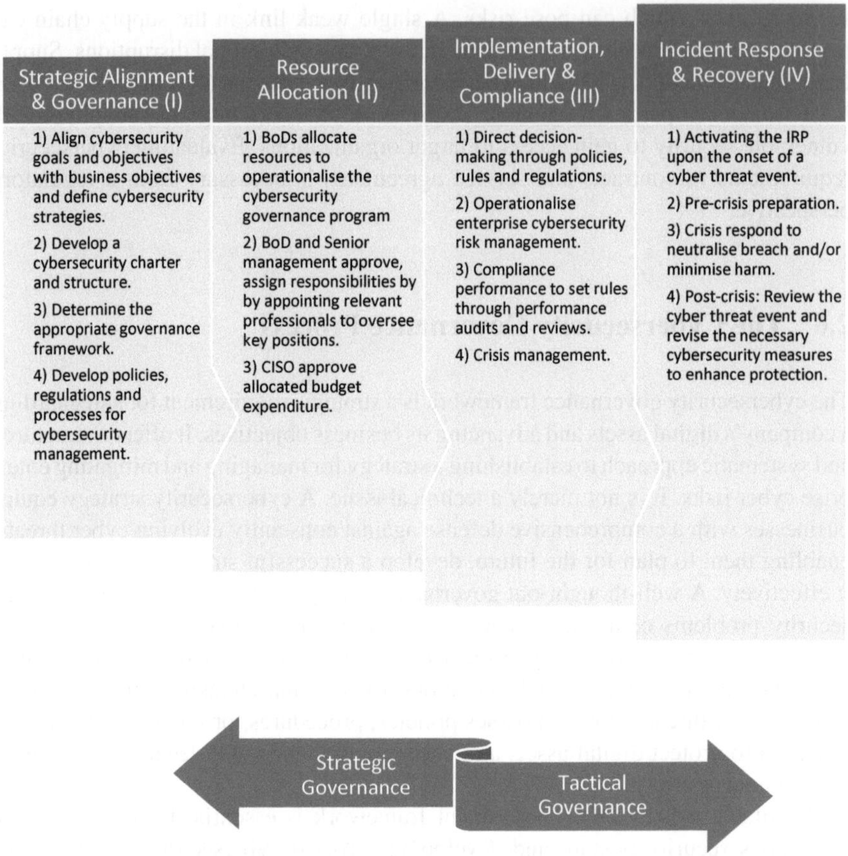

Fig. 2.3 Cybersecurity governance process

systems, and sensitive data at risk are likewise identified and documented. This alignment promotes operational efficiency, as security solutions crafted with business operations in mind reduce disruptions and boost productivity. A robust cybersecurity plan that corresponds with business goals can enhance operations, customer satisfaction, regulatory compliance, competitive advantage, brand reputation, and investor confidence, among other benefits. Therefore, companies must clearly define the objectives of cybersecurity and how they support the business plan to improve compliance, strengthen security, and encourage efficient operations.

By recognizing the key elements that connect an organization's business goals to its cybersecurity measures, strategic alignment facilitates the development of effective cybersecurity policies, enhances risk management, and supports informed investment decisions. Therefore, strategic alignment involves defining the firm's cybersecurity goals and objectives that protect and strengthen its business objectives while considering its current cyber risk exposure.

This section will discuss how an organization aligns its cybersecurity governance strategy with its business objectives and how to implement and deliver that strategy.

2.6.1.1 Align and Define Cybersecurity Strategies Vis-À-Vis Goals to Business Objectives

The organization must ensure that its cybersecurity strategy aligns with and supports the company's overall objectives. The security team must inform board members about the impact of security breaches on the company and emphasize the importance of strategic alignment between security and commercial objectives. The goal is to strike a balance between productivity and security, as increasing connectivity can potentially enhance efficiency, but sensitive systems and data must remain protected. Alignment is achieved through risk identification, assessment, and gap analysis, which enable the firm to pinpoint which vital digital or data assets require the most security based on the company's overarching business objectives. Cybersecurity standards such as the NIST CSF or ISO 27001 can guide this risk assessment process.

2.6.1.2 Establish a Cybersecurity Charter and Structure

The firm must establish a cybersecurity charter that clearly defines and outlines its commitment to cybersecurity, including the responsibilities, duties, and accountability of the executive-level team. The charter will promote and foster a security-focused culture throughout the company. The organization should emphasize the use of automation and technology to enhance cybersecurity effectiveness wherever possible. It can automate routine business tasks to increase efficiency while maintaining security. This chapter also captures the tactical capabilities of the charter.

The structure outlines the decision rights and responsibilities assigned to each node in the organizational hierarchy, which varies significantly due to its different purposes and functions. In cybersecurity, a centralized, hierarchical structure fosters uniformity in security protocols. It enhances effective threat detection, while a decentralized strategy allows for flexibility in responding to specific local conditions and threats.

We propose an ERM cybersecurity governance structure that combines hierarchical and matrix elements. The hierarchical component ensures a robust risk control protocol, while the matrix aspect enhances adaptability, cross-functionality, and effective responses to the diverse range of cyber threats (Fig. 2.4). The Board of Directors, risk committee, and senior management operating at the strategic cybersecurity risk governance (SCRG) level maintain the authority to establish and approve strategic measures, while the departments are responsible for the tactical cybersecurity risk management (TCRM) activities of the E-CyG process.

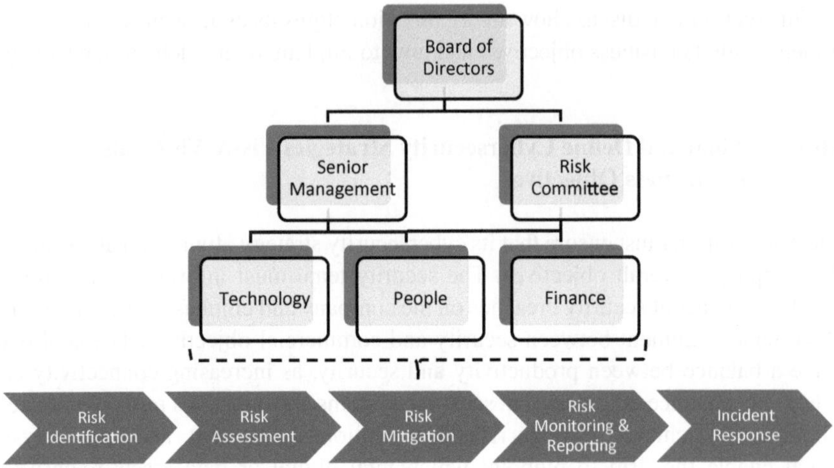

Fig. 2.4 Enterprise cybersecurity governance structure

2.6.1.3 Determine the Appropriate Cybersecurity Governance Framework

Companies aim to utilize governance for the cautious and efficient execution of their cybersecurity programs. To achieve this, the organization develops a cybersecurity framework by adopting and implementing a comprehensive structure, such as COBIT, NIST, or ISO/IEC 27001, to guide its overall cybersecurity strategy. To align cybersecurity with business operations, the company's cybersecurity team will collaborate to identify the cybersecurity governance framework that provides the most business value with the least possible risk.

The adopted framework will significantly influence the company's daily operations and risk management efforts. Therefore, it must align with relevant laws, regulations, industry standards, and best practices to maximize its effectiveness. By selecting the right framework, the company can enhance its protection against cyber risk while ensuring that its stakeholders are confident in the business's safety from cyberattacks and that they have access to a stable, well-managed digital environment throughout the entire value chain.

2.6.1.4 Develop Policies, Regulations, and Procedures

Planning and drafting policies occur after vulnerable assets are identified and the cybersecurity governance strategy and framework have been established. The cybersecurity governance strategy directs the organization's cybersecurity program, and effective security policies are a reflection of it. Policies represent high-level declarations from an organization's senior leadership for management purposes. They constitute strategic, not technical, decisions; they are business decisions. Organizations must develop robust cybersecurity policies to protect their resources, comply with legal requirements, and maintain the trust of their stakeholders.

Well-structured policies take into account the organization's environment, human aspects, and financial and technical factors. The policies, procedures, and practices must be clear and specific, outlining the strategies and actions for managing cyber risk. They reflect the actions that align with the organization's cybersecurity goals, mission, and structure. These policies should be thorough yet easy to understand, enabling staff members to grasp and follow them effectively. Policies typically aim to guide the organization toward its desired outcomes and inform internal decisions, while external requirements, such as regulations, also play a role. The following elements should be included in the policy document's structure:

- Policy subject title;
- The risk item or items that the policy pertains to, along with their risk register identification;
- The introduction outlines the goal, objective, parameters, and terminology;
- The principles, norms, and rules of risk governance are detailed in the policy statements;
- The roles and responsibilities of the relevant staff members involved in overseeing and managing the risks associated with enterprise risk management;
- Information about the penalties for violations is included in the compliance and enforcement regulations;
- The review and update process includes details about the stakeholders conducting the review, its objective, and who from executive leadership approves it; and
- Status of the policy, including its version and enforcement date.

In cybersecurity, the implementation of policy is primarily guided by technology. To effectively implement policies, practices, and procedures, they must align with established standards and best practices, be documented, and communicated to both executives and operators. This ensures uniformity and awareness of the procedures. While standards and regulations inform and enforce policies, tactical procedures apply them in a way that creates accountable and executable processes. Tactical procedures translate policy into action through their implementation and deployment. These procedures should include steps for assessing policies and processes, such as compliance and performance reviews, and providing feedback to enhance and strengthen the organization's cybersecurity posture continually. Figure 2.5 summarizes the policy implementation cycle, highlighting the key nodes in the process that influence the effectiveness of cybersecurity policies.

2.6.2 Resource Allocation (II)

The governance structure should ensure that appropriate resources are allocated to achieve corporate objectives. Additionally, management must determine whether

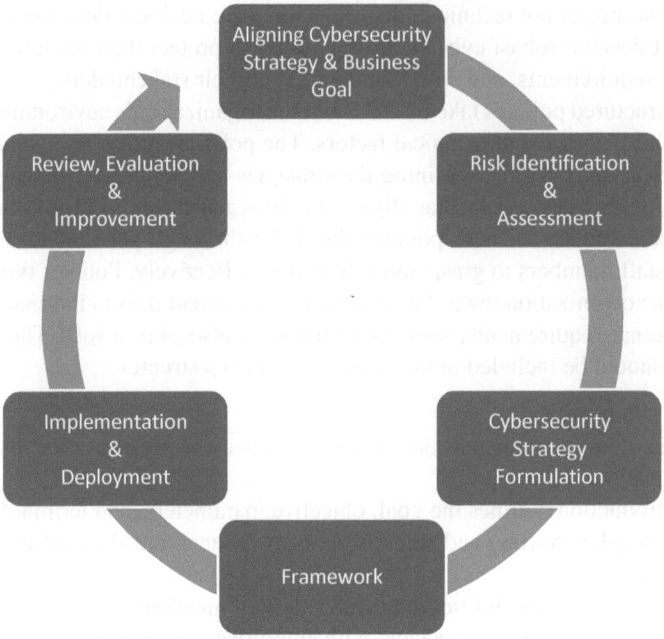

Fig. 2.5 Policy implementation cycle

sufficient resources are available to meet the company's goals. Applications, infrastructure, labor, and information are among these resources. A firm can effectively manage its resources by carefully monitoring its budget and expenditures.

2.6.2.1 Boards of Directors

As the organization's cybersecurity program champion, the Board of Directors (BoD) is responsible for approving and overseeing the cybersecurity strategy and budget. To implement the cybersecurity program effectively, the BoD must allocate sufficient resources to support and sustain their activities.

2.6.2.2 Senior Executive Appointments and Assigning Responsibilities

While the Board of Directors is responsible for appointing the chief executive officer (CEO), the CEO selects the relevant senior management personnel, including the CISO, CRO, CFO, and CIO positions, to oversee essential functions. The chief executive officer and the senior management team are tasked with implementing and maintaining the cybersecurity program and appointing qualified professionals to key roles within the risk control processes.

2.6.2.3 Ciso

The Chief Information Security Officer (CISO), who plays a critical role in governance, is responsible for approving the allocated budgets for cybersecurity expenditures during the daily management of cybersecurity operations. By serving as a liaison between financial governance and cybersecurity requirements, the CISO ensures that budget approvals are strategic, risk-informed, and aligned with organizational resilience objectives.

2.6.3 Implementation, Delivery, and Compliance (III)

One of an organization's most important responsibilities is identifying cyber hazards. Planning is challenging without this knowledge. The company must establish a robust cyber risk management program, ensuring its governance framework identifies all potential cyber threats that could disrupt business operations. The firm is responsible for detecting hazards, evaluating their severity, prioritizing those that pose the most significant risk, and mitigating them. Review digital threat environments to uncover emerging threats and reassess existing ones by prioritizing and addressing these risks.

In implementing and delivering the cybersecurity program, decisions and actions must be guided by and consistent with regulations and policies. Based on the risk assessment, the process begins by establishing specific implementation goals and focusing initially on high-risk areas. Assigning responsibilities and ensuring the necessary funds and staff are available to support the process are crucial (see Fig. 2.2 above for authority, tasks, and responsibilities).

Implementing technological controls requires coordination with the IT team to install or upgrade firewalls, intrusion detection systems, encryption tools, and other security technologies.

Employees are assigned to supervise adherence, detect risks, and monitor performance, setting rules and procedures through periodic reports and reviews. The performance and oversight management of the governance program necessitates continuous observation of the implementation of cybersecurity value propositions, their efficacy, and their contribution to accomplishing business goals. The company will be able to pinpoint areas that require improvement and attention from this observation.

2.6.3.1 Directing Decision-Making

Cybersecurity governance involves steering decision-making through policies, procedures, and regulations. The cybersecurity governance framework ensures that an organization's digital assets are protected through structured policies, procedures, and practices. Consistent, risk-aware, and business-aligned security decisions define effective cybersecurity governance. It helps organizations prevent violations,

Fig. 2.6 Five ERM cybersecurity tasks

maintain compliance, and manage risks effectively by enforcing policies, regulations, and accountability. Without sound governance, decision-making turns reactive, increasing vulnerabilities and heightening the risk of financial or legal repercussions. Therefore, governance establishes clear cybersecurity policies (such as those related to network access and incident response), which guide management and employees in making security-related decisions.

2.6.3.2 Enterprise Risk Management

The ISO/IEC 27001 (2022) standard emphasizes that cybersecurity must be viewed as an enterprise-wide risk management issue rather than merely a technical or operational concern. The enterprise risk management process consists of five fundamental tasks: identify, assess/prioritize, mitigate threats by selecting and implementing the appropriate security measures, monitor, detect and report, and respond and recover (Fig. 2.6).

2.6.3.3 Compliance and Performance

Regular audits are essential for continuous monitoring to assess efficacy and compliance. Key performance indicators (KPIs), key risk indicators (KRIs), metrics, and audit findings help track progress, pinpoint areas for improvement, and enhance controls and policies. Security awareness training is conducted regularly to instruct on new policies, processes, and security best practices. Ongoing awareness programs also keep employees updated about new developments and emerging threats.

There are two aspects of compliance: internal and external compliance. Internal supervision conducts audits to ensure that all activities adhere to established governance policies and procedures. Additionally, it is essential to verify legal compliance. Compliance ensures that cybersecurity actions align with established regulations through regular audits and reviews.

External compliance in cybersecurity governance refers to adhering to laws, regulations, standards, and contractual obligations imposed by external organizations (such as governments, industry groups, or partners) to ensure that an organization meets required security and privacy criteria. It helps maintain stakeholder trust, safeguard consumer data, and mitigate legal risks. Organizations often utilize audits, compliance frameworks, and third-party assessments to verify they meet these external requirements.

2.6.4 *Crisis Management: Incident Response and Recovery (IV)*

When a cybersecurity incident occurs, the Incident Response (IR) team must promptly implement response actions to neutralize and contain the attack, strictly following established Incident Response Plan (IRP) policies and procedures. The following sections discuss the various stages of the IP process from planning to recovery.

2.6.4.1 Incident Response Plan

Activating the Incident Response Plan (IRP) at the onset of a cyber threat event must follow the structured incident response plans (i.e., pre-crisis, crisis response, and post-crisis) as mandated by governance. All decisions and actions taken during a breach, including response, containment, disclosure, recovery, or review, must align with established policies. The response must be accurate and timely upon identifying the nature of the cyber incident. Response and recovery should adhere to the accepted processes to ensure a swift recovery from the incident, allowing the business to resume normal operations.

Figure 2.6 outlines the steps of the IRP process. To effectively address cyber risk and its consequences, the company should develop and implement a cybersecurity response strategy within an enterprise risk management framework. The steps include enforcing procedures and policies to prepare for, detect, respond to, and recover from attacks on its networks, data, and systems. Once a potential cyber event is detected and identified, its impact on the business must be assessed. If it poses a critical risk, measures should be taken to contain and eliminate the attack. The three stages of the crisis response process are illustrated in Fig. 2.7.

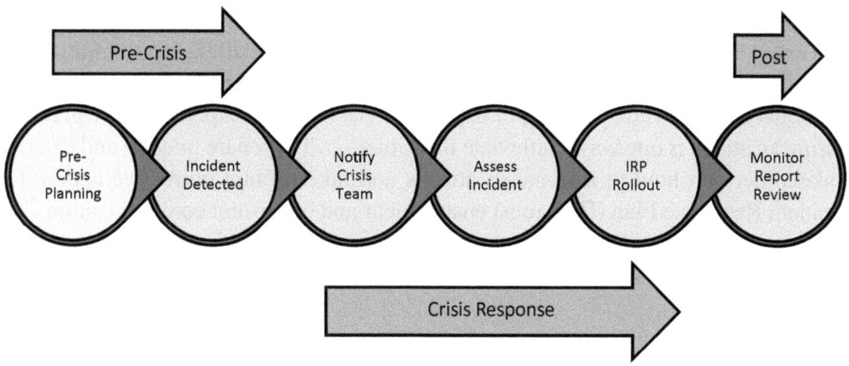

Fig. 2.7 Incident response process

2.6.4.2 Pre-crisis

A corporation's proactive steps to prepare for a catastrophe are known as pre-crisis management. Being prepared means having the skills and information necessary to anticipate, address, and recover from a crisis before it occurs. The Board of Directors and senior management must support and approve the IRP, a component of the enterprise risk management strategy. A budget for the necessary resources to execute the IRP is part of this support. The first step in implementing pre-crisis management is to establish a comprehensive IRP that includes necessary resources, crisis management teams, vigilance and monitoring capabilities, a crisis communication plan, and a recovery roadmap. Implementing a well-thought-out strategy can reduce the organization's losses and minimize downtime, maintain a state of readiness and familiarity with the process, and ensure a coordinated and methodical response during a crisis, thereby minimizing human errors.

Effective disaster preparedness demands a suitable organizational structure, clear policies and processes, and sufficient budgetary allocations for resources. Risk assessment, which involves identifying and evaluating significant risks, hazards, and related vulnerabilities, is the initial step in pre-crisis planning. Organizing resources, including personnel, technology, and equipment, is also essential for the planning phase. For instance, early warning systems that detect these hazards would trigger established crisis plans. As part of the preparation process, crisis response team members undergo training and participate in role-playing and war games based on potential business scenarios to familiarize themselves with the response and recovery systems.

2.6.4.3 Crisis Response

One essential element of a company's cyber risk mitigation plan for crisis response is the Incident Response Plan (IRP). It outlines the procedures for executing incident response and designates the unit responsible for each duty. As cyberattacks cannot be prevented entirely, businesses are increasingly finding it challenging to mitigate the adverse effects of these incidents as the frequency and severity of cyber intrusions rise. Developing an effective response plan that the incident response team can follow during an attack is one way to alleviate this situation. To prepare internal and external stakeholders on how to respond to attacks and take prompt corrective action, the Incident Response Plan (IRP) must ensure clear and consistent communication. The IRP also serves as a defense to minimize the damage to one's reputation and legal liability that a cyberattack can inflict.

2.6.4.4 Post-crisis: Review and Revise

Recovery occurs when an organization resumes normal operations after neutralizing or eradicating a cyberattack. Recovery efforts aim to enhance the organization's preparedness for addressing similar crises by analyzing how the incident or crisis was managed, specifically by identifying and eliminating the root cause of the attack. This approach allows for the implementation of stronger defenses or remedies. Rebuilding trust with suppliers, consumers, employees, and regulators is a key response.

The incident response team and the individuals involved in addressing the incident will review and revise the Incident Response Plan (IRP) during the post-crisis recovery phase, taking into account the lessons learned from the most recent incident. This review must be carried out immediately following the attack. The steps required are analyzing the reasons behind the occurrences and evaluating how well the incident or crisis was managed. Reviewing the cyber threat event and revising the necessary cybersecurity measures to enhance protection. After the incident, a review of the cyber threat event should be conducted to revise and update, as required, the relevant cybersecurity measures that will optimize and enhance the enterprise's cybersecurity posture.

2.7 Governance Frameworks and Regulations

Two common terms in the cybersecurity industry are frameworks and regulations. Cybersecurity governance utilizes established frameworks and regulations to manage cyber threats effectively. The organization's overall strategy for controlling cybersecurity risk incorporates the features of these frameworks and regulations.

Cybersecurity frameworks, or standards, comprise a set of best practices and voluntary recommendations developed by organizations and cybersecurity experts to help businesses strengthen their cybersecurity posture. The ISO 31000, COSO, the National Institute of Standards and Technology Cybersecurity Framework (NIST CSF), the ISO/IEC 27001 standard, and COBIT 5 are essential frameworks relating to cybersecurity governance, which we will specifically refer to as "standards" in this book.

In contrast, cybersecurity regulations are laws enforced by regulatory agencies or government authorities to protect digital information, referred to as "regulations" in the chapters. Cybersecurity laws, which provide legal frameworks designed to safeguard digital systems, networks, and data from cyber threats, unauthorized access, and breaches, are incorporated into these regulations. These regulations outline guidelines for protecting private data, specify the consequences for cybercrimes, and promote best practices for both individuals and businesses. Some examples include the General Data Protection Regulation (GDPR-EU), Network and Information Systems (NIS) Directive (EU), the Payment Card Industry Data Security Standard (PCI DSS, USA), Privacy Act 1988 (Australia), China's Cybersecurity Law (CSL), Singapore's Personal Data Protection Act (PDPA), SOX 2022, and the Health Insurance Portability and Accountability Act (HIPAA). These regulations vary by nation and industry, requiring businesses to adhere to specific cybersecurity best practices and standards to protect user privacy and hold companies accountable for data breaches. Companies operating internationally must navigate a diverse array of laws to avoid legal complications. Those who fail to comply with these regulations may face penalties, fines, or legal action.

As cyber risks are diverse, sector needs vary, and regulatory requirements vary by country, cybersecurity governance encompasses a wide range of standards, structures, and legislation. Therefore, no single framework can address all threats, sectors, and legal requirements; numerous cybersecurity governance standards exist. The widely used international standards include ISO/IEC 27001 (Information Security Management System (ISMS) standard), ISO/IEC 27002 (guidelines for cybersecurity controls), the NIST Cybersecurity Framework (CSF), and COBIT (a governance framework for enterprise IT management, developed by ISACA). The industry-specific regulations we frequently refer to in this book are HIPAA (the Health Insurance Portability and Accountability Act, which governs healthcare in the USA) and GDPR (the General Data Protection Regulation, a European Union data privacy law). In addition, there are regional and national regulations, such as the Cybersecurity Law of China, which mandates data localization and security controls, and Australia's Privacy Act 1988, which governs data privacy. To create a strong security posture, organizations typically adopt a multi-layered strategy, integrating regional legislation (such as the Privacy Act 1988 and the GDPR), industry-specific rules (like HIPAA and PCI DSS), and global standards (like NIST and ISO 27001). We will only reference and discuss the most widely used standards, guidelines, and regulations in this book because there are many more.

2.7.1 Cybersecurity Frameworks or Standards

Cybersecurity standards can be either mandatory or discretionary, encompassing procedures, actions, and configurations designed to achieve governance objectives. These frameworks provide a flexible approach to cybersecurity, allowing businesses to tailor their security protocols to meet their unique needs. Organizations can choose the cybersecurity framework that best aligns with their unique requirements and risk profiles. Cybersecurity standards are intended to be both prescriptive and a guide for companies when designing their processes. They serve as tools for establishing Minimum Security Requirements (MSR), ensuring that processes and practices are developed and maintained with adequate cybersecurity safeguards. In general, frameworks help organizations build effective cybersecurity programs by offering recommendations, best practices, and guidance.

Several standards, regulations, models, and best practices can support or shape the development of a cybersecurity governance plan. The leading frameworks and regulatory standards for cybersecurity controls include ISO 27001, NIST CSF, SOC 2, HIPAA, PCI DSS, and SOX 2002. The firm can integrate these cybersecurity frameworks into its broader governance framework to effectively mitigate cyber risk. Transforming governance frameworks into actionable controls enables businesses to manage incidents proactively, handle risks effectively, and remain audit-ready.

2.7.1.1 NIST CSF

Organizations can utilize the NIST Cybersecurity Framework (NIST CSF), developed by the US National Institute of Standards and Technology (NIST), as part of their established, systematic processes for detecting, assessing, and managing cybersecurity risks. Thus, NIST CSF is relevant throughout the various phases of the cybersecurity governance value chain lifecycle, including planning, design, building or purchasing, implementation, and operation.

NIST is a comprehensive security framework that is widely used and can be tailored to meet the needs of any organization or industry. NIST aligns cybersecurity operations with enterprise risk management processes and business requirements. NIST CSF's cybersecurity framework consists of five categories: Identify, Protect, Detect, Respond, and Recover. These five functions serve as broad categories encompassing other, more complex components. NIST CSF also includes four implementation tiers to help organizations assess their cybersecurity maturity and enhance their cybersecurity practices. However, organizations should recognize that plans may change. Developing a cybersecurity governance strategy requires an understanding of these five NIST-defined functions. A robust governance framework must address essential cybersecurity tasks that are fundamental to all organizations while tackling unique challenges.

NIST CSF version 2 (2024) places a strong emphasis on supply chain risk management for cybersecurity. This risk management program includes recommendations for managing vendors and integrating them properly into a network, without putting the company at unnecessary risk.

2.7.1.2 ISO/IEC 27001 (2022)

The International Organization for Standardization (ISO) developed the ISO 27000 standards (ISO 27001; ISO 27002; etc.), which are a set of best practices designed to enhance business information security. Organizations can integrate these standards into their governance strategies to optimize their Information Security Management System (ISMS). The ISO/IEC 27001 standard is a widely adopted ISMS that systematically manages cybersecurity risks. This series helps businesses navigate the risks associated with cyberattacks and data security threats. Since the ISO 27000 series standards are risk-aligned, companies are encouraged to assess the security risks to their data before implementing various management strategies, prioritizing the most significant risks first.

There are 46 standards in the series, including ISO 27000. It serves as a glossary of terms and concepts while introducing the family. In addition to supporting the broad ideas outlined in ISO 27001, the ISO 27000 series of standards can provide guidance on information security risk management. It aims to ensure that information security is effectively implemented through a risk management approach.

As a leading international standard for Information Security Management Systems (ISMS), ISO 27001 provides a methodology for implementing cybersecurity within an organization. It provides a comprehensive framework for managing cybersecurity threats, protecting sensitive information, and ensuring regulatory compliance. ISO 27001 is the international standard for Information Security Management Systems (ISMS) and provides guidelines for the risk management process. These should be consulted when deciding on and selecting security solutions to address a company's specific threats. Cybersecurity governance is essential for the following reasons:

- It establishes a risk-based approach to security that encourages proactive and systematic risk management to identify, assess, mitigate, monitor, and respond to cybersecurity risks. This approach aligns with the enterprise risk management framework.
- It fosters executive accountability and governance through top-down leadership involvement in security decisions, with explicit policies and roles for outlining governance structures.
- It fosters and promotes the ongoing development and enhancement of cybersecurity measures through the "Plan-Do-Check-Act" (PDCA) cycle.
- Advocating for a comprehensive and holistic protection strategy that addresses individuals, procedures, and technology enhances the organization's security posture.
- Annex A Controls propose 114 security controls across 14 areas, including incident response management and access control.
- It promotes third-party and supply chain security by ensuring that suppliers fulfill security requirements, such as providing contractual assurance for ISO 27001 certification in partnerships.
- It reinforces compliance with legal and regulatory requirements that support, such as GDPR and HIPAA, by mandating data protection controls. This reduces the risks of non-compliance and helps avoid fines and penalties.

2.7.1.3 COBIT Framework

The Control Objectives for Information and Related Technology (COBIT) is a framework developed by the Information Systems Audit and Control Association (ISACA) for IT governance and management. It helps businesses address concerns related to risk management, regulatory compliance, and aligning their IT strategy with organizational objectives. As a general and comprehensive framework, COBIT 5 can be applied to companies of all sizes, including government, non-profit, and for-profit enterprises. It serves as a business framework for enterprise IT governance and management, employing a common language to communicate goals, objectives, and anticipated results to all stakeholders involved. It is based on and integrates industry standards and best practices in the following areas: risk management is conducted throughout the organization; IT is strategically aligned with business objectives; service delivery and project development are prioritized; and risk control performance is regularly reviewed and measured.

The five guiding principles of COBIT 5 are designed to ensure efficient administration and governance, including meeting stakeholder needs, covering the organization from end to end, implementing a single integrated framework, adopting a holistic approach, and separating governance from management. These principles form the foundation of COBIT. The framework offers a set of methods for managing IT risks within an organization to ensure optimal operation. To clarify roles and responsibilities, COBIT 5 distinguishes between governance, which involves decision-making and accountability, and management, which encompasses execution and operational activities.

2.7.1.4 COSO ERM Framework

The COSO ERM cube is a widely used risk management framework for Enterprise Risk Management (ERM), developed by the Committee of Sponsoring Organizations of the Treadway Commission. It emphasizes that ERM is an ongoing process that applies risk management techniques within a strategic framework across the organization. To provide a reasonable level of confidence in achieving business objectives, it aims to incorporate risk mitigation activities, from identifying potential risks to monitoring and managing them within their risk tolerance. This framework presents a systematic and organized method for integrating cybersecurity threats into enterprise risk management.

2.7.2 Laws and Regulations

Firms must comply with regulations that can vary depending on the specific political regime (e.g., sovereign versus multistakeholder) or focus on the digital landscape, as well as the unique conditions and compliance requirements of individual markets or industries. Some regulations apply to all sectors, while industry-specific cybersecurity laws are designed to address the unique threats and requirements of each sector. Prescriptive, enforceable, and mandatory compliance is crucial for regulatory requirements.

> As the healthcare industry continues to embrace digitization, worries about the vulnerability of cloud-based electronic health records (EHR) to cyberattacks have only intensified.

Businesses subject to cybersecurity regulations are legally required to implement specific cybersecurity measures; failing to do so may result in penalties. By conducting audits, inspections, and imposing fines, regulatory agencies hold the authority to ensure compliance with relevant cybersecurity laws and regulations. Typically, regulations outline specific rules, specifications, and security measures that businesses must adhere to.

2.7.2.1 General Data Protection Regulation—European Union

The GDPR regulates privacy and data protection within the European Union and the European Economic Area (EEA). It aims to harmonize European data protection regulations and enhance individuals' control over their personal data. Essential guidelines include data minimization, purpose limitation, and the requirement for express consent before processing data. Violations of the GDPR can lead to substantial fines for organizations.

2.7.2.2 Health Insurance Portability and Accountability Act of 1996 (HIPAA)

The HIPAA law in the USA was established to protect patient health information and ensure privacy in the medical field. It aims to provide guidelines for the secure storage, privacy, and electronic exchange of health information. Violations of HIPAA regulations can result in civil or criminal penalties. It distinguishes between the Security Rule, which outlines measures to guarantee the confidentiality, integrity, and availability of electronically protected health information, and the Privacy Rule, which sets national standards to safeguard specific health information.

2.7.2.3 China's Cybersecurity Law (CSL)

Critical infrastructure operators must store data within China due to strict data localization regulations enforced by China's Cybersecurity Law (CSL). This requirement includes network operators, providers of critical information infrastructure (CII), and companies that process data categorized under this law. China's CSL emphasizes data sovereignty, national security, and governmental authority over the Internet. While it bolsters defenses against cyberattacks, international businesses, in particular, face rigorous compliance obligations. To avoid fines, companies operating in China must ensure data localization, conduct security audits, and coordinate with government authorities.

2.7.2.4 Personal Data Protection Act (PDPA)—Singapore

Singapore's PDPA, enacted in 2012 and updated several times, including a significant revision in 2020, regulates how businesses collect, use, and disclose personal information. It ensures ethical data handling while fostering digital innovation by striking a balance between business needs and individual privacy rights. Organizations must implement strong governance, security measures, and breach response plans to comply.

2.7.2.5 Privacy Act 1988—Australia

The Privacy Act of 1988 is Australia's primary data protection law, governing how private-sector organizations, federal agencies, and certain small enterprises manage personal information. It has undergone significant evolution, with notable updates, including the introduction of the Notifiable Data Breaches (NDB) Scheme in 2017.

In conclusion, when comparing the GDPR, PDPA, and CSL, the GDPR is stricter in protecting individual rights, has a global reach, and imposes heavy fines. The PDPA is a flexible regime that emphasizes and encourages business practicality. The CSL is state centric due to China's adoption of the digital sovereign governance model, which prioritizes data control and national security over privacy.

2.7.3 Other Standards and Regulations

Other selected standards and regulations relevant to cybersecurity governance are presented in Table 2.2.

Table 2.2 Selected standards and regulations

Australian Energy Sector Cyber Security Framework (AESCSF)	AESCSF is a set of cybersecurity standards designed to help owners and operators of energy infrastructure in Australia assess, evaluate, prioritize, and enhance their cybersecurity posture
Systems and Organisation Control 2 (SOC 2)	The American Institute of Certified Public Accountants (AICPA) created the framework to assist service organizations in managing client data with confidentiality, availability, processing integrity, security, and privacy
Payment Card Industry Data Security Standard (PCI DSS)	The PCI DSS was created to safeguard cardholder data and ensure that credit and debit card information is processed, stored, and transmitted securely. It gives banks, service providers, and retailers a common framework for managing credit card transactions
Sarbanes–Oxley Act 2002 (SOX)	SOX cybersecurity compliance entails implementing strong IT controls to protect financial data and guarantee the accuracy of financial reporting

2.8 National Cybersecurity Preparedness

As cybercrime becomes increasingly rampant, complex, and challenging, enterprise initiatives alone may not suffice to ward off cyber threats due to their systemic nature. Therefore, cybersecurity has evolved into a national security issue for the government. Every country must design and implement a comprehensive cybersecurity framework or plan to ensure a safe, secure, and resilient digital environment, thereby maintaining smooth operations. Cybersecurity is a shared national responsibility that requires concerted efforts from all stakeholders in preparedness, response, and recovery from incidents, including the business community, the public sector, and society as a whole.

> An example of shared national responsibility is the revised National Cybersecurity Strategy released by the White House in 2023, which is an attempt by the federal government to help keep US citizens, businesses, and institutions safe from innovative and dangerous cyber threats.

2.8.1 *National Cybersecurity Regimes*

The National Cybersecurity Strategy (NCS) framework is crucial for the USA' cybersecurity initiative.[4] Section 2.8.1 mentioned two fundamentally different approaches by authorities to regulating cybersecurity: the sovereign approach and the multistakeholder approach. Countries associated with the multistakeholder approach are those in the West, led by the USA, while China and Russia advocate for the sovereign model. There are generally no countries at the extremes of the multistakeholder or sovereign continuum, but somewhere in between.

> China is proactively tackling cyberspace governance issues and is essential in bridging the technological divide between nations. Scholars from China, South Korea, the UK, and Australia recently convened in Beijing to deliberate on how China's proposal to establish a cyberspace community of shared future has influenced global cyberspace governance. During the seminar, David Gosset, a French academic and the founder of the China-Europe-America Global Initiative, stated that China promotes collaboration and offers fresh ideas for creating a cyberspace community with a common destiny (Global Times, 2024).

---

[4] National Cybersecurity Strategy, March 2023, The White House. file:///E:/1%20KBO%20Folder/Technology,%20Cyersecurity%20&%20Finance/Articles/US-China/US%20National-Cybersecurity-Strategy-2023.pdf. (Downloaded 20/9/2024).

2.8.2 *Sovereign Versus Multistakeholder*

Deep contrasts in ideals, control systems, and approaches to Internet and cybersecurity policy are reflected in the main concerns between sovereign and multistakeholder cybersecurity governance models. The sovereign model of Internet governance posits that, since cyberspace is an extension of national territory, cyber sovereignty exists, and each state should establish its regulations. In contrast, the multistakeholder approach views the Internet as a "global commons" that ought to be shared and managed through distributed collaboration.

> Because of their profoundly different political ideologies and systems of government, as well as their lack of mutual trust, China and the USA are at opposite ends of the sovereign-multi-stakeholder spectrum. Nations are more likely to maintain strategic stability in cyberspace with open communication and deeper focus on areas of mutual interest (Rosenbach & Chong, 2019).

While the multistakeholder model compromises security, openness, and innovation, the sovereign model prioritizes national security, frequently resulting in tighter censorship and control over digital infrastructure.

2.9 Conclusion

Governance can effectively manage enterprise cyber risk by providing an appropriate framework for managing and mitigating such risks while enhancing a company's business strategy and values. Businesses must understand the specific dangers associated with their cyber environments to choose the most effective cybersecurity governance frameworks, leverage their advantages, and optimize performance. Therefore, cybersecurity framework standards (e.g., NIST CSF, ISO 27001) and regulations (e.g., GDPR, PCI DSS, CSL) offer systematic approaches to addressing cyber threats. They are essential for governance and contribute to business success when cybersecurity governance is treated as a strategic goal, enabling the achievement of long-term resilience and a competitive advantage. In the next chapter, we will discuss how to integrate these cybersecurity standards and regulations into the enterprise risk management framework, developing a holistic approach that can further enhance cyber risk governance.

References

Allen, F., & Gale, D. (2002). *A comparative theory of corporate governance.* https://www.rieti.go.jp/en/events/03010801/pdf/Allen.pdf

Alston, E., Alston, L., & Meuller, B. (2021, July). Leadership within organisational hierarchies. *SSRN Electronic Journal*, July 2021.

Ayuso, S., Rodríguez, M. A., García-Castro, R., & Ariño, M. A. (2014). Maximizing stakeholders' interests: An empirical analysis of the stakeholder approach to corporate governance. *Business & Society, 53*(3), 414–439. https://doi.org/10.1177/0007650311433122

Coase, R. (1937). The nature of the firm. *Economica, 4*, 386–405.

Crisanto, J., Pelegrini, J., & Prenio, J. (2023). *Banks' cyber security—A second generation of regulatory approaches. FSI Insights on policy implementation No 50.* Bank for International Settlement. https://www.bis.org/fsi/publ/insights50.pdf

Eggenschwiler, J. (2018). A typology of cybersecurity governance models. *St Antony's International Review, 13*(2), 64–78.

Eisenhardt, K. (1989). Agency theory: An assessment and review. *Academy of Management Review, 14*, 57–74.

Gilbert, C., & Gilbert, M. A. (2024). Organizational and leadership aspects of cybersecurity governance. *International Journal of Research Publication and Reviews, 5*(12), 1174–1191.

Global Times. (2024). China plays a greater role in global cyberspace governance, narrowing tech gap among countries: Scholars. China plays a more significant role in global cyberspace governance, narrowing tech gap among countries: scholars—Global Times. Accessed 8/9/2024.

Harris, A., Leithwood, K., Day, C., Sammons, P., & Hopkins, D. (2007). Distributed leadership and organisational change: Reviewing the evidence. *Journal of Educational Change, 8*(4), 337–347.

Hillson, D. (1997). Towards a risk maturity model. *International Journal of Project and Business Risk Management, 1*(Spring), 35–45.

Hofstede, G. (1980). *Culture's consequences: International differences in work-related values.* Sage.

Hofstede, G., Hofstede, G. J., & Minkov, M. (2010). *Cultures and organizations: Software of the mind* (3rd ed.). McGraw-Hill.

ISO/IEC 27001. (2022). *Information security, cybersecurity and privacy protection: Information security management systems—Requirements.* https://www.iso.org/standard/27001

Kshetri, N. (2021). *Cybersecurity management: An organizational and strategic approach.* University of Toronto Press.

McKinsey. (2019). *The risk-based approach to cybersecurity.*

Mihm, J., Loch, C., Wilkinson, D., & Huberman, B. (2010). Hierarchical structure and search in complex organizations. *Management Science, 56*(5), 831–848. https://www.researchgate.net/publication/220534200_Hierarchical_Structure_and_Search_in_Complex_Organizations

Onumo, A., Cullen, A., & Awan, I. (2017). *Empirical study of cultural dimensions and cybersecurity development.* Presented at: FiCloud 2017: The 5th International Conference on Future Internet of Things and Cloud. 21–23 August 2017, Prague, Czech Republic.

Ponemon Institute. (2025). *Ponemon Cost of Insider Threat Report.* https://www.linkedin.com/pulse/insider-risk-costing-174m-year-heres-good-news-ruud-grotens-cfcs-qc2ie

Rivkin, J., & Siggelkow, N. (2003). Balancing search and stability: Interdependencies among elements of organizational design. *Management Science, 49*(3), 290–311.

Rosenbach, E., & Chong, S. (2019). *Governing the cyberspace: State control versus the multi-stakeholder model.* Paper-Belfer Center for Science and International Affairs. Harvard Kennedy School.

Senge, P. (2006). *The fifth discipline.* Doubleday, Random House, Inc. The Crown Publishing Group.

Shleifer, A., & Vishny, R. (1997). A survey of corporate governance. *Journal of Finance, 52*(2), 737–783.

Siggelkow, N., & Rivkin, J. (2005). Speed and search: Designing organizations for turbulence and complexity. *Organization Science, 16*(2), 101–122.

Simon, H. (1962). The architecture of complexity. *Proceedings of the American Philosophical Society, 106*, 467–482.

Simon, H.A. (1982). *Models of Bounded Rationality: Empirically Grounded Economic Reason.* Vol. 3, MIT Press, Cambridge.

Slapnicar, S., Axelsen, M., Bongiovanni, I., & Stockdale, D. (2023). A pathway model to five lines of accountability in cybersecurity governance. *International Journal of Accounting Information Systems*, 51. https://www.sciencedirect.com/science/article/pii/S1467089523000349

Spillane, J. (2005). Distributed leadership. *The Educational Forum, 69*(2), 143–150.

Starbuck, W. (2014). Why corporate governance deserves serious and creative thought. *Academy of Management Perspectives, 28*, 15–21.

Taylor, F. (1911). *The principles of scientific management*. Harper and Brothers.

Tirole, J. (2001). Corporate governance. *Econometrica, 69*(1), 1–35. http://www.jstor.org/stable/2692184

Valkenburg, B., & Bongiovanni, I. (2024). Unravelling the three lines model in cybersecurity: a systematic literature review. *Computers & Security*, 139, 103708.

WEF (World Economic Forum). (2025). *The global risks report 2025 20th edition: Insight report*. Switzerland. https://www.weforum.org/publications/global-risks-report-2025/in-full/global-risks-2025-a-world-of-growing-divisions-c943fe3ba0/

Chapter 3
Enterprise Risk Management and Cybersecurity Governance

Abstract This chapter covers the design and implementation of the different forms and processes of cyber risk governance within the Enterprise Risk Management (ERM) framework. We discuss the cruciality of ERM as the foundation for a holistic and integrated risk control mechanism for enterprise cybersecurity governance. We also discuss the need for and implications of governance as a policy tool within the ERM context in strategic cybersecurity planning, risk assessments, security controls, incident response, business continuity, and compliance with legislation and standards. The three basic categories of cybersecurity risks are distinguished, i.e., national security, industrial espionage, and cybercrime. By separating the connotations of cybersecurity and analyzing the various actors and the related governance frameworks, we help create a better understanding of cybersecurity. Another aspect investigated is the difference between strategic and tactical cyber risk management as they pertain to two hierarchical levels of authority, oversight and responsibilities. This dissected approach allows the organization to appreciate the cyber threats it faces and be able to design the appropriate cybersecurity governance measures within the ERM architecture, policies, and procedures to tackle them. A holistic and integrated governance approach is adopted to plan, design, and incorporate cyber risk control measures into the ERM framework for execution from a strategic and tactical perspective.

3.1 Introduction

Enterprise risk management (ERM), also referred to as strategic risk management, enterprise-wide risk management, integrated risk management, holistic risk management, and corporate risk management, is identified in the literature as a comprehensive risk control practice (D'Arcy, 2001; Hoyt & Liebenberg, 2011; Kleffner et al., 2003; Liebenberg & Hoyt, 2003). A thorough understanding of the functions and objectives of enterprise risk management provides valuable insights into effective cybersecurity management. It enables the creation of effective frameworks for risk control measures that can enhance organizational performance (Ho

K. B. Oh et al., *Cybersecurity Governance*,
https://doi.org/10.1007/978-981-95-3865-2_3

et al., 2010). When addressing cybersecurity governance, organizations should adopt an enterprise-wide perspective, as this approach is suitable since cybersecurity affects the entire organization and is not merely a technological or operational issue (ISO/IEC 27001). President Obama, in his speech "On Securing our Nation's Infrastructure" on cybersecurity, said:

> It is not enough for the information technology workforce to understand the importance of cybersecurity; leaders at all levels of government and industry need to be able to make business and investment decisions based on knowledge of risks and potential impacts. (The White House on May 29, 2009).

Enterprise Risk Management (ERM) and corporate governance are intertwined, forming the nexus for effective cybersecurity management. ERM is essential to cybersecurity governance as it provides a top-level, holistic, and integrated platform for protecting the enterprise from cyber risk exposure, thereby achieving long-term business goals (Raghavan et al., 2018; Stine et al., 2020). Therefore, in this book, we propose conducting cyber risk management through a robust system of cybersecurity governance with clearly defined roles and responsibilities within the ERM framework. This framework comprises several documented, agreed-upon, and understood policies, procedures, and practices that govern the management and protection of the firm's information assets. Cybersecurity governance, as a component of Enterprise Risk Management (ERM), provides the structure and framework for codifying policies, systems, and practices that enable enterprises to conduct practical cyber risk management activities.

Since contemporary technology is deeply embedded in all aspects of business operations—from the boardroom to the manufacturing floor and across the entire supply chain—many businesses, regardless of size, consider cybersecurity a critical management priority for protecting against organizational damage. Business interruptions caused by network or system downtime, data loss, intellectual property theft, and reputational harm represent the primary risks associated with corporate cyber risk exposure. This risk fluctuates based on an organization's industry, size, structure, risk profile, posture, and maturity. According to Collier et al. (2013), companies aiming to remain competitive should adopt a risk-based systems approach that integrates the physical, information, cognitive, and social domains to understand better and manage cybersecurity. Identifying and understanding the qualitative differences in organizations' risks is the first step in developing an effective risk management system (Kaplan & Mikes, 2012). Businesses that grasp risk are better prepared to handle unavoidable uncertainty because they can strategically plan for the repercussions of unfavorable events (Jorion & Khoury, 1996).

Business risks can be classified as either alpha, stemming from management's expertise (i.e., unsystematic risk), or beta, arising from market volatility (i.e., systematic risk). Risks related to the firm's operations—such as governance, processes and procedures, supply chain, human factors, frauds, physical factors, systems, and technology—are considered alpha or firm-specific risks. Beta risks originate from events outside the corporate environment or within political and economic contexts. Factors such as macroeconomic conditions, natural disasters, political issues, regulatory changes, social dynamics, legal matters, international complications, competition, terrorism, and criminal activity all fall under the category of beta risks.

> Wide area networks (WANs) can be seen as a source of systematic risk (beta). In contrast, local area networks (LANs) represent the realm of unsystematic risk (alpha) when applying these risk principles broadly to cybersecurity. Additionally, more severe failures, including the collapse of critical infrastructure, may result from the failure of a single component within a digital system or network. For example, an entire nation would face systematic danger if a successful attack targeted the Internet's essential infrastructure, such as the Border Gateway Protocol, which connects and facilitates the data routing of numerous independent systems (Oh & Ho, 2022).

However, cyber risks are not easily categorized as alpha or beta risks because both internal (alpha) and external (beta) technological support infrastructures face varying levels of vulnerability to cyberattacks, which are part of the company's risk environment. For example, a primary source of cyber risk from third parties, including suppliers and service providers, stems from supply chain risk (Starr et al., 2003), which comprises both internal and external components.

3.2 The ERM Framework

ERM is a continuous process that requires the attention of the Board of Directors and senior management (B&SM) to ensure it remains relevant, dynamic, and practical. Its integration into ongoing management initiatives highlights its holistic attributes and importance for sustaining an organization's business. The following ERM framework standards outline the framework's scale and scope.

NIST 8286[1] Series guides risk practitioners in thoroughly incorporating cybersecurity risk management activities into the company's comprehensive risk processes. It defines the word enterprise as covering "all aspects of that organization, spanning the entire breadth and depth of that organization chart." It emphasizes that "ERM" exists at the top level of the organizational hierarchy and spans risk considerations such as mission, financial, reputation, and technical risks.

The ISO 31000 series relevant to ERM includes two supporting documents: the "ISO 31000:2018 Risk Management – Guidelines," which defines a risk management vocabulary, and "IEC 31010:2019 Risk Management — Risk Assessment Techniques," which offers recommendations for the use and selection of methodological

[1] NIST IR 8286 Integrating Cybersecurity and Enterprise Risk Management (ERM) and NIST Special Publication NIST SP 1303 IPD (Initial Public Draft). https://doi.org/10.6028/NIST.SP.1303.ipd.

risk assessment approaches. According to ISO 31000:2018, Risk Management – Guidelines, the ERM framework consists of three parts: risk management principles, a risk management framework, and a risk management procedure, applicable to all types of organizations for managing enterprise risk. ISO 31000 defines the risk management framework as "a set of components that provide the foundations and organizational arrangements for integrating, designing, implementing, evaluating, and improving risk management throughout the organization," and the risk management process as "coordinated activities to direct and control an organization concerning risk." Our approach to Enterprise Risk Management (ERM) for cybersecurity governance is based on the premise of an enterprise-wide strategy to plan, identify, assess, and mitigate the most significant digital risk exposures within an organization.

The COSO (Committee of Sponsoring Organizations of the Treadway Commission) enterprise risk management framework is highly relevant to cybersecurity governance because it provides a structured approach for identifying, assessing, and managing cyber risks as part of an organization's broader risk landscape. COSO ERM ensures that cybersecurity is not merely an IT issue but is regarded as an enterprise-wide risk. The "Internal Control—Integrated Framework" (ICIF) is a central component of the COSO framework, which helps enhance internal controls, governance, and risk management. Although not specifically tailored to cybersecurity, COSO is very relevant to cybersecurity governance for several reasons. The COSO framework for ERM consists of eight key elements: internal environment, goal-setting, event identification, risk assessment, risk response, control activities, information and communication, and monitoring, all of which align with cybersecurity risk management. Even though it is not a dedicated cybersecurity framework, COSO provides a foundation for risk management and governance that enhances cybersecurity oversight. Organizations often combine COSO with NIST or ISO frameworks to ensure robust cyber risk management and compliance.

3.2.1 Enterprise Risks

The ability of a company to achieve its strategic goals, ensure financial stability, maintain operational effectiveness, uphold compliance, and protect its reputation can all be negatively impacted by enterprise risks, which are potential threats or uncertainties. These risks can affect the entire organization, rather than just specific projects or divisions, and can arise from both internal (alpha) and external (beta) factors. The following are some of the enterprise risks addressed by enterprise risk management:

- Strategic risk refers to risks that affect an organization's long-term objectives. These risks encompass market shifts, competition, and changes in the regulatory landscape.

- Operational risk: This risk encompasses hazards such as value chain disruptions, human errors, and system failures stemming from internal and external processes, personnel, and systems.
- Financial Risk: Risks related to monetary loss, including credit, market, liquidity, and cyber risks.
- Compliance risk refers to the risks associated with violating cybersecurity laws, regulations, or corporate policies.
- Reputational Risk: Threats that can harm an organization's reputation include negative publicity resulting from cyberattacks or backlash on social media, which may lead to a loss of revenue or market value.
- Cybersecurity Risk: Threats associated with networks and business systems, data breaches, cyber threats, and various vulnerabilities in information technology.
- Supply Chain Risk: Risks that affect the supply chain, including interruptions or supplier failures.
- Risks related to the destruction or loss of tangible or digital assets, including real estate, computer equipment, and machinery, are known as physical asset risks.
- Environmental Risk: Hazards posed by environmental factors, including climate change and natural disasters.

It is essential to note that cybersecurity in today's digital environment permeates or influences, in some way, all the above risks except the environmental risk. As modern industries increasingly depend on digital systems, cloud computing, IoT, and AI, cybersecurity becomes crucial. A single breach can result in significant financial losses, business interruptions, damage to one's reputation, legal repercussions, and even threats to human safety.

3.2.2 Developing the ERM Framework

The essentials for developing an ERM governance framework include the following attributes and processes presented sequentially. Engaging the right individuals at the board level is crucial for creating a robust governance model. Any Board of Directors will struggle to provide effective corporate governance if its directors lack the necessary skills and qualities. Once the appropriate individuals are on board, there must be consensus on the duties and responsibilities of the BoD, as well as what should be assigned to management. After reaching an agreement, the roles, duties, and delegations should be documented as policies, possibly as part of a more comprehensive board charter.

The Board of Directors is responsible for determining the governance structure, with the primary focus of BoD meetings being the monitoring and evaluation of organizational effectiveness. A chief executive officer (CEO) must be appointed to oversee the organization's operations. The chief executive needs to understand their authorities and the BoD's expectations regarding objectives. The BoD should receive regular performance feedback on the chief executive based on objective criteria.

The CEO is primarily responsible for providing leadership to achieve cybersecurity governance outcomes. A cybersecurity strategy plan is required to outline the goals clearly. Effective cybersecurity governance plans should explicitly state the ideals, expectations, and objectives, serving as the foundation for the successful formulation, implementation, monitoring, assessment, and evaluation of performance at various organizational levels. The CEO, CISO, and other cybersecurity risk representatives are charged with drafting the policies and procedures for the cybersecurity plan.

3.3 ERM and Cybersecurity

The concept of cybersecurity governance stems from "corporate governance." It is a "toolkit" (the Chartered Governance Institute) that comprises policies, rules, and regulations designed to help organizations effectively evaluate and manage cyber risks. It offers a structured approach that enhances the decision-making process through codified policies, rules, and procedures, guiding businesses in mitigating cyber threats.

Cybersecurity governance refers to an entity's policies and controls for managing cybersecurity risks that arise from threats and vulnerabilities associated with the use of cyberspace (AICPA, 2017). It has clear implications for both cybersecurity risk management and enterprise risk management (Bender et al., 2021; Cole & Wood, 2017; Frunza & Gragan, 2018). By integrating cybersecurity into their Enterprise Risk Management (ERM) framework, organizations can more effectively manage cyber risks and protect their assets and reputations (Kim et al., 2019; Mee & Placks, 2016; Nelson & Che, 2020; Radianti & Lubbe, 2018). A robust and integrated cybersecurity framework requires proper regulation to align cybersecurity measures with business objectives and activities. The concept of cybersecurity governance provides a necessary link (Fig. 3.1).

Cybersecurity governance involves identifying potential gaps and threats that an organization may face. Assessing these gaps and threats requires aligning and prioritizing them based on their criticality and impact on business objectives, thus developing appropriate strategies to mitigate and manage them. Here are some steps an organization can take to integrate cybersecurity governance into its Enterprise Risk Management (ERM) framework, collectively referred to as the "Enterprise Cybersecurity Governance Framework" (E-CyG).

3.3.1 Enterprise Corporate Governance

The ERM concept is closely linked to cybersecurity corporate governance through improved information flow between the Board of Directors and various company entities. For example, the BoD and senior management communicate and discuss

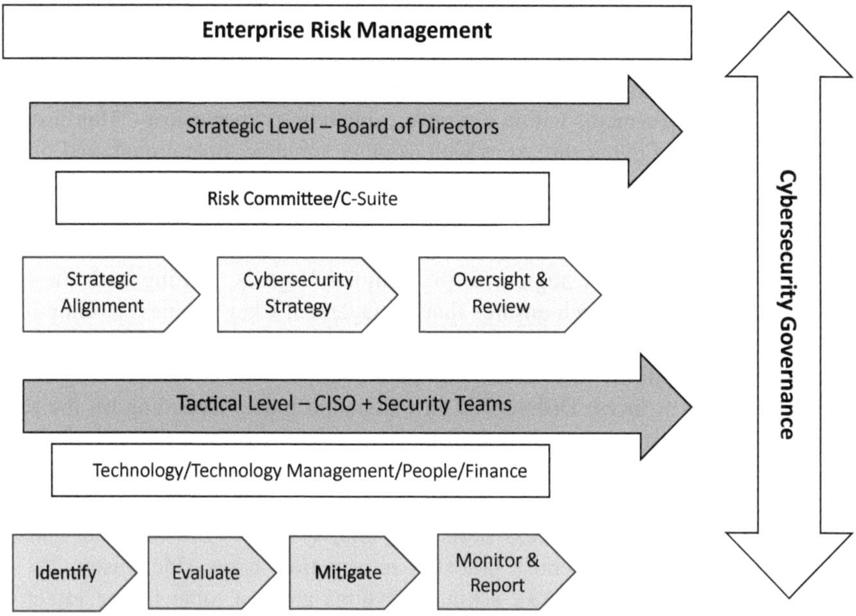

Fig. 3.1 Integrated ERM cybersecurity governance matrix

strategy and associated risks. Similarly, the same occurs between senior management and the business units. Therefore, enhancing corporate governance requires the sharing and communication of risk information to all stakeholders within the organization's hierarchy. We refer to the ERM-embedded cybersecurity governance process as the Enterprise Cybersecurity Governance Framework (E-CyG).

3.3.2 *E-CyG Function*

The broader ERM aims to take a holistic approach to understanding risks, ensuring effective organizational management. Its primary objectives include implementing and maintaining risk control policies and procedures that align with the organization's business objectives and risk tolerance. The E-CyG process outlines strategies and actions that reduce risk exposure to the acceptable levels the company is willing to take on and assume. It outlines the protocols for identification, assessment, mitigation, monitoring, detection, and reporting, as well as incident response policies and procedures related to cybersecurity governance.

3.3.2.1 Risk Identification

ERM frameworks provide an integrated and comprehensive approach to identifying risks across all departments within a company, including cybersecurity. This ensures the identification of cyber threats as well as other strategic, operational, and financial risks. This step aims to identify potential threats to vulnerable assets, such as networks, business systems, and data, thereby gaining an understanding of the weaknesses these threats could exploit.

The risk strategy must align with the company's goals, starting with the risk identification process, which ensures that management's key business assumptions are understood to capture as many cyber risk variables as possible. Understanding a company's operations, objectives, and threat contexts is essential for recognizing the cyber threats it faces. Different assumptions are made depending on the type of business. For instance, a utility firm may be concerned about power outages, a retail business about its customer-facing websites, and a healthcare organization may worry about electronic health record (EHR) outages.

The risk identification process starts with an overview of the company and its business value chain to identify essential information assets (McKinsey, 2017). According to Gregersen (2018), asking questions about a topic is one effective strategy for generating ideas during brainstorming sessions. Risk identification can be carried out as a company's initial risk assessment or as a continuous assessment function to pinpoint new or emerging risks resulting from changes in the operational environment (Robin et al., 2002).

Risk identification aims to recognize all relevant threats that may affect the business. By identifying and classifying as many of the company's digital risk factors as possible, risk identification offers a visual representation and insight into the main sources of uncertainty.

3.3.2.2 Risk Assessment

An organization's networks, business systems, and data are all vulnerable to cyberattacks and should be regularly assessed for security. After identifying cyber threats, the Board of Directors and senior management must assess these cybersecurity threats to determine their criticality based on their probability and potential impact on the company, including the likelihood of various outcomes or losses. Evaluating the possible effects of a threat exploiting a vulnerability on the organization—such as financial loss, damage to its reputation, and operational disruption—is crucial in determining the likelihood of the threat's success. This evaluation also allows for ranking dangers according to their probability and severity.

This evaluation is crucial to the comprehensive ERM process, enabling the prioritization of risks and effective allocation of resources. Risk quantification allows management to prioritize and manage cybersecurity risk mitigation options, enabling the company to control identified risks through its risk strategy and support its business objectives.

3.3.2.3 Risk Mitigation

Cybersecurity governance utilizes controls recommended by established frameworks to minimize recognized risks and incorporates them into its mitigation strategy. The implementation of controls and procedures designed to reduce the likelihood or impact of risks is referred to as risk mitigation. Prioritizing high-risk areas ensures efficient allocation of resources. The actions taken to lessen the effects or neutralize an attack can also be described as risk mitigation. Risk mitigation aims to foresee and reduce the impact of threats before they jeopardize the organization's business objectives. Key controls include firewalls, encryption, access restrictions, and employee training. Risk reduction is crucial for achieving cybersecurity goals and objectives.

3.3.2.4 Monitor, Review, and Report (MRR)

E-CyG promotes MRR by the ongoing evaluation of cybersecurity threats and the effectiveness of mitigation techniques, facilitating timely adjustments to governance procedures. Therefore, continuous monitoring of risks, gaps, weaknesses, and control effectiveness is essential for effective cybersecurity governance. Risk reviews should be conducted regularly, and control measures updated to reflect environmental changes, including emerging threats, business process modifications, and new technologies. This aligns with ERM's focus on continuous risk assessment and adapting to the changing digital landscape.

E-CyG ensures that the inherent nature of the risk (i.e., frequency and/or impact) remains unchanged and that the measures are adequate. The organization must continuously monitor and detect risks after they have been identified, evaluated, and mitigated. Additionally, it must report risks at regular intervals regarding the state of exposure and the effectiveness of the measures to the Board of Directors and senior management as part of the organization's broader risk reporting procedure. At the highest levels, this guarantees transparency and well-informed decision-making.

3.3.2.5 Incident Response

When a danger arises, a crisis could seriously harm the organization if not handled promptly and efficiently (Ho et al., 2010). E-CyG mandates that preparations for responding to cybersecurity incidents be integrated into the organization's comprehensive disaster recovery and business continuity plans. This approach minimizes operational disruption by ensuring a coordinated response to cyberattacks.

The incident response plan aims to establish an internal process for responding to cybersecurity events. The "Response" function, according to NIST,[2] guarantees

[2] Source: National Institute of Technology & Science, Cybersecurity Framework. https://www.nist.gov/cyberframework/online-learning/five-functions.

that cyberattacks and other cybersecurity scenarios are handled promptly and effectively. The objective of NIST CSF's "Respond" function is to assist organizations in developing and implementing governance practices that empower response team members to take action in response to a cybersecurity occurrence when it is detected. The specific areas include response strategy, communications, analysis, mitigation, and improvements.

The primary goal of NIST's "Recover" function is to restore, build, maintain, and enhance a company's resilience after a cybersecurity event. Recovery operations implement strategies for cyber resilience and preserve business continuity in the event of a cyberattack, security breach, or other cybersecurity incident. Among the recovery activities are improvements to communications and recovery planning. Additionally, lessons learned from cybersecurity incidents are integrated into the E-CyG process to strengthen risk management and governance procedures for the future.

In summary, the IRP's key components include a statement of the incident response plan's objectives, outlining clearly defined roles, responsibilities, and levels of decision-making authority. Information and communication must be shared with internal and external stakeholders to satisfy disclosure, awareness, and regulatory requirements. Guidelines for minimizing damage and addressing any identified flaws in information systems and related controls must be accessible.

3.3.2.6 Lessons Learned

E-CyG establishes feedback loops to ensure that future risk management governance initiatives benefit from lessons learned in previous events. Thus, reporting and documentation of cybersecurity events, along with related incident response activities, are essential for evaluating and revising the incident response plan after a cybersecurity event.

3.3.2.7 Performance Metrics

Performance metrics in cybersecurity are quantitative indicators that assess the effectiveness, efficiency, and general condition of a company's security programs, controls, and incident response capabilities. These indicators enable organizations to assess their progress, pinpoint areas for improvement, and make informed, data-driven decisions to strengthen their security posture. Table 3.1 presents some primary performance statistics at the top of the enterprise cybersecurity risk governance value chain for threat identification, detection, and response.

Table 3.1 Performance evaluation metrics

Risk Exposure Score	This score measures total risk based on vulnerabilities, threats, and the criticality of assets
Quantity of Critical Vulnerabilities	This metric tracks high-risk vulnerabilities that remain unfixed
Mean Time to Detect (MTTD)	The average time needed to detect a security event
Mean Time to Respond (MTTR)	The average time needed to contain and clean up an event
Number of Incidents Detected	Monitors volume over time to spot patterns
False Positive Rate	The false positive rate is the percentage of warnings that are not real threats
Patch Latency	The amount of time it takes to apply important patches after release
Vulnerability Remediation Rate	The proportion of vulnerabilities found and addressed in a predetermined time

3.4 Defining Cyber Risks

One of the most effective ways to understand cybersecurity is to examine its various governance frameworks by clarifying their meanings. First, we differentiate among the three primary categories of cybersecurity—national security, industrial espionage, and cybercrime—as they vary significantly in scale, actors, stakeholders, timeframe, and social importance (Friedman, 2011).[3]

In E-CyG, it is essential for board members and top managers who make decisions about cyber risk to gain the necessary knowledge about cybersecurity. The primary objective of cybersecurity governance is to analyze cyber threats and understand their impact on business operations by examining the motivations of attackers. The types of cyberattacks are numerous, and the concerns surrounding data and privacy breaches have received considerable attention from corporations. However, the new risks in the corporate cyber environment are more varied and complex (Fig. 3.2). Businesses are already facing threats from cyber risk exposures, including intellectual property theft, business interruption, and cyber extortion, which may result from potential cyberattacks. These cyber threats can lead to financial losses due to fraud, damage to reputations and brands, operational disruptions, additional expenses for restoring compromised systems, and failure to notify the relevant authorities of a breach. The most frequent threats include ransomware, malware, supply chain attacks, compromised credentials, malicious insider threats, vulnerabilities in third-party software and applications, and hacked emails. All of these can cause irreversible harm, resulting in business losses of millions of dollars. However, eliminating cyber risk in terms of security is almost impossible. Minimization and mitigation may be the most effective approaches.

[3] Friedman, A. 2011, "Economic and policy frameworks for cybersecurity risks," Center for Technology Innovation at Brookings, July 2011.

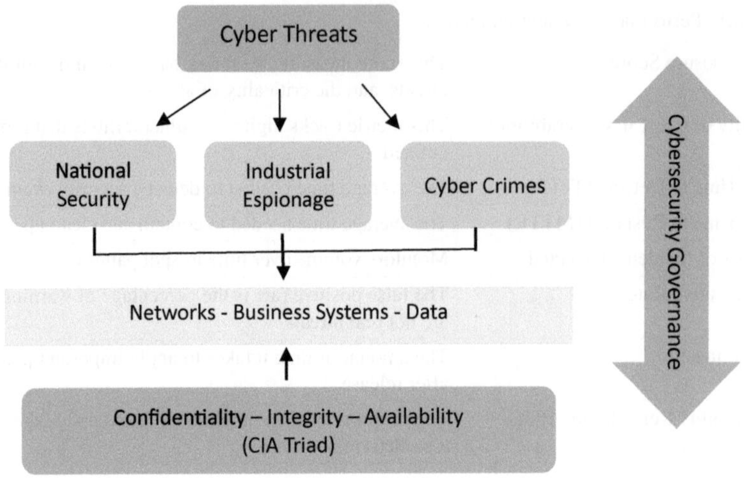

Fig. 3.2 Cyber threats, governance, and actors

Cyber hazards within a company can take various forms, affecting operations, finances, reputation, and compliance. These threats arise from vulnerabilities in technology, processes, or human behavior, which threat actors often exploit. Cyber hazards in businesses manifest through technological, financial, operational, and reputational channels. To reduce exposure and maintain resilience, proactive risk management demands the integration of technology, regulations, and personnel training. Clearly defined risk management governance responsibilities are vital for organizations to identify, assess, and mitigate cybersecurity threats. Risk management governance in cybersecurity encompasses many different forms, including:

Risk Evaluations: The risk assessment process involves identifying potential cybersecurity risks, evaluating their likelihood and potential impact, and prioritizing them for mitigation and remediation. Organizations can conduct risk evaluations at various levels, ranging from the organizational level to the specific system or application level.

Security controls: Organizations implement technical and procedural security measures to mitigate cybersecurity risks. These safeguards include firewalls, intrusion detection systems, access controls, encryption, and employee training programs.

Preparation: Preparing for and addressing cybersecurity issues is referred to as incident response planning (IRP). IRP involves establishing communication channels, defining key stakeholders and their roles, and developing procedures for identifying and resolving issues.

Recovery: Business continuity planning ensures that an organization can continue to operate during a cybersecurity incident or other disruptive event. This involves identifying critical data and systems, developing strategies to resume operations, and implementing backup and recovery processes.

Compliance: Effective risk management in cybersecurity relies on adherence to relevant laws and regulations. Organizations must adhere to various regulations and standards, such as the GDPR, PCI DSS, and the NIST Cybersecurity Framework, to mitigate cybersecurity risks and prevent breaches.

The E-CyG process is essential for facilitating effective cybersecurity, allowing organizations to identify, assess, and mitigate cybersecurity threats. Risk assessments, security controls, incident response planning, business continuity planning, and compliance with relevant regulations and standards are all critical components of a comprehensive risk management strategy. By implementing a robust risk management program, organizations can decrease the likelihood and impact of cybersecurity incidents, protecting their assets, reputation, and clients.

3.4.1 National Security

The "national security" case stands out among the three because it involves actions that disrupt a country's vital infrastructure and assaults on the military, which are extraordinary situations characterized by a high level of social importance, enormous scale, specific stakeholders (typically states and terrorist organizations), and a complex timeframe calculus (Friedman, 2011). National security cyber risks encompass cyberattacks carried out by governments or state-sponsored organizations, often with the intent of sabotage or espionage (Table 3.2). This effort to sway the balance in favor of their national interests may lead to an increase in government-led commercial cyber espionage operations (WEF, 2025).

> An attack on Ukraine's power infrastructure in December 2015 resulted in approximately 230,000 customers losing power for up to six hours. An alleged Russian advanced persistent threat group, "Sandworm," was said to be responsible for the attack, which occurred amid the conflict between Russia and Ukraine.

Table 3.2 State-sponsored attacks

Sabotage	The 2013 National Security Agency hack was a political sabotage that targeted US surveillance programs
Political espionage	Political cyberattacks are state-sponsored espionage targeting elections, political leaders, or governments. Different ideologies or the collection of intelligence that will be used in international negotiations, policy decisions, or political outcomes could be the motivation
Military espionage	Military espionage primarily involves gathering intelligence to understand a rival country's military capabilities, including its technology, activities, and strategies

Table 3.3 Types of industrial espionage

Supply Chain Attacks	This entails compromising a target's less secure supply chain components (e.g., Stuxnet was an advanced cyberweapon developed through a US-Israel collaboration against Iran's nuclear program, and the SolarWinds Orion software hack, which gained access to sensitive systems of US government agencies). It can also attack supply chains to gain insight into cost structures, marketing strategies, or supplier contracts
Industrial Espionage/IP Theft	The theft of business-related data, such as financial information, trade secrets, proprietary technology, and intellectual property, from a company that would be considered a rival is known as industrial espionage. Intellectual property theft involves the loss of research and development (R&D) data, patents, designs, and product technology

Nation-states are investing considerable time and resources in gaining a strategic cyber advantage through espionage, disruption, and theft to enhance their military capabilities, intelligence collection capabilities, and national objectives.

3.4.2 *Industrial Espionage*

Cyber industrial espionage is a form of cyberattack in which an unauthorized user attempts to access intellectual property (IP) or sensitive, classified information for financial gain and to gain a competitive edge. The two common types of industrial espionage are explained in Table 3.3. The long-term implications of industrial espionage are significant, as the theft of intellectual property can affect the enduring interests of businesses, shareholders, and society. Furthermore, when a company's stored data is compromised, hackers can access and control that information, jeopardizing the confidentiality, integrity, and availability of the affected data. Evaluating the extent of industrial espionage is difficult, as "both governments and companies are understandably reluctant to disclose details"; therefore, information about it is primarily based on assumptions and judgments (Friedman, 2011).

Business competitors commit cybercrimes to cause disruptions or unlawfully obtain data to gain a competitive advantage, resulting in significant financial losses for the target organization.

3.4.3 *Cybercrime*

Cybercrime involves the risks associated with threats, harms, and illegal activities. Recently, the rise in cybercrime has been fueled by the increasing popularity of Internet of Things (IoT) devices, which often lack sufficient security measures, making them easy targets for hackers. Additionally, the absence of cyber risk awareness among users contributes to IoT vulnerabilities. Consequently, from an enterprise

Table 3.4 Cybercrimes

Phishing Attacks	Cybercriminals use deceptive emails and websites to steal sensitive information, such as login credentials and credit card details
Advanced Persistent Threats (APTs)	These are long-term, targeted cyberattacks in which an attacker gains access to a network and remains undetected for an extended period
Distributed Denial of Service (DDoS) Attacks	These assaults flood a network, service, or server with Internet traffic, making it unreachable to users
Cloud Security	Ensuring data security in the cloud is challenging, particularly given the shared responsibility for vulnerability between cloud service providers and their clients
Ransomware	This malware encrypts and locks a victim's data, requiring a ransom to regain access
Social Engineering	When people are coerced into violating standard security protocols and best practices to obtain unauthorized access to systems, networks, or physical locations
Insider Threats	These dangers originate from employees, former employees, contractors, or business partners who possess and exploit insider knowledge about the company's computer systems, data, and security procedures

perspective, concerns about safeguarding mobile devices from various threats are escalating as more individuals use them for work. Table 3.4 highlights the common crimes perpetrated by cybercriminals.

3.4.4 Cyber Threat Actors

Cybercriminals, rival companies, insiders, and nation-states are the most common types of cyber threat actors that have emerged from the cyber realm, jeopardizing an organization's cybersecurity by gaining unauthorized access to technology. Financial gain drives cybercriminals, who threaten organizations by stealing information, funds, and data through ransomware, extortion, and theft. Professional and well-organized cybercriminals operate independently or in groups to carry out malicious acts.

One of the biggest social media networks in China is Sina Weibo. In March 2020, an attacker stole a portion of its database, which included information on 538 million Weibo users, and sold it for $250 on the black market.

Employees, suppliers, subcontractors, and other partners currently or previously associated with a company's business networks are referred to as insiders. They may engage in illegal activities out of malice for financial gain or due to emotional distress. Other cyber disruptions caused by insiders can stem from inadequate knowledge, carelessness, or human error, resulting in unintentional actions.

3.5 Cybersecurity Governance Framework Standards

This section extends the discussions in Chapter Two on standards and regulations to highlight how they provide valuable guidance on integrating these frameworks into cybersecurity governance structures across various organizations. As part of the process, risk control mechanisms, performance measurements, routine audits, and ongoing improvement plans are necessary to enhance and maintain the effectiveness and relevance of cybersecurity governance. The prominent governance standards for guiding the design of enterprise cybersecurity frameworks include:

3.5.1 Coso

In 2004, the Treadway Commission's Committee of Sponsoring Organizations (COSO) released an Enterprise Risk Management (ERM) standard. A more robust risk control framework can be achieved by aligning organizational cybersecurity governance with the Enterprise Risk Management (ERM) framework; however, most organizations find this challenging because no standard method exists for implementing ERM (Rubino, 2018). The COSO ERM and ISO 31000 risk management recommendations are two ERM frameworks that are frequently referenced in the literature (Agarwal & Ansell, 2016; Ahmad et al., 2014). The COSO ERM enterprise risk management standard offers comprehensive recommendations for all types of businesses. The widely adopted risk management framework for Enterprise Risk Management (ERM) is the COSO ERM Cube.

3.5.2 *Nist*

One example of a cybersecurity risk governance framework is the National Institute of Standards and Technology Cybersecurity Framework (NIST CSF). Developed by the National Institute of Standards and Technology, this framework helps organizations manage and mitigate cybersecurity risks. It offers guidelines for effectively managing and reducing these risks. Guidelines for incorporating cybersecurity governance into Enterprise Risk Management (ERM) are provided by the NIST Cybersecurity Framework (CSF). The CSF is a perfect fit for ERM integration, as it is designed to help organizations manage cybersecurity risks in alignment with broader business objectives. The NIST CSF comprises five core functions that organizations can utilize alongside the Framework's related auxiliary functions to mitigate risks to their business operations. A strong and comprehensive cybersecurity infrastructure is built on these five essential functions: Identify (ID), Protect (PR), Detect (DE), Respond (RS), and Recover (RC) (Fig. 3.3). All other significant cybersecurity components are organized around these five interdependent categories and functions, which operate continuously and simultaneously. The valuable references in the NIST CSF create a clear connection between its functions, classifications, and subcategories and the security measures of other frameworks. The following sections discuss the core functions.

3.5.2.1 Identify

The cybersecurity team must have a thorough understanding of the organization's most valuable assets and resources to safeguard the business against cyberattacks. This function involves comprehending the organization's assets, identifying potential vulnerabilities and threats, and assessing the potential impact of a cybersecurity incident. This role includes asset management, business environment governance, risk assessment, risk management strategies, and supply chain risk management.

3.5.2.2 Protect

This function entails developing and implementing safeguards to protect the organization's assets from cybersecurity threats and vulnerabilities. The protect function includes essential physical and technological security measures necessary for creating and implementing appropriate safeguards, thus protecting vital infrastructure. The categories encompass data security, information protection methods and procedures, encryption, identity management and access control, maintenance, protective technology, and other security measures.

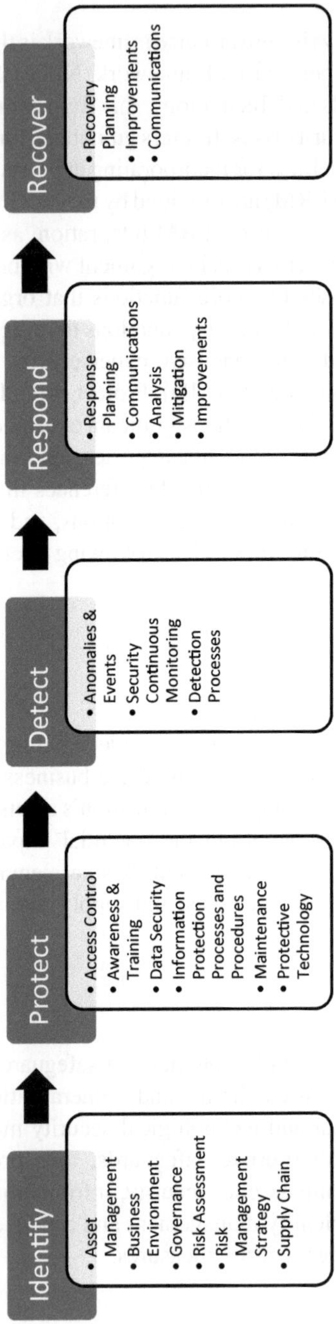

Fig. 3.3 NIST CSF core

3.5.2.3 Detect

In the event of a cyberattack, the Detect function activates countermeasures. This function involves developing and implementing strategies to identify cybersecurity incidents as they occur. It includes monitoring networks and systems for unusual activity and establishing incident response procedures. The categories encompass incidents and abnormalities, ongoing security monitoring, and detection procedures.

3.5.2.4 Respond

This function involves developing and implementing a plan to respond promptly and effectively to cyberattacks and cybersecurity incidents. It includes isolating affected systems, containing the damage, and restoring normal operations as swiftly as possible. The specific components of this action are response strategy, communications, analysis, mitigation, and upgrades.

3.5.2.5 Recover

Recovery operations implement strategies for cyber resilience and maintain business continuity in the event of a cyberattack, security breach, or other cybersecurity incidents. Among the recovery activities are enhancements to communication and recovery planning. It involves developing and implementing strategies to recover from cybersecurity incidents, including restoring data and systems, evaluating the effectiveness of incident response procedures, and making necessary improvements.

The NIST CSF offers a flexible and adaptable approach to managing cybersecurity risks, suitable for organizations of all sizes and types. It is widely recognized and utilized by government agencies, businesses, and other organizations as a best practice for managing cybersecurity risks. Rather than providing specific instructions on inventory software platforms, applications, or physical equipment and systems, the NIST CSF presents a checklist of tasks to be completed. Businesses can select technologies that best align with their cybersecurity risk management needs. If further information is required, a company can refer to useful references in other complementary standards for guidance on comparable controls.

3.5.3 ISO/IEC 27001/27002

ISO/IEC 27001 is an international standard for Information Security Management Systems (ISMS), providing a framework for managing and protecting sensitive information through a risk-based approach. The ISO 27000 family of standards offers guidance to help businesses manage the risks associated with cyberattacks and data security threats. Since the ISO27000 series standards are aligned with risk management, companies are encouraged to assess the security risks to their data before implementing various management strategies, starting with the most significant risks. Commonly referred to as the ISO 27000 series, the ISO 270001 family of standards comprises best practices to help companies enhance their information security.

In addition to addressing policy topics related to network services and user authentication for external connections, ISO/IEC 27002 offers guidelines on network access control. Security policy, asset management, communications and operations management, access control, and information security incident management are just a few of the controls and processes that this model was developed to provide worldwide standards and best practices for information security management.

ISO 27005:2011 aligns with the risk management standard ISO 31000 to simplify the integration of enterprise risk management techniques with information security risk management.[4] In addition to providing explicit instructions on risk scales, it offers valuable guidance on conducting the risk assessment required by ISO 27001, presenting advice on risks, weaknesses, opportunities, and consequences. ISO 31000 outlines common principles and guidelines for implementing risk management, rather than prescribing a specific system. Establishing the context and identifying the scenarios in which domain-specific risk management strategies, methodologies or approaches are necessary are crucial steps in implementing risk management within an organization.

3.5.4 Cobit 5

By ensuring compliance and mitigating risks and security threats through effective IT governance and management, COBIT 5 helps businesses maximize the value of their intellectual property. The general information security standards provided by COBIT 5 address the needs of stakeholders and the enterprise's integrated, end-to-end framework, allowing for a comprehensive approach and the separation of governance from management. Information security is managed by COBIT 5 as an integrated framework of multiple standards, utilizing a series of enablers tailored to an organization's specific environment. These enablers help organizations transform their cybersecurity management by focusing on the non-technical aspects of cybersecurity. The methodology can be employed to integrate systems and initiate the comprehensive changes necessary to address cybersecurity concerns. The framework offers methods for managing organizational IT risks to ensure optimal operational performance. It is based on and incorporates industry standards and best practices in the following areas: risk management is implemented across the organization; IT is strategically

[4] ISO 31000 provides guidelines and concepts for enterprise-wide risk management. It describes a comprehensive method for identifying, assessing, managing, tracking, and communicating hazards to all members of an organization. The standard aims to enhance the organization's ability to effectively manage risk and can be applied to any activity, including decision-making at all levels.

aligned with business objectives; service delivery and new project development are valued; and risk control performance is regularly reviewed and measured.

COBIT 5 is a comprehensive framework that can be integrated with other standards, such as the ISO/IEC 27000/27002 frameworks, which provide best practices and standards. It offers flexibility and broader coverage concerning standards. To effectively manage and mitigate information security risks, organizations must establish and maintain an Information Security Management System (ISMS). COBIT APO13.01 is a vital part of the COBIT 5 strategy and an essential component of the COBIT framework for IT governance and management, addressing emerging cyber risks.

3.6 Cybersecurity Governance Regulations

These regulations offer a framework for managing cybersecurity risks within an enterprise risk management context. Organizations can utilize them as a reference to develop their broader ERM-based cybersecurity governance programs and demonstrate compliance with industry best practices and regulatory requirements.

3.6.1 General Data Protection Regulation (GDPR)

This regulation, created by the European Union, governs the protection of personal data for EU residents. It establishes a framework for managing and safeguarding personal data using a risk-based approach. The GDPR was created to ensure accountable data management. Early in the design process, data protection must be taken into consideration. Data security is integrated by default, and control methods for the data type, data source, and data minimization techniques must be established. The GDPR mandates that organizations assign data protection responsibilities to individuals who collect, use, and retain data; a data protection officer should be appointed if needed. Data processing agreements must be in place when collaborating with third parties.

The company will employ operational and technical measures, including end-to-end encryption and two-factor authentication, to ensure the security of its data. Operational precautions include staff training, a data privacy policy, and restricted access rights to personal information. Processing personal data is generally prohibited under the GDPR unless it is expressly permitted by law or obtained with the explicit consent of the data subject.

3.6.2 *Health Insurance Portability and Accountability Act*

The Health Insurance Portability and Accountabilty Act (HIPAA) Security Rule is a set of standards established by the US Department of Health and Human Services that govern the security and privacy of electronic protected health information (ePHI). It prevents sensitive patient health information from being disclosed without consent. HIPAA establishes national standards for the privacy, security, and integrity of protected health information (PHI), which apply to healthcare providers, health plans, healthcare clearinghouses, and their business associates. HIPAA ensures that patient health information is kept private and secure while permitting critical healthcare activities.

3.6.3 *Centre for Internet Security*

The Centre for Internet Security (CIS) created this set of guidelines for securing computer systems and networks. It provides a prioritized list of security measures to minimize cybersecurity risks by developing best practices, tools, and resources that enhance cybersecurity defenses for both public and private organizations. It is best known for its CIS Controls® and CIS Benchmarks™, which are widely adopted as industry standards for securing IT systems and data. Example CIS controls include "Inventory and Control of Hardware/Software Assets" (CIS Control 1), "Secure Configuration for Systems" (CIS Control 2), "Continuous Vulnerability Management" (CIS Control 3), and "Incident Response & Management" (CIS Control 17).

3.7 Conclusion

By integrating ERM into cybersecurity governance, organizations can ensure that cybersecurity risks are comprehensively, proactively, and strategically managed, in alignment with their overarching risk management goals (Vyskoc et al., 2019). This integrated strategy protects the organization's value, fosters compliance, and enhances resilience in an increasingly complex threat landscape (Zhu et al., 2019). Therefore, ERM and E-CyG play a vital role in cybersecurity governance by providing practical, consensus-driven guidelines to help enterprises defend against cyber threats.

References

Agarwal, R., & Ansell, J. (2016). Strategic change in enterprise risk management. *Strategic Change, 25*(4), 427–439.

Ahmad, S., Ng, C., & McManus, L. (2014). "Enterprise risk management (ERM) implementation: Some empirical evidence from large Australian companies. *Procedia-Social and Behavioral Sciences, 164*, 541–547.

AICPA (American Institute of Certified Public Accountants). (2017). *Reporting on an entity's cybersecurity risk management program and controls.* https://www.aicpa.org/cpe-learning/publication/reporting-on-an-entitys-cybersecurity-risk-management-program-and-controls-attestation-guide-OPL

Bender, A., Turner, A., & Daniels, J. (2021). The intersection of enterprise risk management and cybersecurity: Lessons from the pandemic. *Journal of Business Continuity & Emergency Planning, 14*(1), 1–12.

Cole, E., & Wood, T. (2017). Cybersecurity risk management and enterprise risk management: Is there convergence? *Journal of Cybersecurity, 3*(1), 13–22.

D'Arcy, S. (2001). Enterprise risk management. *Journal of Risk Management of Korea, 12*(1), 207–228.

Collier, Z., Linkov, I., & Lambert, J. (2013). Four domains of cybersecurity: A risk-based systems approach to cyber decisions. *Environment Systems and Decisions, 4*(33), 469–470.

Friedman, A. (2011, July). *Economic and policy frameworks for cybersecurity risks.* Center for Technology Innovation at Brookings.

Frunza, M., & Dragan, G. (2018). Cybersecurity and enterprise risk management: An exploratory study. *Journal of Economic Computation and Economic Cybernetics Studies and Research, 52*(2), 165–178.

Gregersen, H. (2018, March–April). Better brainstorming. *Harvard Business Review.* https://hbr.org/2018/03/better-brainstorming

Ho, B., Oh, K., Durden, G. & Slade, B. (2010). *Crisis decision making.* Nova Science Publishers.

Hoyt, R. & Liebenberg, A. (2011). The value of enterprise risk management: Evidence from the U.S. insurance industry. *Journal of Risk and Insurance, 78*(4), 795–822.

ISO 31000:2018 Risk Management—Guidelines. https://www.iso.org/standard/65694.html

Jorion, P., & Khoury, S. (1996). *Financial risk management: Domestic and international dimensions.* Blackwell Business.

Kaplan, R., & Mikes, A. (2012, June). *Managing risks: A new framework.* Harvard Business Review.

Kim, J., Ghose, A., & Grossman, R. (2019). Integrating cybersecurity risk into enterprise risk management: A Research Framework. *MIS Quarterly, 43*(2), 471–494.

Kleffner, A., Lee, R., & McGannon, B. (2003). The effect of corporate governance on the use of ERM: Evidence from Canada. *Risk Management and Insurance Review, 6*(1), 53–73.

Liebenberg, A., & Hoyt, R. (2003). The determinants of ERM: Evidence from the appointment of CRO. *Risk Management and Insurance Review, 6*(1), 37–52.

McKinsey & Company. (2017). *Protecting your critical digital assets: Not all data and systems are created equal.* McKinsey. Accessed 11/9/2021.

Mee, P., & Placks, S. (2016). The convergence of enterprise risk management and cybersecurity: A practical guide for boards of directors. *Harvard Business Review, 94*(10), 74–81.

Nelson, R. R., & Che, X. (2020). Integrating cybersecurity risk into enterprise risk management: A case study of a financial services company. *Journal of Business Continuity & Emergency Planning, 14*(2), 138–147.

Oh, K., & Ho, B. (2022). *Cybersecurity risk management: An enterprise risk management approach.* Nova Science Publishers.

Radianti, J., Dietz, J., & van der Lubbe, J. (2018). Integration of cybersecurity into enterprise risk management: A conceptual model. *International Journal of Information Management, 39*, 80–86.

Raghavan, V., Rietschel, M., & Sanders, J. (2018). Enterprise risk management and cybersecurity: A Review of the literature and a proposed research agenda. *Journal of Information Systems, 32*(3), 63–89.

Robin, A., Campbell, D., Preedy, D. Paschino, E., Born, M., Haynes, P., Kazmi, P. Oikawa, R. & Getchell, S. (2002). Microsoft solutions framework risk management discipline. *Researchgate.* https://www.google.com/search?q=(5)+(PDF)+Microsoft+Solutions+Framework+Risk+Management+Discipline+(researchgate.net)&rlz=1C1GCEA_enIN1184IN1184&oq=(5)+(PDF)+Microsoft+Solutions+Framework+Risk+Management+Discipline+(researchgate.net)&gs_lcrp=EgZjaHJvbWUqBggAEEUYOzIGCAAQRRg70gEHMjgzajBqNKgCALACAA&sourceid=chrome&ie=UTF-8

Rubino, M. (2018). A comparison of the main ERM frameworks: How limitations and weaknesses can be overcome implementing IT governance. *International Journal of Business and Management, 13*(12), 203–214.

Starr, R., Newfrock, J., & Delurey, M. (2003). Enterprise resilience: Managing risk in the networked economy. *Strategy and Business, 30*, 70–79.

Stine, K., Witte, G., Quinn, S., & Gardner, R. (2020). *Integrating Cybersecurity and Enterprise Risk Management (ERM)*, NISTIR 8286, National Institute of Standards and Technology.

Vyskoc, J., Krejcar, O., & Macik, M. (2019). Enterprise risk management and cybersecurity: An empirical study of the relationship between the two fields. *Journal of Systems Integration, 10*(1), 41–54.

World Economic Forum (WEF). (2025). *The global risks report 2025* (20 ed.). Insight Report.

Zhu, L., Li, W., & Zhang, Q. (2019). A framework for enterprise risk management of cybersecurity. *International Journal of Security and Its Applications, 13*(3), 67–76.

Chapter 4
Integrated Cybersecurity Governance and ERM Framework

Abstract This Chapter discusses technology advances and why we must maintain our efforts to secure it from cyber threats. Information technology (IT) is the practical use of knowledge, resources, and skills to solve problems, boost productivity, and improve everyone's quality of life. It is essential in guiding and forming society and economic growth. IT applications employed for cyber risk control act as a strategic and tactical instrument in organizational information security management. Information technology (IT) and cybersecurity are inextricably linked; therefore, governance is integral to this relationship for cyber risk control. By leveraging proprietary knowledge and know-how, IT helps develop, maintain, and improve the firm's competitive advantage.

4.1 Introduction

This chapter builds on the cybersecurity governance framework established in Chapter Three, utilizing the Enterprise Risk Management (ERM) approach to examine key components of cyber risk management. We focus on the integration process and why enterprise cybersecurity governance is crucial for holistic risk management, enabling organizations to identify, assess, and mitigate cybersecurity threats within their Enterprise Risk Management (ERM) framework. A comprehensive examination of cyber risk governance reveals how governance serves as a policy tool in risk assessments, security controls, incident response planning, resilience, business continuity planning, and compliance with laws and standards. This chapter highlights the framework's structure, hierarchy, and essential components. A key aspect is comparing strategic and operational cyber risk management in the enterprise cybersecurity governance (E-CyG) framework, which features a two-level hierarchical structure for managing cybersecurity risks. By breaking down the approach, organizations can design a practical governance framework to assess cyber threats, plan security measures, document policies, and implement and maintain them within an ERM architecture.

K. B. Oh et al., *Cybersecurity Governance*,
https://doi.org/10.1007/978-981-95-3865-2_4

4.2 Essentials of Enterprise Cybersecurity Governance

Every department within a business organization relies on a strong cybersecurity posture to shield itself from cyber threats. Cybersecurity governance should address cyber risks alongside other risks; therefore, the cybersecurity strategy must incorporate relevant governance components into the organization's Enterprise Risk Management (ERM) framework. The ISO 31000 relationship between the principles, framework, and process indicates that these core elements are interdependent. The principles, including best practices and objectives, are crucial to risk management; they need to be clearly defined and represented within the framework and process. The framework expresses the risk management arrangements that will be integrated at every level of the organization. The effectiveness of the framework will dictate the success of risk governance. Risk governance policies and procedures should be tailored to the firm's specific requirements and environment, and should be an integral part of ERM and the corporate culture (Fig. 4.1).

The components of the core elements in Fig. 4.1 are listed in Table 4.1, and the key components are discussed in Sect. 4.2.1. Other components not specifically covered in this section have been addressed in previous chapters.

The steps an organization can take to integrate cybersecurity governance into its ERM framework, based on the core elements, are outlined below.

4.2.1 Strategic Components

ERM is a strategic, proactive, and collaborative approach to managing cyber risk, which is essential for optimizing enterprise cybersecurity and minimizing business disruptions. At its core, Enterprise Risk Management (ERM) is a systematic method for identifying, evaluating, and prioritizing an organization's operations and

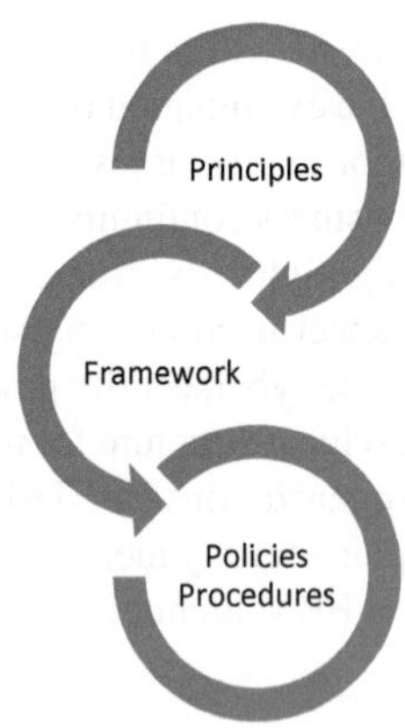

Fig. 4.1 ISO31000 core elements

Table 4.1 Components of the ISO31000 core elements

Principles	Framework	Policies & Procedures
Vision & Mission	Design architecture	Scope, Context & Criteria
Goals & Objectives	Standards	Communicate & Consult
Strategic alignment	Regulations	Risk identification
Holistic & Integrated	Leadership & commitment	Risk assessment
Structured and comprehensive	Strategies	Risk mitigation
Customized	Integration	Risk monitoring & reporting
Inclusive	Implementation	Incident response
Dynamic	Evaluation	
Best available information human and cultural factors	Improvement	
Continual improvement		

goals. Our rationale for advocating an ERM approach is that, as a business issue, cyber risk poses a critical risk management challenge that requires attention and action at all levels of the organization (Stine et al., 2020). Implementing a unified risk-based framework for organizational governance activities enhances efficiency, improves business decisions, and strengthens strategic planning. The acceptable degree of cybersecurity risk is defined by the organization's risk culture and tolerance, which are developed through Enterprise Risk Management (ERM) and influence decision-making in cybersecurity governance. Consequently, the organization's strategic objectives and risk tolerance are aligned with its cybersecurity governance.

ERM ensures that corporate priorities—such as operational efficiency, continuity, reputation management, and regulatory compliance—are addressed when evaluating cybersecurity risks. It demands a dynamic, strategic, holistic, collaborative, and integrated approach, utilizing governance as the common thread to enable the company to tackle the issue at multiple levels by employing various risk management measures. Consequently, our cybersecurity management plan leverages enterprise risk management principles, best practices (e.g., standards), corporate governance, technology, human resource management, and finance to create a robust cybersecurity posture. ERM can guide the security team in developing a cybersecurity governance process that outlines specific steps for planning, designing, codifying, implementing, and administering the entire cybersecurity value chain. This risk management approach establishes and defines clear goals, objectives, strategies, procedures, and performance metrics.

Both the NIST CSF and the ISO 31000 standard for ERM can be customized to align with a company's specific goals, objectives, culture, structure, and industry. Its application involves a systematic and methodical approach to assist the organization in managing uncertain risks. As a comprehensive and integrated strategy for managing cyber risks within an organization's cybersecurity framework, the key business goals for cybersecurity in ERM are as follows:

4.2.1.1 Vision, Mission, Goals, and Objectives

Vision, mission, goals, and objectives are essential components of corporate principles that shape an organization's direction and decision-making. They also reflect how the organization envisions its business path and cybersecurity governance as a catalyst for achieving that path. The vision is a long-term, aspirational statement outlining what the organization aims to achieve in the future. At the same time, the mission is a concise statement defining the company's purpose, core values, and primary business operations. Goals are broad, high-level outcomes the company seeks to achieve in the medium to long term, and objectives are specific, measurable, and time-bound actions that support the attainment of those goals.

4.2.1.2 An Integrated, Holistic, and Systematic Approach

Incorporating cybersecurity governance within the ERM enables management to conduct enterprise-wide cyber risk assessments, identifying and prioritizing cybersecurity risks in alignment with the organization's risk appetite and business objectives (Stine et al., 2020). The ERM offers a comprehensive, established, and systematic method for developing the organization's cyber risk management strategy and tactical response.

4.2.1.3 Strategic Alignment

ERM ensures that governance supports long-term business objectives by aligning cybersecurity risk management with the organization's strategic goals. It also promotes a balanced approach to managing both risk and opportunity, ensuring that cybersecurity measures do not hinder growth and development. ERM is traditionally classified into four stages: identification, evaluation, mitigation, and reporting. ERM mandates that businesses clearly define their goals at every organizational level where risks are identified. The initial phase of the ERM framework requires understanding and clarifying the strategy, including its vision, mission, and goals. Business risks stemming from technology are increasing, manifesting differently within an organizational environment depending on how they interact with one another and with other risks present in the organization. To fulfill its vision, risk management must focus on risk control strategies within an organizational context that aligns with its business mission, objectives, and core values (Oh & Ho, 2022). A vision reflects the company's future position, whereas a mission outlines its aims and objectives and how it intends to achieve them.

Figure 4.2 illustrates a taxonomy of the organization's cyber risk governance alignment. The corporate vision emphasizes and outlines the company's desired future state (e.g., under the NIST CSF framework, a future state could be any of the more advanced tiers that the organization aims for). At the same time, the mission statement clarifies why it exists and its current position. Goals are broad, abstract, and

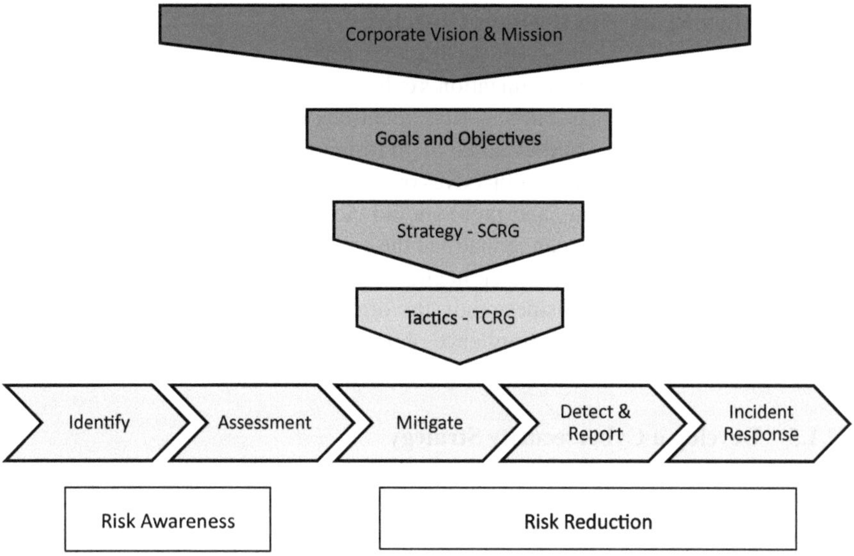

Fig. 4.2 Strategic cybersecurity governance alignment

purposeful statements that outline the expected outcomes of a specific plan or action. Objectives are defined, time-bound, and measurable actions that help an organization achieve its goals.

In cybersecurity governance, strategy and tactics play distinct yet complementary roles in risk management and mitigation. At the Strategic Cyber Risk Governance (SCRG) level, strategies are the approaches used to achieve specific objectives and form policies that guide the pathways to desired outcomes. A cybersecurity strategy is a comprehensive, long-term plan that aligns with overarching security objectives and business goals. It involves adopting risk management standards (e.g., ISO 31000, COSO, COBIT 5, NIST CSF, ISO 27001) and complying with relevant regulations (e.g., GDPR, HIPAA), defining security frameworks, governance structures, policies, and procedures, allocating budgets, and planning for risk resilience and business continuity.

Tactics are operational or actionable activities within a strategy. In Tactical Cyber Risk Governance (TCRG), the operational procedures for risk identification, assessment, mitigation, monitoring, detection, communication, and incident response are documented, outlined, and implemented. The five steps in the TCRM can be classified as actions relating to "risk awareness" and "risk reduction, monitoring, and response." Risk awareness identifies and assesses business risk exposures to recognize potential organizational risks. Risk reduction, monitoring, and response involve implementing risk controls to decrease or mitigate the frequency or severity of possible losses and assessing their effectiveness. Risk response refers to actions or measures that enhance preparedness, respond to an incident, or recover from a crisis (Fig. 4.2).

4.2.1.4 Align Risks with Business Objectives

The first step is to identify an organization's cybersecurity risks by analyzing its assets to uncover potential vulnerabilities. Risk identification aims to create a comprehensive inventory of risks and evaluate them to pinpoint the primary threats to the company. A company's business objectives outline the digital engagement and opportunities it chooses to pursue, and these should closely align with its cybersecurity approach. Since cyber risks can jeopardize the achievement of company objectives, identifying risks is a crucial first step in aligning objectives with strategy. The goals may pertain to a strategic business unit, the organization as a whole, or a specific process, function, activity, or compliance obligation.

4.2.1.5 Develop a Cybersecurity Strategy

Based on the identified risks, the organization should develop a comprehensive cybersecurity plan with specific goals and objectives, along with a detailed strategy for implementing and managing cybersecurity controls. A cybersecurity strategy is effective only if it is holistic and comprehensive, featuring a clear architecture and an awareness of interdependencies. Organizations require an effective enterprise risk management strategy to swiftly identify, quantify, mitigate, report, and respond to risks, thereby achieving cybersecurity objectives that align with the organization's overall goals. Fig. 4.2 depicts this risk control motivation by aligning the five stages in a cybersecurity context within a strategic governance framework. ERM supports this process as an integrated approach to examine which cybersecurity risks are relevant to the company's performance and why. It is a continuous, forward-thinking process that combines business management with technology, human, and financial resources to address cyber risk issues that may jeopardize the achievement of critical goals.

4.2.1.6 Governance Framework and Oversight

An enterprise cybersecurity governance framework integrates an organization's business management and cybersecurity governance components to ensure effective management of both. The objective is to ensure sound risk management practices align with strategic goals. The enterprise's cybersecurity risk management framework is referred to as its governance structure, encompassing its objectives, policies, procedures, responsibilities, and task allocation. Maintaining control over the cyber risk management process enables it to function seamlessly and align with the cybersecurity strategy plan. Chaudhary and Hamilton (2016)[1] identify five essential elements for effective cybersecurity risk governance. To be effective, these five

[1] "The Five Critical Attributes of Effective Cybersecurity Risk Management", Raj Chaudhary and Jared Hamilton (2016), BankDirector.com, Charting a Course for America's

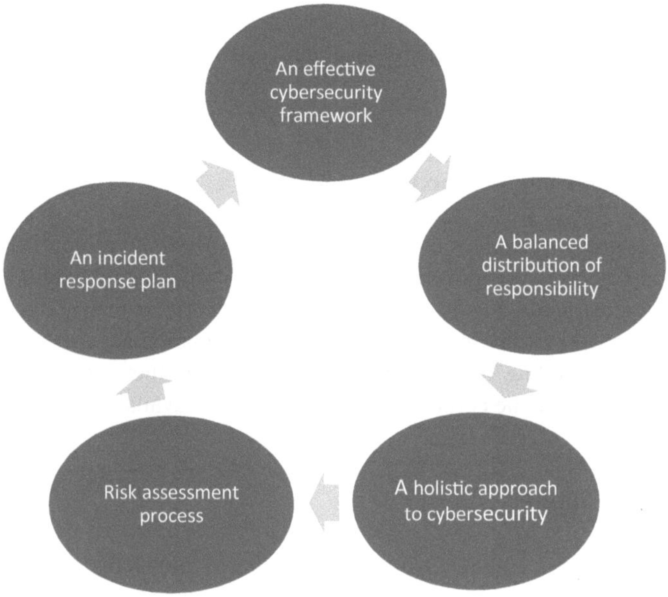

Fig. 4.3 Five attributes of cybersecurity risk management

characteristics must be integrated into a company's strategy for mitigating the risk of business disruptions and data breaches. The characteristics may need adjustment and adaptation, as there is no one-size-fits-all solution for cybersecurity risk management due to the diversity of industries and organizational settings, as well as the scope, complexity, and ever-changing nature of attacks. Fig. 4.3 illustrates the five critical attributes for effective cybersecurity governance, as outlined by Chaudhary and Hamilton (2016).

At the highest level, ERM specifies that the Board of Directors and upper management design an "effective governance framework" and a practical approach aligned with the corporate vision, goals, and objectives to protect the company's information assets. This will help ensure and maintain adequate oversight of cybersecurity risks and functions, secure sufficient funding, and keep cybersecurity a high priority. It outlines the policies, procedures, and regulations for the cybersecurity process that will be used to achieve the firm's cybersecurity goals. A "balanced distribution of responsibility" defines each member's role and responsibility. A "holistic approach to cybersecurity" will guarantee that technological, human, physical, and intangible asset protection measures are evaluated, addressed, and implemented to safeguard the firm's essential assets against cyber threats (Gerber & Von Solms, 2005). An effective "risk assessment process" will accurately identify the cyber risks to which the company is vulnerable and estimate the negative impact on vital business processes.

Banking Leaders. https://www.crowe.com/-/media/Crowe/LLP/folio-pdf/The-Five-Critical-Attributes-of-Effective-Cybersecurity-Risk-Management_FS-16003-202A.pdf

Lastly, a detailed "incident response plan" is critical for responding quickly and efficiently to a cyberattack to minimize damage and recover from the event (Chaudhary & Hamilton, 2016).

4.2.1.7 Safeguarding Resources

One of the primary objectives of ERM for cybersecurity is to protect the organization's assets. Cybersecurity governance is essential for safeguarding digital resources, as it provides a structured and comprehensive framework for managing, protecting, and mitigating risks to an organization's critical information networks and systems. This includes defending against online threats such as theft, data breaches, and cyberattacks to ensure the confidentiality, integrity, and availability of data.

4.2.1.8 Risk Culture

An organization's risk culture encompasses the shared knowledge, values, attitudes, and beliefs of its stakeholders concerning risk and its governance. Enterprise Risk Management (ERM) promotes a practical cybersecurity governance framework that fosters a culture of risk awareness and management throughout the organization. All staff members receive education on enterprise cybersecurity policies and threats, as well as their role in mitigating these risks. Training initiatives that align with ERM's goal of integrating risk management into the organization's culture are essential components of cybersecurity governance.

4.2.1.9 Risk Appetite and Tolerance

An organization's risk appetite and tolerance for cyber risk indicate the level of risk exposure it is willing to accept. The Board of Directors approves these, the highest cybersecurity governance body or those with decision-making authority, and communicated to all organization members. ERM assists in prioritizing cybersecurity threats based on their likelihood and potential financial impact by assessing the organization's risk appetite and tolerance levels. Organizations must align their cyber risk mitigation or response strategies with their risk appetite.

4.2.1.10 Maintaining Business Continuity

Effective cybersecurity governance aligns security strategies with business objectives to ensure that digital assets are safe, compliant, and resilient against evolving cyber threats, thereby promoting business continuity. Without it, businesses face risks of monetary losses, fines, and damage to their brand. In a cybersecurity crisis, Enterprise

Risk Management (ERM) aims to ensure that the organization's operations continue by developing plans for incident response, disaster recovery, and business continuity.

4.2.1.11 Retaining Customer Confidence

ERM for cybersecurity protects consumer confidence by safeguarding customer information and ensuring that the company takes necessary precautions to reduce cybersecurity threats. Cybersecurity governance is crucial for maintaining consumer trust by ensuring that a company secures sensitive data, upholds compliance, and adheres to security best practices. Clear frameworks, security policies and processes, data protection and privacy assurance, and customer communication can all contribute to achieving this.

4.2.1.12 Reputation Risk Management

The foundation of a company's reputation rests on a robust cybersecurity governance system, which influences investor and consumer confidence, competitive advantage, and regulatory compliance. A significant cybersecurity incident can damage an organization's reputation. Cybersecurity risk management aims to safeguard this reputation by implementing effective security controls, responding promptly to incidents, and communicating transparently with stakeholders. By demonstrating effective risk management, a well-organized cybersecurity governance framework attracts investors and partners, avoids legal and financial penalties, ensures compliance, prevents breaches that erode confidence, establishes security as a brand asset, and creates a competitive edge by differentiating itself in the market.

4.2.1.13 Minimizing Financial Risk

Cybersecurity events can have a significant impact on an organization's finances. Enterprise risk management (ERM) for cybersecurity aims to mitigate financial risk by implementing appropriate security controls, creating incident response and business continuity strategies, and identifying potential economic risks associated with cybersecurity incidents. Cybersecurity governance is crucial in mitigating financial risk by implementing structured policies, controls, and monitoring procedures to safeguard an organization's digital assets. Cybersecurity governance minimizes financial risk by avoiding breaches, ensuring compliance, maintaining confidence, and maximizing the return on security investments. Organizations with a robust governance framework are better equipped to manage threats and avoid costly mistakes.

4.2.1.14 Regulation and Standards Compliance

Compliance refers to following standards, regulations, or policies; the two main categories of compliance are external and internal. External compliance refers to standards or regulations established by industry peak bodies, regulators, or legislation, which can be either mandatory or voluntary. Internal compliance refers to adhering to an organization's established policies, procedures, and practices. Enterprise Risk Management (ERM) for cybersecurity ensures the company complies with all relevant cybersecurity laws, rules, and guidelines, including the GDPR, PCI DSS, and NIST Cybersecurity Framework. ERM helps identify and manage cybersecurity compliance risks, while cybersecurity governance ensures that procedures and controls are in place to meet these discretionary and legal obligations. Cybersecurity procedures are regularly audited both internally and externally as part of the Enterprise Risk Management (ERM) process to ensure effectiveness and compliance.

ERM's critical cybersecurity corporate goals encompass protecting assets, ensuring business continuity, complying with regulations and standards, maintaining consumer confidence, managing reputational risk, and mitigating financial risk. Comprehensive Enterprise Risk Management (ERM) programs enable organizations to tackle cybersecurity threats and protect their customers, reputation, and assets. The ERM cybersecurity governance approach consists of five steps or functions to address risk. Figure 4.4 illustrates the key elements organizations typically follow when adopting the ERM method.

4.2.1.15 Implementation

After organizations conduct a comprehensive cyber risk assessment and develop a strategy, the next step is to implement the security plan. This implementation phase is the final and critical step in creating a cybersecurity program plan. During this phase, cybersecurity governance moves from theory to practice. Implementing a cybersecurity governance plan is crucial because it ensures the effective application of security policies and procedures, controls, and risk management techniques. Even the strongest governance framework is ineffective without proper implementation, leaving organizations vulnerable to cyberattacks. Executing a cybersecurity governance framework involves several management components to ensure that cybersecurity risks are accurately identified, managed, and monitored, while remaining aligned with business objectives. Additionally, testing all elements that will ultimately form the complete cybersecurity strategy is vital during implementation.

4.2.1.16 Risk Assessment and Mitigation

Once risks are identified and aligned, they are evaluated and prioritized based on their likelihood and the potential impact of a cybersecurity incident. Creating a comprehensive inventory of risks and assessing them helps identify the primary

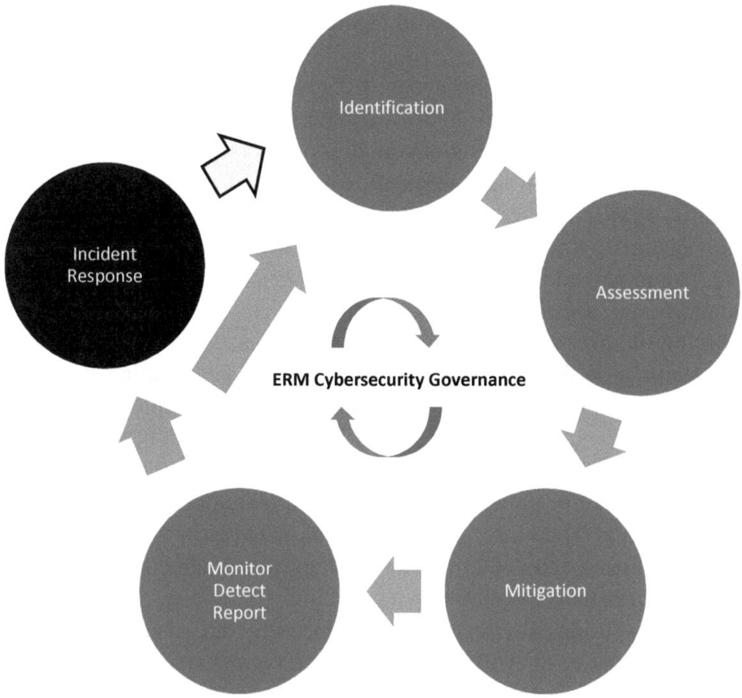

Fig. 4.4 ERM cybersecurity governance nexus

threats to the company. It is essential for ERM to understand which risks the business can control and which it has little to no control over. Utilizing risk assessment to determine a risk's significance helps improve resource allocation and management. This allows the organization to focus on the most significant and manageable risks. The firm must consider the rigor of the method when selecting from the assessment techniques. A list of evaluation tools and techniques suitable for different settings or assets could be included in the policy.

Management must determine how to respond to identified and assessed risks. The "4Ts" method[2] is among the steps management may take in response to a particular risk. The impact of a choice, the probability of the risk, and the costs and benefits of the action are all factors that management must consider when deciding how to respond to a risk. The risk-return balance is used to determine the acceptable level of risk. The mitigation procedure begins once management has established expectations regarding the degree of risk. Mitigation is selecting the proper risk control option, which includes the selective application of numerous technologies and approaches to safeguard the organization's assets.

[2] The 4Ts method refers to "Treat," "Transfer," "Terminate," or "Tolerate" risk, which form the foundation for risk governance.

4.2.1.17 Continuous Oversight and Management

Effective cybersecurity oversight ensures that governance is actively enforced, which requires comprehensive risk awareness, regular communication, transparency, and accountability. ERM is a continuous process. Cybersecurity risks are constantly evolving, so it is essential to continually oversee and monitor the organization's cybersecurity strategy and governance framework to ensure it effectively addresses new and emerging threats. Oversight ensures that cybersecurity governance is effective, compliant, and aligned with company objectives. It involves monitoring, accountability, and decision-making at multiple levels.

The Board of Directors and C-suite executives must consistently focus on maintaining Enterprise Risk Management (ERM), while incorporating it into ongoing management activities to emphasize its significance to employees at all levels. The BoD must provide strategic oversight by establishing cybersecurity priorities that align with the company's risk appetite, which requires regular risk reporting, reviewing cybersecurity policies and procedures, and allocating adequate budgets for security projects. Therefore, gathering feedback and ideas from key stakeholders, along with disclosing cybersecurity plans, will ensure alignment among department heads and senior management.

Maintaining a strong cybersecurity governance structure ensures it stays effective, current, and responsive to evolving threats and changing business needs. The maintenance process includes regular reviews of policies and procedures to ensure regulatory updates and framework alignment, threat intelligence responses to stay ahead of evolving attack patterns, and updates to the supply chain. Additional focus areas involve updates to security technology and controls, reinforcement of training and awareness, maintenance of audit and compliance, and insights gained from incident response and recovery.

4.2.1.18 Incident Response Plan

An effective cybersecurity risk strategy relies on the company's ability to avert crises that impact the business, employees, and stakeholders (Ho et al., 2010). Companies should incorporate a comprehensive incident response plan (IRP) into their cybersecurity strategy to effectively address security breaches and mitigate their impact. A cybersecurity Incident Response Plan (IRP) is a documented, systematic approach to identifying, responding to, and recovering from cybersecurity incidents. Its goal is to minimize damage and restore normal operations as quickly as possible. The plan outlines roles, responsibilities, procedures, and communication methods for handling incidents, including data breaches, ransomware attacks, and system hacks. IRP governance can be divided into pre-crisis, crisis response, and post-crisis processes (Ho et al., 2010). Pre-crisis governance refers to a company's proactive approach to preparing for a crisis, encompassing risk management policies and procedures. Preparedness encompasses roles, responsibilities, and processes for acquiring information and skills before a disaster, enabling effective anticipation, response,

Table 4.2 IRP components

Steps	Ho et al. (2010)	Perry & Lindell (2004) Evaluations
1. Preparation and implementation: Policies, training, tools, and procedures are in place.	Pre-crisis	VA, CA, TR
2. Detection and analysis: Identifying and evaluating breaches, and determining the necessary actions to be taken.		
3. Containment - preventing short- and long-term harm.	Crisis response	
4. Eradication - eliminating the underlying cause (e.g., ransomware attack, malware).		
5. Recovery is the process of securely restoring systems and data.	Post-crisis	TR & FS
6. Lessons learned - conduct a post-incident review to identify areas for improvement.		

and recovery from a crisis. Crisis response involves mitigating or containing the breach and preventing escalation. Post-crisis governance refers to the procedures a company implements to recover and resume normal operations after neutralizing or eliminating a cyberattack.

Perry and Lindell (2004) evaluate an organization's crisis preparedness using four criteria: a risk assessment (vulnerability assessment, VA), a capacity assessment of the organization's ability to respond to crises (capacity assessment, CA), the training and retention (TR) of qualified staff, and a flexible system (FS) that can be quickly deployed during a crisis. In the event of a potential cyberattack, organizations must establish multiple teams, processes, and procedures to initiate the response and recovery efforts. If a security issue arises, everyone will know the immediate actions to take. The main components of an incident response plan are presented in Table 4.2.

By following these steps, organizations can gain a comprehensive understanding of their cybersecurity risks and implement effective strategies to mitigate them, thereby safeguarding their critical assets.

4.2.1.19 Performance Review

Performance reviews are essential to cybersecurity governance because they ensure that staff, security policies, and procedures align with the organization's risk management goals. Proactive risk management, reviewing the effectiveness of security controls, measuring personnel and security awareness, coordinating cybersecurity with business objectives, and ensuring compliance with rules and standards are all important. In cybersecurity governance, performance reviews help ensure that security measures remain efficient, compliant, and responsive to emerging threats. They foster a culture of accountability, strategic risk management, and continuous improvement. The ERM review process involves revising policies and procedures, updating risk assessments, and considering cybersecurity risks during routine risk reporting and monitoring activities.

4.2.2 Tactical Components

Under cybersecurity governance, actions are classified as either tactical (short-term, operational) or strategic (long-term, high-level) to ensure effective risk management and organizational resilience. Tactical actions are immediate, operational responses to address threats, vulnerabilities, or incidents, focusing on execution (e.g., implementing specific controls or responses) and are time-sensitive to handle urgent risks (e.g., blocking a malicious IP address, patching a zero-day flaw, conducting a phishing simulation for employees). The governance role in tactical oversight ensures that daily security operations align with policies and support strategic objectives by mitigating immediate risks. The integration of cyber risk management plans at the C-suite level is where tactical governance occurs, which is integral to and leverages the ERM operational process. It involves implementing responsibilities, assigning accountabilities, and maintaining the plans. Cybersecurity operational or tactical risk management in a corporate digital environment typically involves several key steps:

4.2.2.1 Identify Assets

Identify the organization's critical assets, including hardware, software, data, and other resources that need protection. Assessing vulnerabilities involves conducting a vulnerability assessment to uncover potential weaknesses in the organization's systems, applications, and network infrastructure, as well as in critical assets (e.g., payment systems, supply chains, customer data) and their vulnerabilities. This process may include penetration testing, vulnerability scans, or other evaluations.

4.2.2.2 Assess Threats

The risk assessment process involved evaluating potential threats identified that could impact the organization's assets, including malware, phishing attacks, ransomware, and insider threats. The cybersecurity risk tolerance must align with the organization's risk appetite to establish acceptable cyber risk thresholds, such as the maximum tolerable downtime for networks, business systems, or data availability.

Cybersecurity threats are abstract concepts that do not provide sufficient information for decision-makers to initiate a proactive risk management process unless they are calibrated and translated into a quantifiable format that reveals an imminent risk to their exposure and potential impact on business processes and operations. To quantify threats, a financial impact analysis or assessment is conducted to estimate possible losses from incidents (e.g., data theft, system downtime, regulatory penalties, fraud losses, reputational damage). An evaluation of the likelihood and potential impact of each threat on the organization's assets is performed, or other risk analysis methods, such as Factor Analysis of Information Risk (FAIR), can be employed to quantify cyber risks in financial terms to ascertain the potential impact of each threat. The final step in risk assessment is to prioritize or rank risks based on their likelihood and potential impact. By prioritizing, the organization can concentrate on addressing the most significant risks. Organizations may also conduct scenario analysis, such as value at risk or stress testing, to assess cyber resilience against high-impact incidents.

4.2.2.3 Mitigate Risks

Prioritizing risks based on their business impact directs resources toward risks that threaten strategic business objectives, such as prioritizing supply chain security over less critical systems. To develop risk mitigation strategies for the prioritized risks, these strategies include implementing security controls, such as firewalls, intrusion detection systems, or other measures, to reduce the likelihood and impact of potential threats. Implementing cybersecurity risk mitigation strategies requires leveraging ERM controls to integrate cybersecurity into existing ERM processes for risk monitoring, detection, reporting, continuous improvement, and business continuity planning. Adopting the NIST CSF or ISO 27001 frameworks will support aligning cybersecurity strategies with ERM requirements.

4.2.2.4 Monitor, Detect, Review, and Report

This step requires ongoing vigilance and monitoring of the organization's systems, applications, and network infrastructure for evolving and potential vulnerabilities or threats. As cyberattacks are unpredictable and constantly changing, it is vital to consistently monitor both the technological landscape and the nature of cyberattacks. As digitization advances, ensuring that the implemented security controls, such as SIEM (Security Information and Event Management) tools, provide real-time risk data to ERM controls remains crucial over time. Key risk indicators (KRIs) must be utilized to track and monitor performance, regularly evaluate controls through internal audits, and align with ERM review cycles. Firms should frequently review and update their risk management strategies to effectively address emerging risks.

4.2.2.5 Incident Response and Recovery

An effective incident response requires proper preparation, accurate assessments to conduct forensics correctly and avoid false positives, rapid action to contain the breach, well-coordinated collaboration between executives, security, IT, legal, and PR teams, and resilience through resource allocation, patch management, and ongoing training and education to prevent future occurrences. Therefore, it involves activating the incident response process following a cyber breach to neutralize and contain the threat while promptly minimizing the damage caused by the attack. Once completed, the security team will restore the affected systems to ensure they return to normal operations and mitigate further business losses. Additionally, the incident is reviewed to enhance the organization's cybersecurity resilience.

4.2.2.6 Culture, Awareness, and Continual Improvement

Effective cybersecurity governance relies on a strong risk culture and a deep understanding of security. It ensures that security is a shared organizational responsibility rather than just a technological one. This approach promotes breach prevention by making employees the first line of defense, ensuring adherence to changing requirements, fostering confidence among investors, customers, and regulators, and reducing the frequency and severity of incidents. Training to educate and raise employee awareness about cyber risks, along with incident response drills to simulate cyberattacks, is part of a broader ERM awareness program. Post-incident evaluations should provide continuous feedback to ERM, allowing for updates to cybersecurity policies and improvements to cyber risk strategies in response to evolving threats.

4.3 Integrating Cybersecurity Governance into ERM

Integrating cybersecurity governance into an Enterprise Risk Management (ERM) framework ensures that cyber risks are identified, assessed, mitigated, monitored, and managed in alignment with overall business goals. The organization's cybersecurity governance process is embedded in the enterprise risk management framework (i.e., E-CyG), functioning as a practical, risk-based, and comprehensive approach that guarantees cyber threats are managed alongside other business risks. This approach ensures that organizations' cyber risk exposures are part of a larger risk landscape, resulting in improved decision-making, transparency, and resilience. By adopting the ERM cycle outlined in Chapter Three and the five critical attributes for effective cybersecurity governance (Chaudhary & Hamilton, 2016) as the foundation, we propose an integrated ERM-based cybersecurity governance framework, as illustrated in Fig. 4.4.

4.3.1 A Holistic Approach to Cybersecurity

The ERM framework provides a comprehensive approach to identifying and addressing cybersecurity risks across a firm's business units. This ensures that cyber threats, along with other strategic, operational, and financial risks, are treated as business risks. By adopting a holistic strategy, cybersecurity risks are prioritized and managed collaboratively, resulting in improved compliance and resilience through optimized oversight, resources, and security protections.

ISO 31000 and COSO ERM are frameworks that guide and support the integration of risk management. They provide a governance structure, principles, and guidelines for effective risk management, defining a generic approach that any organization can apply to various risks. The NIST Cybersecurity Framework (CSF), COBIT, and ISO 27001 focus on cyber threats, each offering a unique approach to managing and securing digital assets. Their core motivation is to help organizations map and align cyber risks with enterprise risks and business outcomes (Fig. 4.6).

4.3.2 An Effective Framework

The first step in integrating cybersecurity governance with Enterprise Risk Management (ERM) is aligning its objectives. This involves synchronizing cybersecurity risk with ERM objectives by mapping cyber risks to business goals. It entails connecting cyber risks to corporate objectives and ensuring that cybersecurity initiatives align with strategic, operational, financial, and compliance risk objectives. The mapping process identifies how cyber threats could disrupt the CIA triad of a business's operations, including networks, systems, and data, as well as its reputation, customer trust, and regulatory compliance. The cyber risk profile and posture are integrated into the ERM framework, where cyber risks are classified and ranked alongside operational, financial, and strategic risks.

Having a uniform risk vocabulary for cyber hazards that includes ERM terminology—such as risk appetite, culture, tolerance, impact, and likelihood—is crucial. ERM aims to understand and manage risks to ensure effective organizational management. Its primary objectives are to identify, evaluate, mitigate, monitor, review, and communicate risks that align with the organization's business objectives and risk tolerance.

4.3.3 A Balanced Distribution of Responsibility

There are multiple layers of responsible cybersecurity, including techno-centric, human-centric, organizational (both intra- and inter-organizational), and societal-centric perspectives. Senior leadership is crucial in promoting responsible cybersecurity across these layers (Panteli et al., 2025). The original Three Lines of Accountability (3 LoA) and later the Five Lines of Accountability (5 LoA) models provide the foundation for defining the structures, responsibilities, and accountability needed for cybersecurity governance (Valkenburg & Bongiovanni, 2024; Slapnicar et al., 2023).

The Three Lines of Defense Model establishes a layered approach to management: the first line is the frontline IT function responsible for implementing security controls; the second line is in charge of risk management policies, monitoring the first line's controls, and ensuring compliance (internally and externally); the third line involves the internal audit role, which provides independent assurance and guidance on the overall quality of cyber risk governance. Executive management represents the fourth line, overseeing the organization and allocating resources for cyber risk management. The Board of Directors constitutes the fifth line, accountable for endorsing the organization's risk appetite and ensuring that executive management's actions align with the organization's risk tolerance.

4.3.4 Governance Structures

The E-CyG helps establish a governance structure that includes the Board of Directors and executive oversight, ensuring cybersecurity is a consistent agenda item at BoD and risk committee meetings. The CISO reports to both the BoD and the risk committee. The E-CyG framework outlines hierarchical roles and oversight while promoting cross-functional collaboration in risk governance. This approach unites the BoD, executive, IT, HR, finance, and operations departments within a collaborative governance model that aligns cyber controls with business processes. To foster shared responsibility, the structure clarifies risk ownership and accountability for cyber threats, as well as control, to the CISO, IT team, cybersecurity team, and business unit leaders.

4.3.5 Risk Assessment and Incident Response

Integrating cybersecurity governance within the ERM framework synchronizes cybersecurity controls (scope, assess, prevent, detect, and correct) with an organization's broader enterprise risk management process of identifying, evaluating, mitigating, monitoring, detecting, reporting, responding to incidents, and reviewing, which represent standard risk governance tactics and practices.

4.4 Enterprise Cybersecurity Governance Frameworks

There is no one-size-fits-all plan for managing cyber risks. However, the National Institute of Standards and Technology's (NIST) "Cybersecurity Framework" serves as a helpful guide for businesses aiming to develop their cybersecurity governance plan. Companies may still need to adjust their security procedures and controls to meet the specific requirements or roles of their particular business sectors, even when following the basic NIST architecture. The "plan" refers to the governance strategy adopted by the organization, and the "structure" denotes the implementation, communication, and reporting chain of the plan, specifying roles, responsibilities, and accountability. All this information must be included in the governance policies and procedures documentation. ERM can assist in designing and regulating these E-CyG documents to ensure they align with the overall risk management plans.

It is critical to distinguish the conceptual differences between governance and management in frameworks for addressing cybersecurity risks within an organization. Strategic governance and operational or tactical management are two distinct actions. In business, "strategic" and "tactical" denote different stages of preparation and implementation. Governance refers to decision-making methods and strategic direction, while management focuses on implementation and operational execution. Governance provides direction for management, while management influences the decisions made by governance. Like other risk exposures within an organization, a cybersecurity strategy emphasizes "what" and "why, "aiming to achieve business goals, whereas tactics concern "how" to accomplish them. Each organization needs both to succeed; strategy provides direction, and tactics ensure efficient execution and performance. This distinction enables organizations to structure their cybersecurity oversight and operational roles properly.

Strategic enterprise risk management represents a higher-level approach that integrates cybersecurity with overall business strategy. In contrast, tactical cyber risk management focuses on an operational level, concentrating on implementing specific cybersecurity controls and procedures—such as technology, processes, physical measures, or a combination thereof—to protect the organization's digital assets. Both strategic and tactical risk management decisions should be integrated into a comprehensive cybersecurity program to effectively address cybersecurity risks. Figure 4.5 illustrates the E-CyG process, which encompasses the ERM-focused Risk Identification, Risk Assessment and Prioritization, Risk Mitigation, Risk Monitoring, Reporting, and Response processes, along with the relevant governance elements of the five critical attributes for effective cybersecurity governance (Chaudhary & Hamilton, 2016). The following subsections elaborate on the distinctions between strategic and tactical risk management.

4.4.1 Strategic Cybersecurity Governance

Strategic planning focuses on long-term goals and an organization's overall position. It encompasses high-level decisions that impact the entire company, including corporate growth, market positioning, and significant investments. Resource allocation—including personnel, finances, and time—is another crucial aspect of strategic cybersecurity planning that helps achieve long-term risk management objectives.

At a high level, the main goal of strategic cyber risk management is to align an organization's cybersecurity strategy with its overall business objectives. This process involves identifying and assessing the company's cybersecurity risks, creating a mitigation plan, and integrating it into the broader business strategy. Strategies guide the business toward its long-term goals by aligning with its vision and mission.

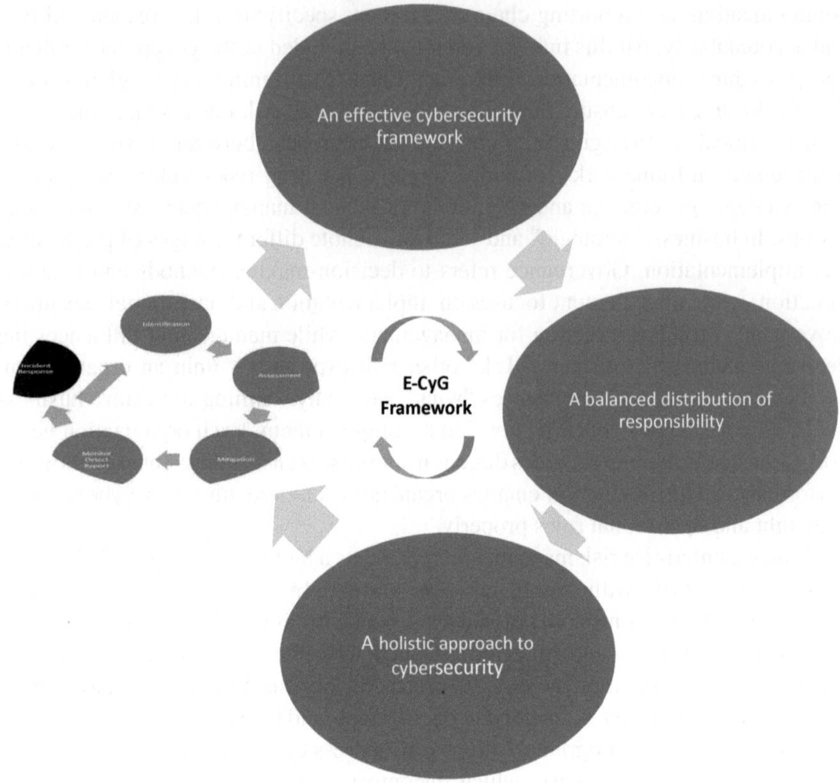

Fig. 4.5 Integrated E-CyG framework

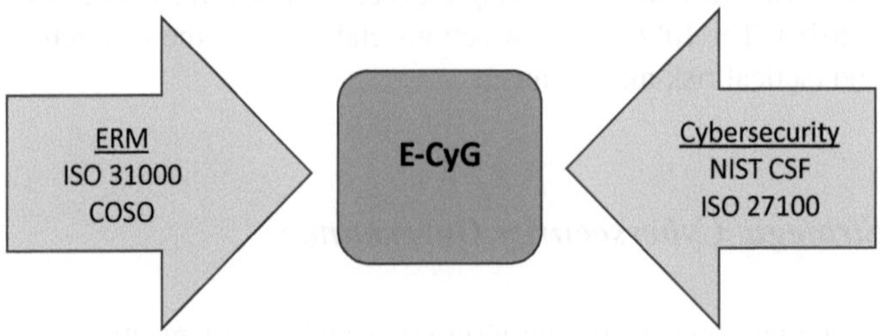

Fig. 4.6 Standards for ERM cybersecurity governance integration

Senior management or the Board of Directors typically oversees strategic cyber risk management, which aims to align the organization's cybersecurity posture with its commercial objectives.

Policies and procedures related to cybersecurity are defined by the organization's core ideals, expectations, and social norms. Therefore, when establishing strategies, the Board of Directors must consider cultural factors (Hofstede, 1980; Hofstede et al.,

2010) that influence the effectiveness of governance (Huang & Pearlson, 2019). It is also important to note that, although technical and system security form the first line of defense in cybersecurity, organizational culture has a significant impact on the effectiveness of cybersecurity governance. Formalizing a strategic cybersecurity policy necessitates a systematic approach to documentation, ensuring clarity, alignment with business objectives, and compliance with regulatory requirements. A discussion of the documentation process follows:

- Establishing the goals and parameters of the cybersecurity governance plan is a crucial first step. The purpose of the policy (e.g., risk reduction, compliance, and response) and its scope (i.e., which networks, systems, and data are covered) must be clearly defined in the documentation. Additionally, the policy should ensure compliance with legal requirements and corporate objectives.
- Documenting the qualitative and quantitative processes and techniques, along with the necessity of conducting a risk assessment to identify critical assets, threats, and vulnerabilities, is essential. The findings are recorded in a risk register that is regularly reviewed and updated.
- The decision-making authority for cybersecurity issues is defined within the governance duties and responsibilities of the BoD, the risk committee, the C-suite, the CISO, the cybersecurity and IT teams, and employees, among others.

4.4.2 Tactical Cybersecurity Management

On the other hand, tactical cyber risk governance is an operational approach that aims to protect an organization's assets by establishing, implementing, and enforcing specific cybersecurity rules and procedures. This level of governance offers oversight and enables quick responses to risks by bridging the gap between strategic policies and operational execution. It involves applying specific security measures, such as intrusion detection systems, firewalls, and access controls, to lessen the likelihood and impact of cybersecurity incidents. The CISO leads the cybersecurity and IT teams to manage operational cyber risk, ensuring the organization's network infrastructure, systems, and data are secure from potential attacks.

Tactical planning focuses on specific targets and short-term objectives. It involves detailed preparation and targeted efforts that support strategic goals, often concentrating on particular divisions or initiatives. Tactics are designed to implement and execute the strategy, ensuring that daily activities align with the overall strategic plan. Improving operational effectiveness and addressing urgent issues are the aims of tactical planning. To accomplish this, monitoring and observing security procedures ensure accountability, consistency, and continuous improvement in tactical cybersecurity governance. In the field of cybersecurity, effective tactics include running detection software, implementing physical security controls, cultivating a strong corporate risk culture, and conducting training programs to raise awareness.

For documenting the tactical cybersecurity governance process, standard operating procedures (SOPs) serve as a step-by-step guide for executing security tasks, including risk detection, patch management, reporting, and incident response. The content of the SOPs addresses activities such as roles and responsibilities (e.g., Cybersecurity and IT teams). It defines the workflows of the enterprise cybersecurity process (e.g., identify, assess, mitigate, and monitor), along with the reporting or feedback function (e.g., risk committee, CISO, departmental heads, and line employees) and incident response (e.g., escalation paths for incidents, vulnerability remediation steps, review). Additionally, the risk register documents relevant information regarding the nature and remediation of the organization's cyber threats, including mitigation actions, assigned responsibilities, and the severity ranking of each threat.

4.4.3 The Integrated Structure

Outlining the distinct roles of technology, human resources (HR), and finance in cybersecurity governance is a crucial strategic decision-making process, as leadership (Board of Directors and executives) relies on input from all three sectors to make informed cybersecurity decisions. It ensures alignment of cybersecurity with business goals; effective risk management—a coordinated approach—minimizes vulnerabilities across people, processes, and technology; clear accountability and responsibility are established by assigning distinct roles, ensuring that each department understands its responsibilities in maintaining cybersecurity; and resource optimization occurs as finance ensures cost-effective cybersecurity spending by preventing wasteful expenditures or underinvestment in critical areas where HR hires and trains skilled personnel and technology deploys solutions efficiently. A structured approach that integrates technology, human resources, and finance ensures a comprehensive and robust cybersecurity posture.

The E-CyG structure, illustrated in Fig. 4.7, represents the integrated ERM and cybersecurity governance hierarchy. The cybersecurity governance framework (E-CyG) is part of the enterprise-wide risk management process. The governance sub-frameworks for the enablers—information systems technology (IT/CyG), technology management (TM/CyG), human resources (HR/CyG), and finance (FIN/CyG)—are incorporated within the E-CyG framework.

The subsequent chapters will examine the cybersecurity governance elements from each enabler's perspective within the integrated framework depicted in Fig. 4.7. A process for each enabler will be discussed, recommending and highlighting the essential components needed to create an optimal cybersecurity governance framework in their respective domains.

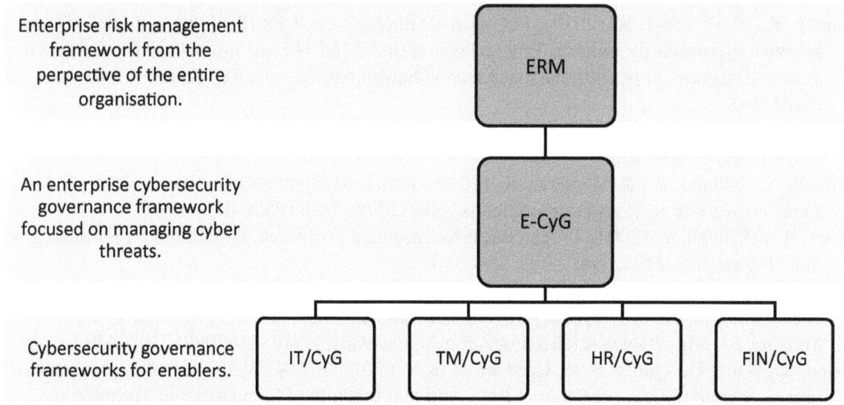

Fig. 4.7 E-CyG structure

4.5 Conclusion

Since cybersecurity risks extend beyond mere IT issues—they can disrupt operations, damage a company's reputation, incur financial losses, and even threaten legal compliance—cybersecurity governance must be integrated into Enterprise Risk Management (ERM). This integration ensures that cyber risks are evaluated alongside financial, operational, and strategic risks, resulting in a cohesive risk posture. The benefits of integration include a holistic risk management approach, enabling executives and board members to make strategic decisions regarding risk appetite, resource allocation, and mitigation techniques. This prevents cybersecurity from becoming isolated and ensures it is recognized as a business enabler. A unified approach promotes efficiency, resilience, compliance, and strategic agility in an increasingly digital and threat-laden environment, safeguarding organizations against fragmented risk management, financial losses, regulatory penalties, and reputational damage.

References

Chaudhary, R., & Hamilton, J. (2016). Charting a course for America's banking leaders. *BankDirector.com.*. https://www.crowe.com/-/media/Crowe/LLP/folio-pdf/The-Five-Critical-Attributes-of-Effective-Cybersecurity-Risk-Management_FS-16003-202A.pdf

Gerber, M., & Von Solms, R. (2005). Management of risk in the information age. *Computers & Security, 24*, 16–30.

Ho, B., Oh, K., Durden, G., & Slade, B. (2010). *Crisis decision making*. Nova Science Publishers.

Hofstede, G. (1980). *Culture's consequences: International differences in work-related values*. Sage.

Hofstede, G., Hofstede, G., & Minkov, M. (2010). *Cultures and organizations: Software of the mind* (3rd. ed.). McGraw-Hill.

Huang, K., & Pearlson, K. (2019). For what technology can't fix: Building a model of organizational cybersecurity culture. Proceedings of the 52nd Hawaii international conference on system sciences. https://scholarspace.manoa.hawaii.edu/items/c2f05c8b-a609-4c08-8dea-2d1c4e453b88

Oh, K., & Ho, B. (2022). *Cybersecurity risk management: An enterprise risk management approach.* Nova Science Publishers.

Panteli, N., Nthubu, B., & Mersinas, K. (2025). Information systems Frontiers. *Springer Nature Link.*. https://link.springer.com/article/10.1007/s10796-025-10588-0

Perry, R., & Lindell, M. (2004). Preparedness for emergency response: Guidelines for the emergency planning process. *Disasters, 27*(4), 336–350.

Slapnicar, S., Axelsen, M., Bongiovanni, I., & Stockdale, D. (2023). A pathway model to five lines of accountability in cybersecurity governance. *International Journal of Accounting Information Systems, 51.* https://www.sciencedirect.com/science/article/pii/S1467089523000349

Stine, K., Witte, G., Quinn, S., & Gardner, R. K. (2020). *NISTIR 8286- integrating cybersecurity and enterprise risk management (ERM).* National Institute of Standards and Technology.

Valkenburg, B & Bongiovanni, I. (2024). Unravelling the three lines model in cybersecurity: a systematic literature review," Computers & Security, 139. https://www.sciencedirect.com/science/article/pii/S0167404824000099.

Chapter 5
Information Technology, Systems Technology, and Cybersecurity

Abstract This chapter discusses technology advances and why we must maintain our efforts to secure it from cyber threats. Information technology (IT) is the practical use of knowledge, resources, and skills to solve problems, boost productivity, and improve everyone's quality of life. It is essential in guiding and forming society and economic growth. IT applications employed for cyber risk control act as a strategic and tactical instrument in organizational information security management. Information technology (IT) and cybersecurity are inextricably linked; therefore, governance is integral to this relationship for cyber risk control. By leveraging proprietary knowledge and know-how, IT helps develop, maintain, and improve the firm's competitive advantage.

On the other hand, it is also an enabler for cybersecurity to enhance digital risk management. As an enabler, IT can assist the firm in shaping and accomplishing its cybersecurity strategic and operational objectives. IT is a vital weapon in the fight against cyber threats. It enables cybersecurity experts to monitor networks, systems, and servers to look for anomalies that can point to a cyberattack using cutting-edge tools and techniques like artificial intelligence and machine learning. We look at governance issues, challenges, and essentials to help align and design the organization's cybersecurity program vis-à-vis its IT capabilities.

5.1 Introduction

This chapter discusses technological advances and the necessity of continuing our efforts to protect them from cyber threats while utilizing them to enable cybersecurity. In the context of this book, we define information technology as the business processes that encompass hardware and software technologies, as well as information (i.e., networks, business systems, and data) utilized in a business environment. Information technology (IT) and cybersecurity are fundamentally intertwined; therefore, effective cybersecurity governance is essential to managing cyber risk within this relationship. IT plays a crucial role in developing, maintaining, and enhancing the firm's competitive advantage by leveraging proprietary knowledge and know-how.

K. B. Oh et al., *Cybersecurity Governance*,
https://doi.org/10.1007/978-981-95-3865-2_5

IT represents the practical application of knowledge, resources, and skills to address problems, boost productivity, and enhance the quality of life for everyone. It is vital in guiding and shaping social and economic growth.

On the other hand, as a tool for managing cyber risk, technology can help the firm shape and achieve its strategic and tactical cybersecurity objectives. Technology serves as a vital weapon in the fight against cyber threats. It enables cybersecurity experts to monitor networks, systems, and servers for anomalies that may indicate a cyberattack by utilizing advanced tools and techniques such as security applications, artificial intelligence, and machine learning. We examine the issues, challenges, and essentials of aligning an organization's IT with its cybersecurity governance. A holistic and integrated ERM framework is adopted to plan, design, and incorporate cybersecurity governance into the execution framework, considering both strategic and tactical perspectives.

Technology enables businesses to become industry leaders by helping them develop, maintain, and continually enhance their competitive advantage. Knowledge and expertise must be leveraged and applied in design, innovation, tools, machinery, systems, processes, engineering, and science to create technology. This concept encompasses a broad range of applications, including software, algorithms, networks, information technology, biotechnology, communication technology, transportation technology, medical technology, industrial technology, and databases, along with tangible items such as computers, cell phones, cars, medical equipment, and more, all of which fall under the umbrella of technology.

Technology continually develops and advances as discoveries, creations, and innovations emerge. This evolution enables growth and transformation in several aspects of human existence, including commerce, entertainment, education, healthcare, and transportation. Porter (1985) suggests that technology can alter existing industrial structures and create new industries. The benefits of technology in business include cost reduction, the creation of new products and services, improved customer service, expansion into new markets, facilitation of business scope and scale adjustments, and the integration and automation of business operations and systems.

By the end of the 1990s, Internet technology had replaced the so-called age of perimeter security (OECD, 2012; OECD, 2002), which had begun earlier in the same decade, ushering in a new cybersecurity paradigm to counter breaches that could occur anywhere, requiring continuous verification. According to the OECD (2012), in this new environment, "seamless interoperability and interconnectivity enabled the various, previously siloed IT components of organizations to morph into joined-up information systems, within which information could flow freely" beyond organizational and even national boundaries.

Apart from the Internet, IT environments are increasingly vulnerable due to the convergence of numerous emerging technologies, including genomics, artificial intelligence (AI), cloud computing, 5G connectivity, quantum computing, digital twins, the Internet of Things (IoT), and machine learning (ML). We are witnessing the emergence of sophisticated information technology (IT) and operational technology (OT) that can extraordinarily generate, collect, and process digital data as the use of the Internet of Things (IoT), powered by AI and machine learning, continues to grow in commerce. IT systems are inherently connected as they primarily focus on data and communication. In contrast, operational technology mainly interacts with the physical world, using hardware and software to control industrial devices and equipment. Since technology can both create and mitigate cybersecurity issues, these two fields are closely linked. Although technology has made our lives more convenient and manageable, it has also introduced new security risks that did not exist before.

On the one hand, actors can now exploit new vulnerabilities and attack surfaces introduced by technological advancements. For example, the growing use of cloud computing, mobile devices, and Internet of Things (IoT) devices has heightened the potential for cyberattacks. The risk of social engineering attacks has also risen with the expansion of social media. However, technology remains a crucial tool in the fight against cyber threats. Cybersecurity experts monitor networks and search for anomalies that indicate a cyberattack, using cutting-edge tools and techniques such as artificial intelligence, quantum computing, and machine learning. They also utilize encryption and other security measures to protect private information and prevent unauthorized access.

In summary, there is an inseparable connection between technology and cybersecurity. As technology evolves, our efforts to protect it from cyber threats must also advance. Technology is the practical application of knowledge, resources, and skills to solve problems, enhance productivity, and improve the quality of life for everyone. It plays a crucial role in guiding and shaping society and economic growth. As a tool for managing cyber risk, technology can help the firm shape and achieve its strategic and tactical cybersecurity objectives.

5.2 How Technology Creates Cybersecurity Issues

What is the difference between information security, cybersecurity, and network security? Information security focuses on maintaining the confidentiality of digital information and documents. Network security is crucial for safeguarding the integrity and availability of electronic network infrastructure for vital systems, as modern companies increasingly adopt computer networks and systems. The introduction of the Internet fundamentally changed everything, offering previously unimaginable technological possibilities while also introducing new challenges and risks (Table 5.1). It also led to the emergence of cybersecurity, which forms a vital new sector of the economy.

Cybersecurity professionals must remain vigilant and proactive in identifying and mitigating potential threats as technology continues to evolve. The likelihood of cybersecurity threats and vulnerabilities has dramatically increased due to advancements in technology and connectivity. The blurring of boundaries between IT and OT intensifies the interaction among the components of the CIA triad, thereby heightening the complexity and exposure to cyber risk. As businesses, governments, and individuals adopt new technologies, they become more susceptible to cyberattacks. Here are some examples of how technology gives rise to cybersecurity problems:

Table 5.1 Cybersecurity challenges

Increasing attack surfaces	The attack surface grows as more devices, networks, and applications connect to the Internet, introducing new vulnerabilities that hackers can exploit. Every network or device is a potential entry point for hackers to exploit.
Human factors	Insufficient user awareness and human mistakes are the primary causes of many cybersecurity issues. Users could unintentionally download malware or click on phishing links, allowing hackers to gain access to their systems and devices.
Mobile device proliferation	People use mobile devices widely for both personal and professional reasons. As a result, they possess a significant amount of private information that hackers can exploit. Furthermore, mobile devices are susceptible to attacks since they are frequently linked to unprotected networks.
Hardware and software shortcomings	No hardware or software is flawless, and cybercriminals exploit these flaws to gain unauthorized access to systems and devices.
Cloud computing	This method of processing and storing data has grown in popularity. However, it also poses security risks, such as the possibility of unauthorized access to data and data breaches resulting from incorrectly configured security settings.

5.2.1 Defining Product Versus Process Technologies

In the realm of technology and innovation, there are two distinct concepts: product technology and process technology. Both product and process technology have significant cybersecurity implications, as they create vulnerabilities, attack surfaces, and risks that enterprises must manage. Below is a summary of their differences:

5.2.1.1 Product Technology

"Product technology" refers to the skills, methods, and equipment used in creating, designing, and manufacturing a specific product or range of products. It encompasses software, hardware, and embedded systems that constitute a product, with an emphasis on the quality, features, and functionality of the final product. Additionally, product technology focuses on the finished product's qualities, features, and performance. It involves research and development (R&D), design, engineering, and innovation processes aimed at creating new or enhanced products that fulfill consumer needs, meet market expectations, and align with technical advancements.

Product technology can benefit every industry and sector that develops tangible commodities, such as IoT devices, industrial machines, and smart appliances, as well as intangible products like software. It spans various fields, including software development, appliances, consumer electronics, automobiles, and pharmaceuticals. The goal of product technology is to create competitive, innovative, and marketable goods. It involves the development of physical products or software programs with specific characteristics, features, and capabilities. Measuring profitability, sales volumes, customer satisfaction, and market acceptance is essential for evaluating the performance of product technology.

5.2.1.2 Process Technology

Process technology encompasses the systems and workflows used in manufacturing, automation, and business operations. It employs tools, machinery, and systems to transform inputs into outputs. This field emphasizes the operational methods and strategies necessary for effectively producing products or delivering services, with a focus on the efficiency and optimization of production and service delivery processes. It includes all techniques, instruments, machinery, and systems that turn inputs or raw materials into final goods or services. The goal of process technology is to increase output, lower costs, reduce waste, enhance quality, and streamline processes.

Process technology has applications across sectors that utilize production, manufacturing, or service delivery processes. It influences manufacturing, energy, chemicals, food processing, healthcare, logistics, and other industries. Process technology streamlines production lines, supply chains, workflows, and operational procedures to boost productivity and efficiency.

Process technology leads to improved operational performance, more efficient workflows, increased productivity, lower costs, reduced waste, and enhanced quality control. Metrics such as production efficiency, cycle time reduction, defect rate reduction, resource optimization, and overall process improvement are employed to evaluate the effectiveness of process technology.

In conclusion, process technology emphasizes the systems and procedures used to create goods or deliver services efficiently. In contrast, product technology pertains to the knowledge and methods for developing specific products. Both process technology, which enhances production or service delivery processes, and product technology, which focuses on the outcome, are essential in various aspects of a corporation.

5.2.2 Product and Process Technology Cybersecurity

Cybersecurity issues with both process and product technology require attention and are discussed in the following sections.

5.2.2.1 Product Technology Cybersecurity Concerns

Software Vulnerabilities: Product technology involves creating software applications to power the product, and hackers can exploit vulnerabilities in the software. Common issues include insecure software configurations, improper input validation, and coding flaws. This risk can be mitigated by implementing secure coding practices to address these issues, conducting thorough security testing, and regularly applying software patches and updates.

Data Protection: Products often handle sensitive data, including client or private information, such as user, financial, and proprietary details. Cybercriminals may attempt to access and exploit this data by compromising product systems. To protect against data breaches, it is essential to implement strong data encryption, secure authentication procedures, adequate access controls, and robust data loss prevention strategies.

Malware and Ransomware Attacks: Product technology systems are vulnerable to ransomware and other malicious software, which can corrupt data or disrupt normal operations. Firewalls, intrusion detection systems, strong endpoint security, and regular system updates can help prevent malware infections.

Supply Chain Security: For product technology security, supply chain security is crucial in preventing tampering, counterfeiting, or the introduction of hostile components during manufacturing and distribution operations. Maintaining control over the supply chain, implementing secure development and testing procedures, and thoroughly screening vendors are all vital.

User Security and Privacy: Solutions focused on users must address security and privacy concerns. This entails implementing secure authentication processes, safeguarding private information, ensuring secure communication channels, and providing transparent privacy policies along with clear user consent procedures.

Unpatched Vulnerabilities: Exploitable vulnerabilities arise when security patch updates are not implemented. Regular software updates should be included in the policy and adhered to rigorously.

5.2.2.2 Process Technology Cybersecurity Concerns

Security of Industrial Control Systems (ICS): Supervisory Control and Data Acquisition (SCADA) and Distributed Control Systems (DCS) are industrial control systems that monitor and manage critical infrastructure, which is often essential to the operation of process technology. However, these systems can be vulnerable to cyber threats, including sabotage, data manipulation, and unauthorized access. If these systems are compromised, it may lead to environmental harm, safety risks, or operational problems. To secure ICS environments, organizations must implement intrusion detection systems, network segmentation, system hardening, and strict access controls.

Compliance Risks: Failing to comply with standards or regulations (NIST, ISO 27001, GDPR, HIPAA) heightens legal risks. A structured governance system that regularly monitors and updates security measures while coordinating technological controls, staff training, and budget allocation with regulatory requirements will mitigate cybersecurity compliance risk.

Security of Physical Infrastructure: Process technology relies on physical components like machinery, sensors, and actuators, which are susceptible to manipulation or unauthorized access. Implementing physical security measures such as environmental monitoring, access controls, and surveillance systems can help reduce these risks.

Human Factors: Employees or contractors involved in process technology systems may unintentionally introduce security vulnerabilities through social engineering attacks, weak passwords, or improper handling of sensitive data. Implementing strict access controls, conducting user awareness campaigns, and providing regular cybersecurity training are crucial to reduce these risks.

Insider Threats: Process technology settings may be susceptible to insider threats when employees or contractors deliberately compromise systems or misuse their privileges. Strict access controls, role separation, user behavior monitoring, and conducting background checks can help mitigate insider threats.

Operational Technology Disruption: Cyberattacks targeting process technology can significantly disrupt business operations, leading to financial losses, heightened security risks, or service outages. Nonetheless, the effects of cyber incidents can be mitigated by developing incident response strategies, regularly testing backup and recovery procedures, and implementing redundant systems.

Connectivity and Remote Access: Process technology systems often provide remote access features for monitoring and maintenance. However, if these remote access points are not adequately protected, they may be vulnerable to cyberattacks. To prevent unauthorized access, multi-factor authentication, encryption, and secure remote access protocols must be implemented.

Disruption and Ransomware Attacks: These potential breaches or attacks on high-value targets and critical infrastructure—such as energy, healthcare, banks, and aviation—are likely to disrupt operations. Ransomware interferes with business operations by encrypting data, locking critical databases, or making IT infrastructure (servers, endpoints, cloud apps) inaccessible, thereby halting workflows. This leads to downtime costs when operations cease, resulting in lost productivity and revenue. Additionally, it damages reputation by eroding customer trust following public breaches.

Cloud Services Risks: Cloud services expose sensitive data to hackers. Data breaches and misconfigurations pose threats associated with cloud services due to shared responsibility models; however, these risks can be minimized through rigorous access controls, encryption, constant monitoring, and adherence to cloud security best practices such as Center for Internet Security (CIS) standards or the Cloud Security Alliance (CSA) framework. The CIS benchmarks and CSA frameworks are industry standards for protecting IT systems and cloud environments. CIS benchmarks provide guidelines for minimizing vulnerabilities in systems, networks, and cloud services. The CSA Framework (e.g., Cloud Controls Matrix—CCM) focuses on cloud-specific security, helping enterprises assess risk and comply with legislation such as the GDPR and HIPAA.

Artificial Intelligence and Machine Learning Manipulation: Cybercriminals can exploit and manipulate machine learning models to their advantage. AI and

ML systems possess unique cybersecurity vulnerabilities due to their data-driven nature and inherent complexity, as attackers can manipulate input data to deceive AI models. Some vulnerabilities include data poisoning, where attackers compromise training data to distort model behavior (for example, spam filters accepting malicious emails); insider threats, in which malicious insiders manipulate models or training pipelines; and supply chain risks that arise when pre-trained models are introduced with backdoors.

Cybersecurity issues related to product and process technologies require a multi-faceted strategy that includes a practical governance framework, technical safeguards, personnel training and awareness, regular risk assessments, and a proactive approach to emerging threats. Organizations must evaluate their specific product and process technology environments, identify cybersecurity threats, and implement appropriate security measures to safeguard their systems. Maintaining a strong cybersecurity posture in these areas necessitates frequent security evaluations, staff training, incident response planning, and awareness of new threats. In other words, to reduce risks in an increasingly interconnected world, a defense-in-depth strategy that integrates secure design, continuous monitoring, and staff expertise is essential.

5.2.3 Information Versus Operational Technologies

Operational technology (OT) and information technology (IT) are distinct disciplines focusing on different aspects of technology within organizations. The primary purpose of IT lies in communication, data processing, and business operations (i.e., networks, systems, and data), while OT is centered on monitoring and controlling physical processes (e.g., utilities, manufacturing, and industrial systems). The following sections highlight the key differences between the two.

- The primary focus of IT is to maintain and utilize computer systems and digital information to support data archiving, retrieval, processing, and communication. It typically encompasses information management, network administration, cybersecurity, data analysis, and software development. Conversely, OT concentrates on managing and regulating the physical equipment, systems, and infrastructure directly related to the operation of industrial systems, including production facilities, power grids, transportation networks, and other essential infrastructure. OT involves robots, sensors, actuators, industrial control systems (ICS), supervisory control and data acquisition (SCADA) systems, and process automation.
- The objectives of IT are to support business operations by providing reliable and secure information based on efficient communication and storage systems, which help organizations in their decision-making processes. The focus is on the CIA triad's attributes of data management, productivity, collaboration, and digital transformation. Conversely, OT primarily seeks to improve and optimize efficiency and effectiveness, particularly in enhancing the safety, reliability, and availability of physical processes in industries. This includes monitoring and

regulating processes and equipment to ensure regulatory compliance, minimize downtime, and reduce disturbances in industrial operations.

- When it comes to systems and applications, IT covers a wide array of technologies, including web servers, cloud computing, artificial intelligence, computer networks, servers, databases, software, and other related technologies. IT solutions facilitate the optimization of business operations, boost productivity, improve communication, and efficiently store and analyze data.
- Industrial-specific operational technology (OT) systems and applications employ technologies such as programmable logic controllers (PLCs), distributed control systems (DCS), human-machine interfaces (HMIs), industrial sensors, actuators, industrial robotics, and other specialized hardware and software. The primary objectives of OT are to ensure the reliability, safety, and efficiency of industrial processes.
- IT cybersecurity mainly prevents unauthorized access, data breaches, malware attacks, and other cyber threats to digital information, networks, systems, and software applications. Some IT security measures include firewalls, antivirus software, encryption, access controls, and security policies and procedures. Industrial cybersecurity and OT security safeguard critical infrastructure and industrial control systems from online dangers. The three main challenges in OT security are preventing unauthorized access to physical devices, defending against malicious code that could disrupt industrial operations, and ensuring the security and reliability of the OT environment.

The implications for cybersecurity governance indicate that IT governance is centered on protecting networks, systems, and data to ensure compliance (e.g., HIPAA, GDPR), as well as the confidentiality, integrity, and availability of information. OT governance emphasizes safety, efficiency, and continuity (e.g., NIST SP 800–82,[1] IEC 62443[2]). A cyberattack on OT could result in physical harm (e.g., manufacturing disruptions, power grid failures). The Industrial Internet of Things (IIoT) and the integration of digital technology into industrial processes are driving the convergence of IT and OT, which have traditionally functioned as separate domains. This fusion, also referred to as IT-OT convergence, seeks to leverage the benefits of both fields to improve productivity, efficiency, and security in industrial environments. While IT cybersecurity governance concentrates on information security, OT cybersecurity aims to prevent physical and operational disruptions. Effective governance necessitates supporting the CIA triad of IT while maintaining OT's safety, reliability, and availability attributes, especially as systems converge. To

---

[1] NIST Special Publication (SP) 800–82, Guide to Industrial Control Systems (ICS) Security, provides guidance on how to secure Industrial Control Systems (ICS), including Supervisory Control and Data Acquisition (SCADA) systems, Distributed Control Systems (DCS), and other control system configurations such as Programmable Logic Controllers (PLC). https://csrc.nist.gov/pubs/sp/800/82/final

[2] IEC 62443 is a set of standards that address the security of operational technologies in automation and control systems.

achieve the ideal balance between the two, organizations must adopt a comprehensive cyber-physical risk governance framework.

5.3 Technology as a Cybersecurity Enabler

Technology has always been a key component of the conventional approach to cybersecurity mitigation. Organizations view technology as a vital tool in defending against cybersecurity threats, making it a primary solution for addressing information security issues. The nexus between cybersecurity governance and technology is illustrated in Fig. 5.1 in the context of the E-CyG context. The solutions to cybersecurity risk fall into two distinct categories: "techno-regulation" and "security by design." "Techno-regulation" intentionally influences individuals' behavior by building norms into technological devices (Van den Berg & Leenes, 2013). Systems that automatically update or back up, segment networks, enforce strong password policies, and utilize artificial intelligence (AI) to detect cybersecurity risks are all examples of security-by-design solutions.

5.3.1 Techno-Regulation

Techno-regulation utilizes regulatory frameworks and policies specifically designed for sectors or industries that heavily rely on technology. It refers to the use of technical tools, frameworks, and automated systems to enforce rules, policies, and laws, often with minimal human intervention (Zaccagnino et al., 2021). These rules aim to mitigate risks, safeguard consumer rights, foster innovation, and ensure fair competition. Technology, in general, can act as a "regulator" by influencing (or even coercing) people to adopt certain desirable behaviors and courses of action, or it can function as its own "regulator" or be "secure by design, " as in the case of automatically updating software. Techno-regulation enhances efficiency and consistency in cybersecurity governance, but it also raises ethical concerns (e.g., surveillance overreach), legal issues, and operational challenges. However, the ultimate goal of technological control is to persuade or even compel people to follow morally righteous or desirable paths. Consequently, it has a closer connection to nudging than to security-by-design techniques. Instances of technological regulation include laws governing privacy, such as those requiring organizations to adhere to standards regarding the collection, use, and protection of personal data under regulations like the Health Insurance Portability and Accountability Act of 1996 (HIPAA) in the USA and the General Data Protection Regulation (GDPR) in the European Union. Companies must implement appropriate governance on data privacy and security safeguards to comply with these requirements. The most effective approach likely involves a hybrid governance model, where computerized enforcement is balanced with human judgment and oversight.

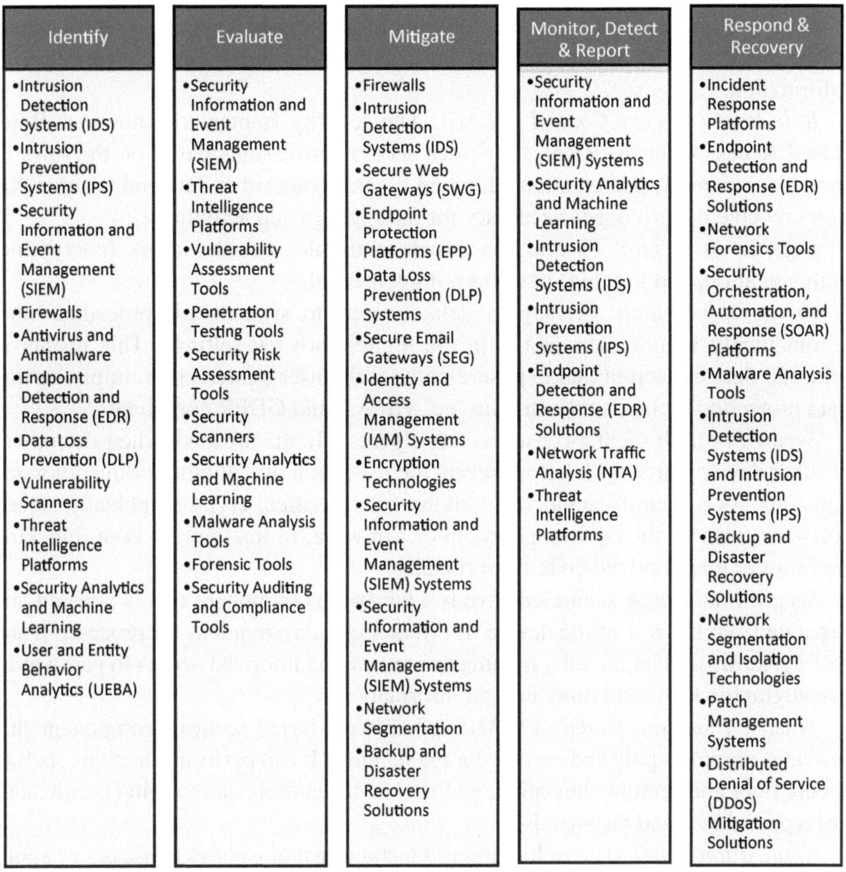

Fig. 5.1 Cybersecurity technologies for E-CyG processes

5.3.2 "Security-by-Design" Technology

Security by Design (SbD) is a strategy that integrates cybersecurity throughout the lifecycle of a system, product, or infrastructure, from initial design to deployment and maintenance. Rather than treating security as an afterthought, SbD addresses security at the earliest stages of development, ensuring that protections are built in from the start. This approach to software and hardware design and development aims to create systems that are as attack—and vulnerability-free as possible from the outset, utilizing techniques such as continuous testing, authentication safeguards, and best programming practices. The core principle is to incorporate security considerations throughout the design and development process, resulting in robust and secure systems. Examples of security-by-design strategies and technologies include the following:

Least Privilege and Zero Trust: Systems implement strict access controls, verifying every request to ensure that only authorized users can access sensitive information.

Role-Based Access Control (RBAC): The security framework known as Role-Based Access Control (RBAC) provides access permissions based on the roles of individual users. It prevents unauthorized access to sensitive data and ensures that users receive the privileges necessary for their designated activities.

Defense in Depth: To mitigate threats, multiple security layers (encryption, authentication, and logging) have been implemented.

Privacy by Default: Privacy by default refers to systems and procedures that automatically secure user data with the highest privacy settings. This results in minimal data collection and exposure without the user's interaction, implying that data protection methods are intrinsic (i.e., HIPAA and GDPR compliant).

Secure Boot: This feature ensures that only trusted software loads when a computer or other device starts up. It helps prevent the execution of malicious or unauthorized software. As a security standard, it allows only verified, cryptographically signed software, such as the operating system or firmware, to load during boot, blocking malware or unauthorized code from running.

Secure Enclave: A secure enclave is a hardware component that is isolated and separate from the rest of the device. It offers a safe environment for processing and storing sensitive data, thereby helping to prevent unauthorized access to passwords, cryptographic keys, and other critical information.

Trusted Platform Module (TPM): A hardware-based security component that provides cryptographic and secure storage features. It can perform functions such as secure boot and remote attestation, and is used to securely store digital certificates, encryption keys, and passwords.

Application Sandbox: Sandboxing is a technique that isolates a process or application from the rest of the system, thus limiting its ability to interact with other applications and access resources. It helps prevent malicious code from compromising the entire system.

Encryption: Encryption involves transforming data into a format that can only be read or accessed with a decryption key. It is often used to protect data in transit and at rest, ensuring that it cannot be read without the correct key, even if intercepted.

Intrusion Detection and Prevention Systems (IDPS): Intrusion Detection and Prevention Systems (IDPS) are security systems that monitor system activity and network traffic for signs of malicious activity or unauthorized access. They help defend against attacks by quickly identifying and responding to potential security threats.

Threat Detection and Prevention: To monitor networks and identify irregularities that may signal a cyberattack, cybersecurity experts utilize advanced technological techniques, including machine learning, artificial intelligence, and behavioral analytics. They also employ intrusion detection and prevention systems to stop unauthorized access and block harmful communications.

Multi-Factor Authentication (MFA): This security measure requires users to provide multiple forms of identification to access a system or application. User knowledge, possessions, and identity can all be included in this. MFA adds an extra layer of protection to prevent unauthorized access.

Patch Management: Preventing cyberattacks requires regular patch management. Patches are software updates that address hardware and software vulnerabilities. Cybersecurity experts can reduce the likelihood of hackers exploiting these vulnerabilities by managing fixes across multiple devices and systems.

User Awareness: Training can also be delivered through technology, such as phishing simulation exercises, password hygiene tips, and best practices for secure browsing. Organizations can lower the risk of a cyberattack stemming from human error by educating users about cybersecurity threats and offering strategies to mitigate them.

Artificial intelligence: AI has the potential to significantly enhance cybersecurity, as "security techniques ranging from phishing detection and surveillance systems to fundamental cryptographic algorithms are becoming increasingly powerful and intelligent with the help of AI" (Fang et al., 2018).

In summary, security by design has a significant impact on how governance manages cybersecurity risks, compliance, and policy enforcement, shifting the approach from a reactive to a proactive security model. SbD enhances cybersecurity governance by reducing attack surfaces through built-in safeguards, adhering to standards and regulations, and transferring accountability to developers and manufacturers, rather than solely relying on end users. To be effective, it requires strong policy frameworks, ongoing oversight, and investments in security development.

5.3.3 Protection, Detection, Verification, and Reaction

Whether you are a large multinational corporation with hundreds of locations or a smaller business with just one site, the following are the basics of effective security for any location.

Physical barriers, such as walls and fences that isolate a property from the outside world, are known as "protection." They serve as a visual and physical deterrent to criminals, acting as a first line of defense against trespassing or intrusion on your property. Sometimes, technological devices support this function by alerting security personnel if someone attempts to breach the walls or perimeter fences. The CCTV system and a Perimeter Intrusion Detection System analyzer help determine the precise threat that an intrusion presents when it breaches a firm's perimeter. "Reaction" can be as simple as calling the local police or involving a security team for more extensive facilities. When an intrusion incident is detected by the perimeter intrusion detection system and confirmed by the CCTV system, a security crew will patrol the property and respond accordingly.

5.4 Technological Options and Evaluation

E-CyG assists in identifying and evaluating new cybersecurity threats arising from emerging technologies (such as cloud computing, AI, and IoT). Keeping up with cybersecurity advancements demands a thorough understanding of the latest trends and technologies. The growing adoption of Internet of Things (IoT) devices by enterprises makes it crucial that current technologies are fully scoped, analyzed, and understood. Nowadays, businesses must protect their IoT ecosystems from malicious actors. To choose the right technologies for implementation, organizations need to assess their existing technology stack to mitigate the risks of obsolescence and potential vulnerabilities, thereby improving asset lifecycle management. Cybersecurity governance should ensure that these risks are addressed by establishing appropriate controls and procedures, supported by the latest technology. The list below highlights only a few of the most recent developments in cybersecurity technology.

5.4.1 Artificial Intelligence

The cybersecurity sector is undergoing a transformation driven by artificial intelligence (AI) and machine learning. As technology advances and evolves rapidly, cybersecurity vulnerabilities are likely to increase. AI-based machine learning solutions can effectively tackle cybersecurity challenges (Srinivasan et al., 2023). Artificial intelligence can enhance and bolster cybersecurity. These tools analyze vast amounts of data, identify patterns, and predict future threats. These technologies can detect threats and anomalies, allowing cybersecurity professionals to respond more promptly and accurately. Security teams can uncover security vulnerabilities before they escalate into issues by using AI to identify these threats and discrepancies. Both artificial intelligence and cybersecurity are technological applications. Cybersecurity often utilizes AI, which is applicable across various cybersecurity solutions.

The primary difference between artificial intelligence and cybersecurity is that the former requires a solid understanding of coding and algorithms. At the same time, the latter necessitates some familiarity with networking and computer systems. Artificial intelligence employs intelligent machines to perform specific tasks based on their perception and understanding. In contrast, cybersecurity safeguards computer networks and systems from unauthorized access and data theft. Although cybersecurity data analysis produces numerous data points, firms can leverage artificial intelligence to organize and analyze these points. The cognitive functions performed by human brains are not analogous to those of artificial intelligence.

Governance can leverage AI to enhance risk management evaluations and better understand the threats posed by malicious actors. By automating repetitive processes that would otherwise consume significant time and resources, teams can focus more on higher-value projects. Additionally, AI can be used more effectively to assess risk, enabling teams to make more informed decisions regarding mitigation strategies and security investments. AI can automate specific tasks, such as incident response and patch management, to streamline these processes.

Although AI and ML can enhance cybersecurity defenses, attackers can also employ them to develop more sophisticated malware and advanced attack strategies. The vulnerabilities associated with personal online footprints could be further exploited by those with access to advanced AI or generative AI (GenAI) models.

5.4.2 Behavioral Biometrics

In a novel approach to cybersecurity known as behavioral biometrics, machine learning algorithms analyze user behavior. Behavioral biometrics enhances cybersecurity risk management by examining individual user behavior patterns to detect and prevent fraud, unauthorized access, and insider threats. It provides continuous and passive authentication by identifying trends in user behavior through real-time monitoring of user interactions, including keyboard movements, dynamics, mouse movements, touchscreen gestures, typing speed, and navigation patterns, to detect abnormalities even after the initial login, thereby eliminating the need for passwords or tokens. By examining these patterns, behavioral biometrics can identify potential threats, such as hackers with access to a user's account. Behavioral biometrics improve cybersecurity by providing real-time, seamless risk control and enhancing the detection of sophisticated attacks. It complements standard security methods, making defenses more comprehensive, adaptable, and resilient.

5.4.3 Zero-Trust Architecture

According to the Zero-Trust Architecture (ZTA) security concept, an organization's network must undergo strict identity verification for every individual or device attempting to access it. This approach shifts risk management from perimeter-based defenses to identity-centric, adaptive security. It minimizes exposure, enhances threat detection, and is compatible with modern IT systems (cloud, remote work, IoT). ZTA represents a risk-based security strategy that adheres to the philosophy of "never trust, always verify." Unlike traditional perimeter-based security, ZTA posits that threats can arise from both inside and outside the network, necessitating least privilege access, stringent identity verification, and continuous monitoring. Even when individuals are within the organization's networks, this paradigm operates on the premise that nobody can be trusted by default. With the rise in cyberattacks targeting businesses and organizations, zero-trust architecture has gained increased prominence.

5.4.4 Blockchain

Although blockchain technology is often linked to cryptocurrency, it also has the potential to transform cybersecurity capabilities. Blockchain enhances cybersecurity by incorporating decentralization, immutability, transparency, and cryptographic security, which helps prevent data breaches, fraud, and unauthorized access. By eliminating central trust points, blockchain reduces security threats, ensures data integrity, and facilitates secure decentralized systems. This technology allows for secure data storage of sensitive information by creating a decentralized database that is not governed by a single entity, making it significantly harder for hackers to gain unauthorized access. It boosts security, especially in supply chains, finance, identity management, and the Internet of Things (IoT).

5.4.5 Quantum Computing

Quantum computing is a technique that processes data using the principles of quantum physics. It can solve complex problems significantly faster than traditional computers. Quantum computing introduces new threats and innovative cybersecurity solutions. While it poses risks to conventional encryption, it also enables improved threat detection and ultra-secure communication. It offers unbreakable security, rapid threat detection, and post-quantum defenses.

5.4.6 Cloud Security

Cloud security strengthens an organization's cybersecurity posture by integrating modern technology, centralized controls, and scalable defenses that are often more effective than traditional on-premises solutions. It enhances cybersecurity by providing scalable, automated, and AI-powered solutions that surpass conventional defenses. Many firms rely significantly on cloud computing, which introduces new security vulnerabilities. Innovative cloud security technologies, such as multi-factor authentication, encryption, and access controls, are emerging to address these challenges. By utilizing these technologies, businesses can ensure that their data remains secure in the cloud. As a result, organizations can minimize risk, enhance compliance, and respond to threats more rapidly by leveraging these tools and shared responsibilities.

5.4.7 *Internet of Things (IoT) Security*

Internet of Things (IoT) devices are increasingly common in homes and businesses. However, they can be targets of cyberattacks, making IoT security essential for comprehensive cybersecurity governance. It addresses specific vulnerabilities in networked devices and ensures compliance with organizational rules, legal frameworks, and risk management strategies. IoT security enhances cybersecurity governance by providing visibility, standardization, and risk mitigation tailored to the IoT ecosystem. Organizations can create robust, compliant, and collaborative security postures by integrating IoT-specific solutions like AI-driven anomaly detection and aligning with frameworks such as NIST's IoT Programme. IoT security solutions include encryption, access controls, and monitoring.

5.4.8 *Data Analytics*

Data analytics (DA) transforms cybersecurity by enabling proactive threat detection, automated responses, and risk prediction through the analysis of large datasets. It converts raw security data into actionable intelligence, resulting in faster detection, more informed prioritization, and automated defense. Organizations can shift from reactive to predictive cybersecurity by integrating AI, machine learning, and threat intelligence. Data analytics significantly enhances an organization's ability to anticipate and mitigate cybersecurity threats. By utilizing analytics to identify vulnerabilities before hackers can exploit them, organizations can transition to proactive cybersecurity management. The multidisciplinary field of data analytics employs various analytical methods, including computer science, statistics, and mathematics, to extract insights from datasets. The following highlights how DA can assist in cybersecurity governance:

- SIEM (security information and event management) systems analyze log data from various sources to detect threats in real time.
- User Behavior Analytics (UBA) monitors user behavior to detect irregularities that may indicate compromised accounts or insider threats.
- Performance metrics analysis reviews KPI data over time to assess the effectiveness of security measures and inform decision-making.
- Threat intelligence analysis is the process of gathering and examining information about possible threats to spot trends and anticipate future assaults.

5.5 Cybersecurity Technology Governance (IT/CyG)

Collectively, technologies provide threat visibility, ensure regulatory compliance, and streamline risk management, thereby enhancing cybersecurity governance. Cybersecurity technology governance (IT/CyG) aims to ensure the ethical, secure, and compliant use of cybersecurity technologies, aligns security technology investments with business risk appetite, and establishes accountability and oversight for security technology deployment. It also promotes continual improvement by monitoring, auditing, and ensuring resilience against evolving cyber threats. The process for IT/CyG involves rigorous preparation and implementation to integrate cybersecurity governance frameworks with the existing IT infrastructure, with participation from key units, including IT, risk management, HR, finance, and legal, to ensure comprehensive and inclusive coverage. The IT/CyG framework (Fig. 5.2) establishes a structured approach for managing security technologies in cybersecurity, ensuring alignment with organizational goals, legal requirements, and industry best practices. It defines roles and responsibilities, risk management techniques, and compliance measures to optimize the implementation of security technology.

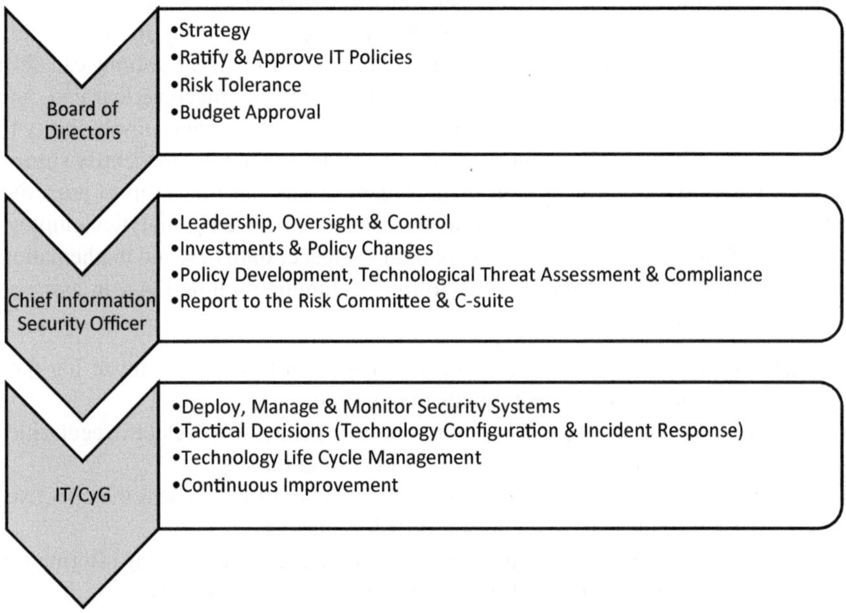

Fig. 5.2 IT/CyG structure

5.5.1 Structure

The governance structure establishes a hierarchical framework for powers, roles, and duties among personnel. The Board of Directors is responsible for cybersecurity strategy, risk tolerance, and budget approval, while the CISO, as the cybersecurity leader, has organizational oversight and control of the role. The CISO may recommend strategic investment decisions and policy changes but will require BoD approval. The CISO develops security policies, assesses technological threats, and ensures compliance in collaboration with the C-suite, cybersecurity team, and IT/CyG representatives. The IT and cybersecurity teams are responsible for deploying, managing, and monitoring security systems. The CISO is primarily responsible for reporting to the risk committee and the C-suite.

This governance framework encourages the systematic, risk-based, and compliant use of security technology in cybersecurity. By integrating accountability, lifecycle management, and continuous improvement, organizations can enhance their cyber resilience while aligning with business goals.

5.5.2 Governance Process

The process begins by evaluating the digital inventory of the firm's systems and assets related to digital operations to gain insight into its current security posture. This step involves identifying all hardware, software, networks, systems, and databases to detect gaps and vulnerabilities by comparing existing controls with framework requirements.

The gap assessment creates a technical implementation plan with specific goals, prioritizing high-risk areas first. It ensures that current technical policies align with the framework's specifications. Duties are assigned, and the necessary funds and staff are made available. Implementation typically involves installing or upgrading technological security measures, including intrusion detection systems, firewalls, encryption tools, and other security technologies.

Part of the technology governance process involves educating staff on new security best practices, policies, procedures, and technological developments. Through ongoing awareness campaigns, employees are informed about the latest advancements and emerging threats.

Governance is essential for establishing a procedure to monitor development and identify areas for improvement. This process requires continuous Board of Directors and management oversight and review through regular internal and external audits to assess efficacy and compliance, utilizing relevant metrics, key risk indicators (KRIs), and key performance indicators (KPIs).

Performance measurement is a crucial component of technology governance, enabling the monitoring and targeting of vulnerabilities for remedial actions. Technology operations metrics, such as Endpoint Protection Coverage, which measures the percentage of devices with active security controls (including Security Information and Event Management (SIEM), Endpoint Detection and Response (EDR), and antivirus), serve as key performance indicators for those actions.

5.6 Conclusion

This chapter elaborates on the use of technology as an enabler and explores the role of technology governance as a mechanism for achieving optimal effectiveness in cybersecurity risk management. In summary, adopting the ERM framework as the foundation for cybersecurity governance promotes a comprehensive and systematic approach to managing cyber risk (Nelson & Che, 2020; Kim et al., 2019; Raghavan et al., 2018). Security technology is a crucial component of cybersecurity governance solutions, as it effectively complements and supports other measures, such as user education, policies, and procedures, in addressing cybersecurity threats. The IT/CyG process must view technology as a strategic tool, and cybersecurity professionals must stay updated with the latest technologies and use them proactively to defend against cyber threats.

References

Kim, J., Ghose, A., & Grossman, R. (2019). Integrating cybersecurity risk into enterprise risk management: A research framework. *MIS Quarterly, 43*(2), 471–494.

Nelson, R. R., & Che, X. (2020). Integrating cybersecurity risk into enterprise risk management: A case study of a financial services company. *Journal of Business Continuity & Emergency Planning, 14*(2), 138–147.

OECD (Organization for Economic Cooperation and Development). (2002). *OECD Guidelines for the Security of Information Systems and Networks: Towards a Culture of Security*. http://www.oecd.org/sti/ieconomy/15582260.pdf

OECD (Organization for Economic Cooperation and Development). (2012). *The Role of the 2002 Security Guidelines: Towards Cybersecurity for an Open and Interconnected Economy*. http://www.oecd.org/sti/ieconomy/2002-security-guidelines/review.htm

Porter, M. (1985). *Competitive advantage*. The Free Press.

Raghavan, V., Rietschel, M., & Sanders, J. (2018). Enterprise risk management and cybersecurity: A review of the literature and a proposed research agenda. *Journal of Information Systems, 32*(3), 63–89.

Srinivasan, R., Kavitha, M., Kavitha, R., & Uma, S. (2023). Cybersecurity and artificial intelligence: A systematic literature review. In D. Sugumaran, P. Souvik, L. Dac-Nhuong, & N. Jhanjhi (Eds.), *Recent trends in computational intelligence and its applications*. Routledge.

Van den Berg, B., & Leenes, R. (2013). *Abort, retry, fail: Scoping techno-regulation and other techno-effects* (pp. 67–87). Comparative Perspectives.

Zaccagnino, R., Capo, C., & Guarino, A. (2021). Techno-regulation and intelligent safeguards. *Multimedia Tools and Applications, 80*, 15803–15824. https://doi.org/10.1007/s11042-020-10446-y

Chapter 6
Cybersecurity Technology Management

Abstract In this chapter, we define and explain the concept of Cybersecurity Technology Management (CTM) and how it applies to cybersecurity governance. CTM is a multidisciplinary area of study that embraces engineering, science, and management disciplines to design a set of rules and procedures for technology utilization to develop, maintain, and improve a company's cybersecurity and competitive advantage. Because IT is such a powerful force, CTM emphasizes the governance policies and procedures for efficiently applying risk control processes and technologies to meet organizational objectives, boost revenue, and gain an edge over competitors. The CTM process provides a comprehensive approach and guidelines to connect strategic governance and technical components with the organization's overarching business objectives. It entails various activities, including planning, organizing, and controlling the multiple parts of the CTM governance. It covers the entire value chain of cyber risk control activities under an overarching ERM umbrella.

Keywords Security-Default-Systems · CTM & Cybersecurity Overlap · CTM Solutions · Technology Architecture · Technology Strategy · Technology Implementation

6.1 Introduction

Technology management involves applying "engineering, science, and management disciplines" (National Research Council, 1987) to systematically design a set of policies and procedures that develop, maintain, and enhance a company's competitive advantage through the effective use of technologies. To produce goods or services and achieve goals, firms collectively combine various techniques, skills, methods, and processes known as technology. Technology encompasses multiple disciplines, including engineering, electronics, biotechnology, information technology, and other related fields. Solving problems and achieving specific objectives requires understanding and applying the right tools, equipment, materials, and systems. Because

K. B. Oh et al., *Cybersecurity Governance*,
https://doi.org/10.1007/978-981-95-3865-2_6

technology is such a powerful force, technology management emphasizes the efficient application of technologies to meet organizational objectives, increase output, and gain a competitive edge.

Cybersecurity technology management (CTM) involves the foundational governance policies and procedures that allow organizations to guide and sustain their daily technical and physical cyber risk control functions. To align cybersecurity technology with the organization's overall business objectives, a focused and thorough approach is necessary to integrate the strategic and technical components of relevant technologies, which are part of the Enterprise Risk Management (ERM) process. It encompasses a range of activities, including planning, evaluation, budgeting, organizing, and managing various aspects of technology. In this chapter, we define and clarify the concepts of CTM governance and their relevance to cybersecurity. Our analysis covers the entire value chain of CTM activities, including strategy, planning, assessment, acquisition, development, implementation, operations, support, evaluation, and review, all under a comprehensive enterprise cybersecurity governance (E-CyG) framework. The components of cybersecurity governance, including strategic planning, investment management, human factor management, and project management, are emphasized and addressed.

CTM governance refers to a company's obligation to manage and control its digital risks to achieve its goals. Establishing cybersecurity governance guidelines is crucial for effective cyber risk management, control, and compliance. This governance function, encompassing both leadership and oversight, is the responsibility of the Board of Directors. Strong leadership and supervision of cybersecurity management are vital to ensure effective cyber risk control. Managing technology is inherently challenging and often disruptive, as it constantly changes and evolves unpredictably.

As cybersecurity encompasses information technology (IT), "the administration of information technology, innovation, and technological business change, is a multidisciplinary area of study in engineering, science and management disciplines" (National Research Council, 1987) is embraced to create a set of strategies, policies, and procedures to systematically develop, maintain, and enhance an enterprise's cybersecurity posture by leveraging technologies. Given that IT is such a powerful force, CTM stresses the efficient use of technology to achieve organizational objectives, enhance productivity, and secure a competitive advantage through improved cybersecurity. Key activities included in this area encompass research and development, product design, manufacturing, marketing, and intellectual property management. Prioritizing and aligning enterprise cyber risk governance with business strategy is essential for facilitating the development and implementation of an effective and practical CTM governance framework.

With the strong connection between IT and cybersecurity, the role of governance and its elements are bound to overlap and intersect. ISO 38500 (2024)[1] offers significant guidance on how cybersecurity governance architecture should be

[1] ISO/IEC 38,500:2024 Information technology—Governance of IT for the organization. It emphasises the importance of participation of the board of directors, senior management, IT specialists and other stakeholders in IT governance, and their roles and responsibilities.

designed, emphasizing the need for leadership, responsibility, strategic alignment, accountability, personnel, compliance, and performance.

6.2 Difference Between Technology and Technology Management

Technology aims to create, enhance, or improve a firm's cybersecurity posture through goods, services, or processes developed via research and development, utilizing engineering and scientific knowledge. Cybersecurity technology management aims to ensure that technology is utilized effectively, aligning with organizational objectives and delivering a competitive advantage. Unlike research and development management, CTM focuses on leveraging cybersecurity technology in business, including its diffusion, usage, and impact. The following are some key distinctions between technology and technology management to help understand and clarify the distinct purposes of both components in cybersecurity:

Scope: Cybersecurity technology includes a wide range of information, tools, methods, systems, and equipment that aid a firm's cyber risk management activities. However, CTM is a more specialized area that focuses on overseeing and optimizing cybersecurity technology within organizations.

Perspective: The development and application of technical knowledge and skills are primary concerns in cybersecurity technology, while technological advancements are crucial for its success. Conversely, CTM takes a managerial perspective, emphasizing the effective use of technology to reduce cyber threats.

Focus: Cybersecurity technology encompasses various professions and fields, including engineering, design, and production. The main areas of emphasis are implementation, functionality, technological efficacy, and innovation. Technology management primarily focuses on the strategic planning, execution, and control of technology-related operations, including technology selection (as discussed in the previous chapter), project management, resource allocation, innovation management, governance, and strategic oversight of cybersecurity technology.

In summary, while CTM is a specialized discipline that focuses on effectively managing and utilizing technology within organizations, cybersecurity technology pertains to the broader concept of technical knowledge and skills. This chapter examines the application of CTM as a discipline for managing enterprise cyber risks, distinct from using available technologies to mitigate cyber risk, as referenced in the previous chapter.

6.3 Cybersecurity Governance and Technology Management Nexus

Technology management encompasses the oversight of technical resources, including hardware, software, networks, and data. Cybersecurity is vital for modern enterprises, intersecting with technology management to protect digital assets, networks, systems, and data from cyber threats. The management of cybersecurity technology is a component of an organization's broader technology management function, which entails defending against both internal and external threats to its technological infrastructures and resources.

Evaluating risks, developing security policies and procedures, implementing security controls, and monitoring networks and systems for signs of cyber threats are all essential elements of a comprehensive strategy for effective CTM. Managing technological resources is involved in each of these operations. To effectively manage cybersecurity, CTM is crucial for reasons presented in Table 6.1.

CTM is essential for cybersecurity management, providing the necessary tools, policies, and procedures to defend against online attacks. By implementing CTM concepts, organizations can create a comprehensive cybersecurity plan that protects against both known and unknown threats.

6.4 How CTM Mitigates Cyber Risk

Cybersecurity technology management can protect organizations from online threats in various ways. The following are the CTM tools and techniques that can enhance cybersecurity:

Security Architect: CTM helps create secure-by-default systems and implement multi-layered defenses in accordance with frameworks such as NIST or ISO 27001. Secure-by-default systems come pre-configured with the highest security settings enabled from the start, minimizing vulnerabilities without requiring user intervention. They incorporate automated encryption, disable unnecessary services and ports, enforce least privilege access (default deny-all policies), and ensure mandatory authentication. A multi-layer design divides a system into distinct, modular tiers (for example, display, logic, and data layers) that interact sequentially, enhancing scalability, security, and maintainability by isolating concerns.

Security Risk Assessment: CTM can help businesses assess the risks associated with online threats. Risk assessment involves identifying the assets that require protection and evaluating the likelihood and potential impact of a cyberattack. Consequently, it uncovers vulnerabilities, monitors threats, configures security tools, and collaborates with security architects to reduce risk through the implementation of technical solutions.

Table 6.1 Success factors for effective CTM

Factors	Effects
Risk Identification	By assessing the technological resources that require protection, CTM can help identify the risks associated with cyberattacks. This process involves estimating the potential impact of a cyberattack and ranking the assets most susceptible to attack
Align cybersecurity objectives to business goals and strategies	CTM assures that the strategic governance and operational control of cybersecurity technologies must align with the company's objectives
Development of cybersecurity governance policies and procedures	CTM requires the creation of security policies and processes that control the use and protection of technological resources. Cybersecurity governance entails creating policies for data encryption, access control, and password management
Implementation of Security Controls	CTM can assist in implementing security measures that protect against online attacks. The controls include implementing intrusion detection and prevention systems, firewalls, antivirus software, and other security technologies
Network and System Monitoring	CTM can assist in monitoring networks and systems for indicators of cyber threats. Monitoring involves identifying anomalies and suspicious activity using techniques such as security information and event management (SIEM) systems
Incident Response Planning	CTM can help create an incident response plan that outlines the steps to take in the event of a cyberattack. This plan involves identifying the incident response team, establishing lines of communication, and determining how to contain and mitigate the attack

Security Planning: CTM can help businesses develop a comprehensive security strategy that outlines the necessary countermeasures in the event of a cyberattack. This strategy involves developing security policies and procedures, identifying security controls, and defining the roles and responsibilities of security personnel.

Technology Network Security Engineering: CTM may help businesses implement the right tools to defend against online threats. This category includes the integration of firewalls, intrusion detection and prevention systems, antivirus software, and other security technologies into practice. It guarantees secure application development and monitors third-party Software-as-a-Service (SaaS) threats.

Security Monitoring: CTM can assist businesses in overseeing their networks and systems for indications of online threats. This involves employing tools like security information and event management (SIEM) systems to detect irregularities and suspicious activities.

Incident Response: CTM can help businesses develop incident response plans that detail the actions to take following a cyberattack. This includes identifying the incident response team, utilizing technical support, establishing communication channels, and outlining steps to contain and mitigate the attack.

Training and Awareness: Organizations can use CTM to educate staff members on cybersecurity best practices and improve their understanding of the risks associated with cyber threats. This includes teaching them about social engineering, password management, and other security-related topics.

Effective, Measurable, and Compliant: CTM connects cybersecurity operations with business strategy, ensuring that security measures are effective, measurable, and compliant. Organizations can enhance their cybersecurity posture and meet regulatory requirements by implementing CTM with structured frameworks and leveraging automation to maintain operational oversight for continuous monitoring of efficacy, performance, and compliance. Technology management is crucial for improving cybersecurity performance reviews and compliance by ensuring that security controls, policies, and processes align with corporate goals and regulatory requirements.

Cybersecurity technology management is crucial for safeguarding businesses against online threats. By implementing technology management principles in cybersecurity, organizations can develop a comprehensive security plan that defends against both known and unknown threats.

6.5 CTM Governance Concepts

Cybersecurity technology management (CTM) involves the strategic control of security tools, techniques, systems, and processes that protect digital assets while aligning with corporate objectives. It ensures that technologies are properly implemented, maintained, and developed to withstand threats, and it maximizes security return on investment (ROI) by integrating technology with organizational resilience. The following discusses the fundamental concepts of CTM governance.

6.5.1 Technology Strategy

A company's cybersecurity technology strategy outlines how it will leverage technology to achieve its cybersecurity objectives. It involves identifying the crucial technologies required, developing a deployment plan, and allocating funds to achieve these goals. Understanding the various types of innovation and their distinct characteristics is essential for effective CTM and for developing a technology strategy that is secure, scalable, and resilient.

6.5.2 Technology Assessment

Technology assessment is the systematic review of a technology's advantages, disadvantages, security risks, benefits, costs, and compliance posture, both before and after implementation. In cybersecurity, this process helps organizations prevent vulnerabilities, ensure regulatory compliance, and mitigate emerging threats. By utilizing financial tools such as cost–benefit analysis, return on investment (ROI), and long-term viability studies, along with technologies like IoT, AI, blockchain, and automation to support technology assessment, it helps businesses make informed decisions about the cybersecurity technology they should adopt and the optimal ways to implement it for a competitive edge. Technology assessment in cybersecurity enables informed decision-making before purchasing or installing technology, avoids costly breaches (e.g., from unvetted software to malware), reduces supply chain risks, and ensures compliance (e.g., GDPR, NIST standards, HIPAA).

6.5.3 Technical Innovation

Businesses will be better positioned to mitigate risks and effectively drive digital transformation if they incorporate governance early in the innovation lifecycle. Technical innovation refers to the development of new technologies or the enhancement of existing ones. It involves creating new systems or products through research, development, prototyping, testing, and implementation. Cybersecurity innovation, a vital component of the security-by-design approach, includes designing and implementing modern architectures and technologies that ensure information security, high availability, disaster recovery, and business continuity. Cybersecurity risks related to innovation must be managed throughout the design, development, testing, deployment, and maintenance phases. Cybersecurity mitigation measures for innovation encompass confidentiality, secrets management, automated security checks, and firmware integrity verification.

Security governance in cybersecurity innovation must ensure that new technologies enhance security rather than compromising it. Maintaining a balance between risk and innovation must align with an enterprise's risk management strategy. Cybersecurity innovation efforts within an organization must be carefully managed in conjunction with security governance to ensure alignment with risk management, compliance, and business objectives. The following are the key security governance challenges that CTM and businesses must address.

- Strategic governance, leadership, and oversight by the CISO, CIO, and Board of Directors are essential for guiding cybersecurity innovation strategically.
- Innovations in cybersecurity, such as artificial intelligence, zero-trust architecture, and cloud-native security, must not expose the organization to unnecessary risk.

- Since new techniques, such as machine learning and AI-based threat detection, must work seamlessly with existing systems, innovative architecture needs to be integrated with the current security stack.
- Implementing cutting-edge solutions for third-party risks could expose startups or inexperienced vendors to unforeseen vulnerabilities. Therefore, governance must assess the security posture of new vendors providing innovative solutions.
- Innovations must adhere to standards (e.g., NIST CSF, ISO 27000) and regulatory requirements, including industry-specific mandates in healthcare (HIPAA), finance (e.g., PCI DSS), and critical infrastructure sectors that have strict governance requirements.
- Budgets and resource allocations for innovation projects may compete with essential security requirements, necessitating the prioritization of investment.
- Employee resistance to change must be addressed through security culture and awareness initiatives, whether it stems from a lack of training, complexity, or reluctance to embrace new security technologies. Since evolving technologies can create a skills gap, management must ensure that cybersecurity teams receive the necessary upskilling within governance frameworks. This way, innovation does not lead to complacency resulting from an over-reliance on, for example, AI-assisted detection systems without human oversight.
- Governance must establish key performance indicators (KPIs), key risk indicators (KRIs), and success metrics to assess performance. To ensure effectiveness, governance should carry out regular evaluations of creative solutions and maintain ongoing audits and reviews.
- Governance must ensure that cutting-edge techniques are integrated into the incident response strategy and tested through simulation or red teaming against unprecedented threat vectors and novel attack surfaces from new technologies, such as AI poisoning and adversarial machine learning.[2]

6.5.4 Technology Transfer

Technology transfer involves moving technology from one organization to another. In cybersecurity risk management, it refers to the exchange or dissemination of technology—such as software, hardware, processes, or knowledge—among organizations, countries, or other entities. While technology transfer can foster innovation and economic growth, it also introduces significant cybersecurity threats that need to be addressed.

---

[2] AI poisoning, sometimes called data poisoning, is a cyberattack in which adversaries purposefully tamper with an AI or machine learning (ML) model's training data. This manipulation aims to change the model's behaviour, frequently producing biased, inaccurate, or dangerous results.

Technology obtained from foreign or untrustworthy sources may include hidden backdoors, viruses, or inadequate encryption. A compromised supply chain software upgrade caused the SolarWinds breach (2020). This hack was a highly sophisticated cyber intrusion that exploited a commercial software product developed by SolarWinds. Advanced persistent threat (APT) actors infiltrated SolarWinds' supply chain and inserted a backdoor into the product, which granted the threat actors global access to government and enterprise networks.

Risk mitigation strategies for managing cybersecurity risks in technology transfers involve conducting due diligence to assess the security posture of vendors and partners before the transfer, implementing Zero-Trust Architecture (ZTA), ensuring that the transferred technology adheres to secure coding and encryption standards, and complying with relevant regulations and data protection laws. Additionally, it is important to monitor supply chains using frameworks such as NIST SP 800–161 for supply chain risk management, and to ensure that individuals responsible for the transfers are familiar with cybersecurity best practices.

6.5.5 Intellectual Property

Intellectual property (IP), which includes patents, trademarks, trade secrets, copyrights, and proprietary algorithms, is a valuable asset for companies. Digital IP necessitates robust intellectual property management in cybersecurity to protect against theft, espionage, financial losses, and competitive disadvantages. Cybercriminals who sell stolen intellectual property on dark web markets, competitors engaged in corporate espionage, nation-state actors involved in economic or military espionage, and insider threats from disgruntled employees and contractors all pose potential threats to intellectual property.

The best practices for protecting intellectual property include data classification, role-based access control (RBAC) to limit exposure, multi-factor authentication (MFA) for IP repositories, digital rights management (DRM) to track IP usage, secure coding practices to prevent reverse engineering, and security information and event management (SIEM) for anomaly detection.

6.6 Essentials of CTM Governance

The relationship between technology management and cybersecurity is crucial in today's digital era, where businesses increasingly depend on technology to operate. Effective CTM is essential for developing, implementing, and maintaining systems and applications that meet the organization's cybersecurity requirements by ensuring security and protecting against cyber risks. Without CTM, organizations may face serious consequences from cyber threats, including data breaches, malware, phishing attacks, financial losses, reputational damage, and legal liabilities. Therefore, technology managers must prioritize cybersecurity and work closely with the CISO, cybersecurity team, and external experts to establish the appropriate safeguards against online attacks. The following are some of the significant areas where CTM management and cybersecurity overlap:

- Risk Management: Technology managers and cybersecurity experts must collaborate to identify, assess, and develop solutions that mitigate the risks associated with technology use within the organization.
- Security Architecture: Integrates security into the Secure Development Lifecycle[3] (SDLC) and enterprise architecture to ensure systems are secure by design, utilizing technologies such as Endpoint Detection and Response (EDR), Zero Trust, Identity and Access Management (IAM), and encryption.
- Resource Allocation: Justifying security expenditures involves analyzing risk exposure and balancing security with cost-effectiveness to ensure optimal allocation.
- Compliance: Legal data security and cybersecurity standards apply to businesses and organizations across various industries. Technology managers have the responsibility to ensure that their systems and procedures align with these standards, while cybersecurity experts can offer guidance on the most effective ways to achieve compliance.
- Response to Incidents: In the event of a cybersecurity incident, technology managers and cybersecurity specialists must collaborate to act swiftly and efficiently, minimizing the impact and preventing further damage.
- Performance Metrics: Assesses the performance of cybersecurity technology and its security effectiveness by utilizing SIEM, thus enabling GRC capabilities and unified reporting.
- Awareness and Training: Ensures that staff members are aware of security guidelines and know how to use technology safely.

The connection between CTM and cybersecurity is essential in today's business environment. Organizations must prioritize cybersecurity in their CTM strategies to develop and implement effective security measures. By considering these factors, businesses can enhance security, optimize IT performance, and foster innovation while facilitating company growth.

[3] The Software Development Life Cycle (SDLC) is a well-defined process that guides software development projects from initiation to completion. It establishes a defined governance structure for planning, developing, and maintaining software, ensuring that development is systematic and meets quality requirements.

6.7 CTM Governance Tools and Techniques

Organizations seeking to guard against cyberattacks and maintain resilience in today's rapidly evolving technological landscape must implement CTM to effectively enhance their creative capacity, improve risk protection, and attain long-term success in cybersecurity. This section explores several CTM governance tools and techniques (Table 6.2).

Organizations utilize CTM to manage technology solutions, safeguard business system security, and tackle various threats and weaknesses. The following list includes essential tools, their primary functions, and examples (Table 6.3).

Implementing CTM governance requires utilizing the aforementioned governance tools and security technology to protect the organization's infrastructure. An essential

Table 6.2 Governance tools and techniques

Road Mapping	A strategic planning tool, technology road mapping aids businesses in identifying and prioritizing technology development projects. It entails identifying critical technologies, assessing their potential advantages, and creating an adoption plan
Scouting	Scouting involves locating and assessing cutting-edge technologies and innovations that may be strategically important to a business. It entails monitoring technological advancements in the sector, attending conferences and trade exhibits, and networking with other companies and research organizations
Forecasting	Technology forecasting involves predicting the future evolution of technologies. It helps businesses forecast future trends, identify new opportunities and technical capabilities, and develop effective plans
Portfolio Management	Managing a company's technology portfolio involves allocating resources, managing risk, and evaluating and ranking technology development initiatives
Innovation	Cybersecurity technology innovations encompass the adoption or development of new tools, techniques, and frameworks to combat emerging cyber threats, enhance data protection, and increase resilience against attacks. Innovation governance refers to the process of managing innovation, encompassing conceptual planning, implementation, and other related activities. It entails establishing an innovation strategy, managing the innovation process, and fostering an innovative culture
Vulnerability Management	Conduct penetration testing to detect system vulnerabilities and provide employee training on phishing, social engineering, and security procedures
Incident Response & Recovery	Create an Incident Response Plan (IRP) with defined responsibilities and escalation paths, and implement backup and disaster recovery (BCP/DRP) techniques
Continuous Improvement	It is critical to use threat intelligence for proactive defense. To enhance security technology and procedures, KPIs and metrics must be utilized to regularly monitor and review their efficacy, considering emerging threats and lessons learned

Table 6.3 Security technology for infrastructure

Network Security	Firewalls (e.g., CISCO Firepower), Intrusion Detection/Prevention Systems (IDS/IPS), Zero-Trust Architecture (ZTA), and DNS Protection
Cloud Security	Cloud Access Security Broker (CASB) to monitor and control the use of cloud applications, secure configurations, and identity and access management (IAM) policies
Endpoint Protection	EDR/XDR, Antivirus/Anti-Malware, patch management, device encryption
Access Control & Identity Management	Multi-Factor Authentication (MFA), Privileged Access Management (PAM), and Identity and Access Management (IAM)
Monitoring & Response	Managed Detection and Response (MDR) and Security Information and Event Management (SIEM)
Data Security	Encryption, Data Loss Prevention (DLP), Email Gateway Security, and data classification
Backup & Recovery	Automated Backup Solutions that ensure data resilience and recovery against disasters and ransomware. Use SIEM and Security Orchestration, Automation, and Response (SOAR) for real-time threat detection and response

aspect of this decision is to consider how to implement a layered defense architecture (Defense in Depth) and incorporate security technologies such as firewalls, EDR, and SIEM for comprehensive coverage. To ensure compliance, tools must also support regulations like GDPR and HIPAA.

6.8 Cybersecurity TM Governance Framework (TM/CyG)

The key relationship between cybersecurity strategy and technology management is interdependence. Effective technology management enables robust cybersecurity and ensures the secure, resilient deployment of technology. This intersection is critical for organizational success in a digitally driven environment. This collaboration between cybersecurity and the technology management function reinforces it as a core component of digital transformation, ensuring a strategic, proactive, and planned approach to security governance.

A practical governance framework in cybersecurity technology management (TM/CyG) requires a process that systematically aligns strategy with security measures and business goals while mitigating risks. TM/CyG involves overseeing the organization's technological resources to ensure they align with its strategic objectives. As part of this, companies must establish policies and procedures for the effective utilization of technology. Additionally, investments and budgets are managed, and regulatory compliance is ensured. The TM/CyG process covers the planning, deployment, and management of technological resources to achieve the organization's strategic cybersecurity objectives, which also include applying technology to foster creativity, enhance operational effectiveness, and establish a stronger cybersecurity posture. The following are the key elements of the cybersecurity and technology management relationship.

6.8.1 *Aims and Objectives*

TM/CyG must ensure that the cybersecurity IT infrastructure supports business objectives, with strategies focused on detecting, preventing, and responding to threats. Technology management involves assessing hazards associated with IT deployment and evaluating the effectiveness of security applications in achieving those objectives. Consequently, technology management must integrate risk frameworks (such as NIST and ISO 27001) into technology lifecycle management to enhance security. For instance, TM/CyG's compliance plan must adhere to standards, regulations, and legislation (GDPR, HIPAA, CCPA) and enforce compliance through controls (encryption), automated monitoring (SIEM), and regular audits. In terms of incident response and recovery, TM/CyG ensures redundancy and disaster response support, provides threat detection and response capabilities, and collaborates with the cybersecurity team to develop and implement incident response strategies, thereby minimizing downtime and data loss.

6.8.2 *Structure*

The TM/CyG framework provides a structured approach to regulating cybersecurity technology, ensuring alignment with organizational goals, regulatory requirements, and industry best practices. It integrates concepts from leading frameworks (such as NIST and ISO 27001) with industry best practices. Several key characteristics and tasks associated with strategic cybersecurity technology management include:

Leadership and Governance Framework: Develop a cybersecurity governance structure with clearly defined roles for the CISO, IT security teams, and Board of Directors oversight. Ensure the BoD is actively involved in cybersecurity governance. Establish policies, standards, and procedures for access control, incident response, and data protection to ensure effective management of these critical areas. Assign responsibilities to security roles for the CISO, TM/CyG team, and system/data owners.

Technology Strategy: Ensure that cybersecurity initiatives align with company objectives and regulatory requirements to maximize effectiveness. This involves creating a roadmap that identifies the technical assets needed to achieve the organization's strategic goals. It also requires assessing the organization's technological needs, identifying gaps in the available technology resources, and determining the necessary technology investments to address those gaps.

Technology Architecture: This involves integrating security into the firm's enterprise architecture and digital transformation initiatives. CTM ensures a purposeful design that makes technology a catalyst for security. Because it provides an organized design for integrating security controls and ensures scalability, resilience, and alignment with business objectives, technology architecture is essential to effective cybersecurity governance. Without a robust framework, cybersecurity governance becomes reactive, fragmented, and ineffectual.

Technology Implementation: This involves implementing the technological assets outlined in the technology roadmap. It includes selecting and acquiring technology resources, setting them up, integrating them with existing systems, testing them, and utilizing them. By integrating proactive, scalable, and automated defenses into an organization's infrastructure, technology implementation simplifies cybersecurity management and transforms theoretical safeguards into practical measures. Technologies that are properly implemented turn policies into active safeguards, reducing the need for manual procedures and addressing the vulnerabilities that attackers exploit.

Innovation: Technology innovation involves leveraging technology to drive organizational innovation. This includes researching cutting-edge technologies, assessing their potential impact on the organization, and evaluating novel technological approaches. Technology innovation strengthens cybersecurity by enabling faster, smarter, and more flexible defenses against evolving threats. Innovation allows firms to stay ahead of hackers by shifting cybersecurity from a reactive to a predictive approach. AI-enhanced teams, autonomous security systems, and quantum-resistant architecture represent the future of security.

The Board of Directors is responsible for approving the cybersecurity strategy, policies, and budgets. In contrast, the CISO, as the cybersecurity leader, oversees TM/CyG leadership, oversight, and control of the function. The CISO develops cybersecurity policies, assesses threats, and ensures compliance with NIST or ISO 27001 in collaboration with the C-suite, the cybersecurity team, and IT representatives. Operationally, the CISO makes TM/CyG decisions in alignment with the board-approved cybersecurity policies and procedures. While the CISO oversees and controls TM/CyG, the IT and cybersecurity teams are charged with deploying, managing, and monitoring security systems. The CISO is primarily accountable for reporting TM/CyG development to the risk committee and the C-suite (see Fig. 6.1).

An organization's risk governance performance will depend on how effectively it plans and implements its strategic TM/CyG. By integrating technological resources with strategic goals and leveraging technology to ensure strong cybersecurity protections, organizations can enhance operational effectiveness, drive innovation, and achieve their corporate objectives.

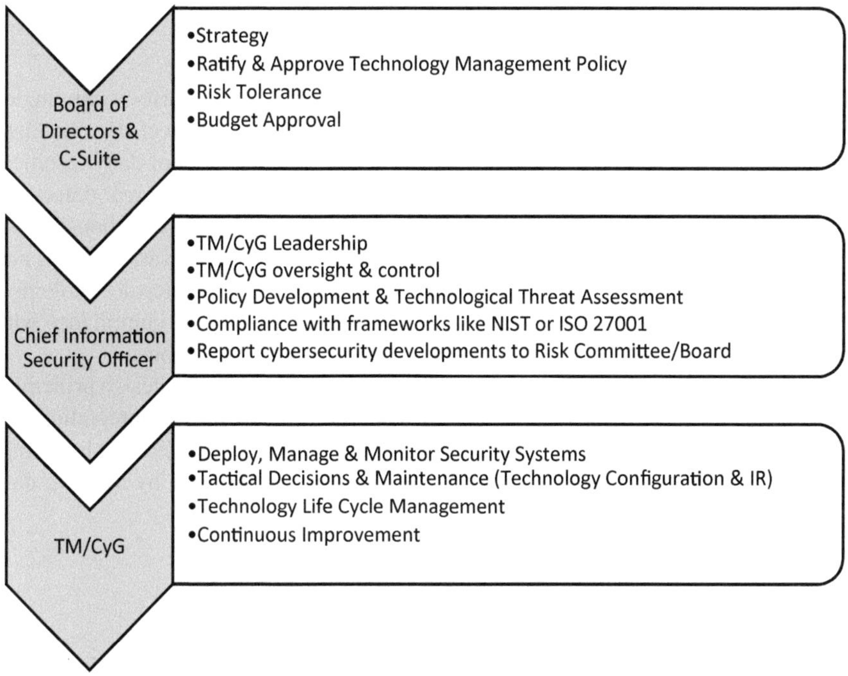

Fig. 6.1 TM/CyG structure

6.8.3 Foundations

CTM manages the planning, procurement, governance, and retirement of technology. Its foundations include adopting a risk-based approach to deployment by prioritizing defenses according to risk assessments (e.g., NIST Cybersecurity Framework, NIST Risk Management Framework), enabling defense-in-depth layered technologies, overseeing technology lifecycle management, and ensuring that technologies are seamlessly integrated and interoperable (e.g., SOAR platforms), while guaranteeing their cohesive and effective operation. CTM promotes innovation by utilizing AI-driven analytics and automated responses. Additionally, CTM complies with and aligns to standards (NIST CSF, ISO 27001) and regulations (GDPR, HIPAA, CIS Controls). It is designed to evaluate third-party tools for vulnerabilities and to perform real-time threat detection for incident response readiness.

6.8.4 Responsibilities

The TM/CyG team conducts regular reviews to ensure that security technologies (e.g., EDR solutions and vulnerability scanners) effectively protect the organization's digital infrastructure. It oversees the IT team's management of daily technical and process operations (e.g., IRP safeguards, patch management, threat detection) while adhering to the organization's technology strategy. TM/CyG is responsible for managing the technology lifecycle, which includes conducting risk assessments and cost–benefit analyses (in collaboration with the finance team) for new technologies, as well as procurement and deployment, and prioritizing vendors' compliance with NIST CSF, ISO 27001, or industry-specific standards and regulations.

TM/CyG ensures that system configuration adheres to secure-by-design principles (e.g., least privilege, zero-trust architecture) and promotes seamless integration and interoperability with existing systems (e.g., SIEM, IAM). During decommissioning, TM/CyG guarantees the secure handling of sensitive information by deleting data and revoking access to retired systems.

6.9 Conclusion

At the strategic level, when defining IT strategy and governance, TM/CyG is responsible for creating technological roadmaps, establishing IT policies and compliance frameworks, managing IT budgets, optimizing costs, and coordinating IT activities with business objectives. In tactical management, TM/CyG oversees the implementation of security policies and controls, ensures compliance, maintains servers, networks, and cloud environments, manages software and applications, and guarantees that disaster recovery and high availability are in place. However, it is always the Board of Directors or CISO who approves policy changes and significant technology investments.

Reference

National Research Council (US). (1987). *Management of technology: The hidden competitive advantage*. National Academy Press.

Chapter 7
People and Human Factors

Abstract Managing cybersecurity solely through technology is always challenging, as dealing with cyberattacks requires a socio-technical strategy. This chapter focuses on this area in the context of governance in human-technology interaction. From a cybersecurity governance perspective, we investigate how firms use people to manage cyber risk effectively. People can assist in identifying and mitigating risks before they have a significant negative impact because they are frequently the first line of defense against cyber threats. The ways that people can support cyber risk management are discussed and include security awareness, training and education, corporate culture, policy compliance, reporting suspicious activity, adhering to established incident response protocols, and aiding in the identification of the issue's origin and breadth, and assisting in the identification of potential risks and vulnerabilities inside an organization.

7.1 Introduction

Businesses are embracing the latest computing technology to achieve their goals. Managing cybersecurity solely through technology is always challenging; instead, addressing cyberattacks requires a socio-technical strategy (Safa et al., 2016). A comprehensive and integrated approach to cybersecurity governance must take human factors into account, recognizing that people are vital to cybersecurity. The human element in cybersecurity refers to incidents and activities whereby ignorance, carelessness, or human error may lead to an incident or breach, resulting in an "unintentional insider" (Hadlington, 2018). Individuals who frequently use technology are more vulnerable to online attacks. Most reported cyber incidents and breaches are the result of human mistakes, a complex security challenge. Human error and human interaction cannot be eliminated.

Most of the time, people are unaware that their activities and behaviors have implications in cyberspace, making them the weakest link in the cybersecurity chain. Consequently, human factors in cybersecurity cannot be overlooked. This

K. B. Oh et al., *Cybersecurity Governance*,
https://doi.org/10.1007/978-981-95-3865-2_7

chapter focuses on this area within cybersecurity governance, particularly on human-technology interaction (Glaspie & Karwowski, 2018). From a governance perspective, we investigate how firms can leverage governance to manage individuals effectively for cybersecurity efficacy.

While addressing human factors in cybersecurity governance is crucial, the significant global deficiency in cybersecurity expertise has made this task even more difficult. Despite the expansion of the cybersecurity industry, a substantial shortage of qualified candidates remains, exposing companies with limited resources to increased cyber risk. Therefore, while humans contribute notably to cyber threats, they are also essential in managing this issue.

> The Malaysian government has called upon technical and vocational education and training (TVET) institutions to train more cybersecurity professionals. There is currently a shortage of 26,000 professionals in the cybersecurity sector. The government has approved a new cybersecurity academy to train more professionals and set up a fund to help partially fund this initiative (*The Star*, 24 September 2024).

While technology can provide adequate security measures, it is essential to recognize that human factors also play a crucial role in maintaining cybersecurity (Glaspie & Karwowski, 2018). Organizations should invest in training and awareness programs to help employees understand their role in protecting sensitive information and developing good cybersecurity habits. When creating policies and procedures, it is essential to consider the end users' requirements, motives, and cognitive traits.

Cybersecurity governance in human resource management (HRM) prevents breaches and cyberattacks on sensitive employee and organizational data, promotes the CIA triad of information, builds trust with stakeholders by demonstrating a commitment to data privacy and security, minimizes the financial and legal risks associated with non-compliance or data breaches, and enhances the company's overall cybersecurity posture.

In human resources (HR) cybersecurity, the enterprise risk management embedded cybersecurity governance (E-CyG) process is essential because it ensures that risks associated with HR systems, data, and procedures are identified, assessed, mitigated, and sufficiently tracked. The E-CyG process provides the structure and oversight required to incorporate governance into HR processes.

7.2 People and Cyber Threats

People and human factors play a significant role in cybersecurity breaches (Schneier, 2000). Human behavior is unpredictable, unlike systems, and mistakes stemming from these behaviors can be costly for individuals and organizations in the online realm. The importance of human elements in cybersecurity is vital, as even the best cybersecurity technology can be undermined by human error or action, despite technology and systems providing a strong defense against cyberattacks. Thus, cybersecurity governance involves more than just technology; it also encompasses people. People's reactions to cyberattacks, unlike those related to technological issues, are cognitive and psychological, influenced by various human factors (Wang et al., 2021). Consequently, while technological measures may adequately address technical challenges, they often fall short in tackling cybersecurity issues that are inherently connected to human nature. Therefore, organizations must adopt a comprehensive approach that encompasses all aspects of cybersecurity, including procedural, human, physical, and technological factors (Corradini & Nardelli, 2020). This prevents the silo or weakest-link effect when addressing risks in our highly interconnected digital environment, making cybersecurity governance an organization-wide effort (Oh & Ho, 2022).

Cybercriminals are increasingly targeting individuals, rather than technology, exploiting their vulnerabilities through criminal intent, psychological manipulation, ignorance, or poor judgment. Studies and reports indicate that human error or behavior is a significant contributor to many cybersecurity incidents.[1] These mistakes can range from simple errors, such as clicking on a suspicious link or falling for a phishing scam, to more complex issues, including weak passwords, misconfigured security settings, or inadequate training on cybersecurity best practices.

Human factors can also lead to more targeted attacks, such as insider threats, where employees intentionally or accidentally leak sensitive information or engage in malicious activities, as listed and explained in Table 7.1. These attacks are often executed through social engineering techniques that exploit human vulnerabilities. A significant contributing factor is employees' lack of awareness and education regarding cybersecurity policies (Li et al., 2019) or a tendency toward complacency (Hadlington, 2017).

Human factors play a significant role in cybersecurity, and effectively managing these elements is crucial for maintaining robust security protocols. To defend against cyberattacks, organizations must prioritize cybersecurity training, education, and awareness, implement strong password policies, and foster a security-conscious culture.

7.2.1 Human Threats to Network and Business Systems

Intentional or unintentional human threats to network systems can harm a network and a business system's security and stability. These threats can significantly impact

[1] The 2020 Cost of Insider Threats Global Report by the Ponemon Institute found that insider threats caused by employee or contractor negligence accounted for 62% of insider incidents. The 2021 Verizon Data Breach Investigations Report found that human error was a contributing factor in 85% of data breaches.

Table 7.1 Some ways in which human factors impact cybersecurity

Phishing and social engineering	Social engineering techniques and phishing attempts exploit human flaws and vulnerabilities. Cybercriminals trick users into disclosing personal information or downloading malware onto their devices using phony emails, calls, or messaging
Lack of security awareness	Many people lack knowledge about cybersecurity threats and how to protect themselves against them. This ignorance and inattention may result in inadvertent security lapses and errors
Weak passwords	One of the most common methods hackers use to access systems and networks is the use of weak passwords. Humans create and manage passwords and occasionally make mistakes, such as choosing easy passwords or using the same one for multiple accounts
Insider threats	Insider threats, in which workers or other insiders inadvertently or intentionally compromise security, can also be caused by human factors. Personal gain, dissatisfaction, or a lack of training are possible causes
Cybersecurity culture	One way to lower the risk of cyberattacks is for an organization to have a strong cybersecurity or risk management culture. The development of this culture entails education and training, encouraging safe security procedures, and cultivating a vigilant and aware work environment among staff members

the confidentiality, integrity, and availability of business systems. Table 7.2 presents several examples of how individuals might compromise a network or business system.

There are various ways in which people can pose a threat to network and business systems, and these risks can significantly compromise network security. Organizations should implement robust password policies, train staff on cybersecurity best practices, mitigate the risk of human threats to network systems, and monitor for suspicious activities.

7.2.2 Human Threats to Data

Human hazards to data can arise from users' accidental or intentional actions when they have access to it. Here are a few examples of data breaches that have been caused by human error (Table 7.3).

Human risks to data can take many forms and seriously compromise the security and privacy of sensitive information. To mitigate these risks, organizations must take proactive measures to educate staff about cybersecurity threats, implement robust password policies, use encryption, monitor for suspicious activity, and enforce access controls.

Table 7.2 Human threats to network and business systems

Phishing and social engineering	Cybercriminals frequently employ social engineering techniques and phishing attacks to compromise a network or system. Cybercriminals use social engineering tactics to deceive individuals into divulging sensitive information or granting unauthorized computer access. It frequently entails coercing staff members into disclosing private information or infecting their equipment with malware. Those tactics include phishing emails, baiting, or pretexting
Weak passwords	Weak passwords make it simple for hackers to enter a network because they can be easily guessed or cracked. Workers who reuse passwords across multiple accounts or use weak passwords may unintentionally compromise networks or business systems
Insider threats	Employees and other insiders who intentionally or unintentionally compromise network security are considered insider threats. These threats may originate from third parties, such as contractors or employees who possess sensitive data or have access to systems. They can involve infecting computers with malware, stealing data, or manipulating them in various ways
Unsecured devices	Cybercriminals may use poorly secured devices as a means of gaining network entry. Devices that are not properly patched or updated, or lack strong passwords or other authentication mechanisms, may fall into this category
Lack of security awareness	Workers who do not understand the dangers of cybersecurity could inadvertently endanger a network. They can do this by downloading malware or clicking on dubious links

Table 7.3 Human threats to data

Social engineering	Cybercriminals frequently employ social engineering techniques, such as phishing and pretexting, to deceive individuals into disclosing sensitive information. These strategies can involve posing as an authority figure or sending phony emails from reliable sources to obtain sensitive information
Insider threats	Insiders with access to confidential information may disclose or steal that information, either intentionally or unintentionally. This can involve transferring data to unauthorized devices, exchanging data with unapproved parties, or inadvertently disclosing data due to negligence or inadequate training
Weak passwords	Weak passwords are easily decipherable or breakable, allowing hackers to access sensitive information. Employees who use easy-to-guess passwords or reuse them across multiple accounts may inadvertently compromise sensitive data
Lack of security awareness	Workers who are unaware of cybersecurity threats risk inadvertently compromising sensitive data. This can involve using unprotected Wi-Fi networks, downloading malware, or clicking on dubious websites
Unsecured devices	Cybercriminals may use poorly secured devices as a point of entry to obtain private information. Devices that are not properly patched or updated or that lack strong passwords or other authentication mechanisms may fall under this category

7.3 People's Role in Enhancing Cybersecurity

The cybersecurity governance of enterprise human resources includes the framework, policies, and procedures that guarantee a company's protection and secure management of data and technology. Aligning HR procedures with cybersecurity principles is essential for protecting data confidentiality, integrity, and availability, thus mitigating risks and ensuring compliance with legal and regulatory requirements.

People can also assist in identifying and mitigating risks before they have a significant negative impact, as they are often the first line of defense against cyber threats. The ways that people can support cybersecurity risk management must be discussed among stakeholders and should include security awareness, training, education, corporate culture, policy compliance, reporting suspicious activity, adhering to established incident response protocols, aiding in the identification of the issue's origin and extent, and assisting in identifying potential risks and vulnerabilities within an organization.

While organizations cannot eliminate human threats to cybersecurity, they can implement measures to minimize the chances of hostile behavior and human error. Below, we outline some strategies and components for this purpose:

7.3.1 Leadership

The Board of Directors and senior management (B&SM) must provide leadership in all cybersecurity initiatives, prioritizing and supporting HR's efforts. For cybersecurity governance to be effective, the BoD needs a strategic vision, and executives must possess agility and effective communication skills when addressing human issues and technical vulnerabilities. Leadership governance is a crucial component of cybersecurity, ensuring that all levels of the organization communicate and collaborate to enable the efficient functioning of processes and essential mechanisms within the cybersecurity value chain. Although it is challenging to control or compel the human factor to change, effective leadership can introduce other incentives and measures to enhance participation in the cybersecurity function, such as recognition, fostering a risk-aware culture, and education. The challenge of cybersecurity governance is compounded by the need for leaders to understand the complexities of both technology and human factors to protect organizational assets (Obi et al., 2024).

7.3.2 Chief Information Security Officer

Businesses should assign a dedicated HR cybersecurity officer and clearly outline their duties and responsibilities regarding cybersecurity within the HR division. The

Chief Information Security Officer (CISO) is primarily tasked with overseeing the organization's cybersecurity function. Key responsibilities of the CISO include:

- Recommending and implementing policies and procedures to protect the firm's data confidentiality, integrity, and availability.
- Coordinating security measures that align with overarching corporate objectives.
- Engaging with the Board of Directors, risk committee, C-suite, and departmental leaders about all aspects of enterprise cyber risk management.
- Developing a cybersecurity strategy and performing risk assessments.
- Ensuring adherence to rules and regulations.
- Collaborating with human resources to prevent data breaches.
- Planning and managing incident response, business continuity, and disaster recovery efforts.
- Communicating with stakeholders regarding the firm's cybersecurity exposure, mitigation efforts, resilience, compliance, and incidents.

7.3.3 Policies and Procedures

A business procedure or process is an interconnected series of actions designed to achieve an organization's strategic or policy objectives. Therefore, they must create and implement HR-specific cybersecurity policies and procedures, including password management, data access controls, and secure communication guidelines. The organization must establish clear guidelines for how staff members should handle sensitive data and utilize business devices and systems as part of its business processes, supported by strict rules and procedures. For example, policies should outline procedures for access, data handling, password creation, and responsibilities for monitoring threats and reporting security incidents.

7.3.4 Education, Awareness, and Training

Organizations can reduce their exposure to cyber hazards by implementing well-structured cybersecurity awareness and training programs (Alghamdi, 2022; Zwilling et al., 2022). Fostering a culture of security throughout the organization can help promote best security practices and decrease the likelihood of human errors. Instilling a security culture should encourage staff members to report potential security incidents and recognize commendable security behaviors, enhancing risk awareness and nurturing a culture of cybersecurity consciousness.

Education and training are the most effective strategies for reducing human hazards and dangers. Employees and business partners should receive cybersecurity risk management training, as recommended by the National Institute of Standards and Technology (NIST CSF). Furthermore, employees, including HR professionals, should undergo regular cybersecurity training provided by their organizations to understand prevalent risks, emerging threats, and preventive measures, such as safeguarding personal devices and identifying phishing attempts, thereby minimizing the likelihood of human errors. The company must inform every employee of its cybersecurity risk management strategy and ensure they are aware of the risks and the significance of the plan. Additionally, ensuring that every employee knows who to contact and what to do in the event of a network, system, or data breach is essential. This training and information must be made easily accessible and comprehensible to all.

7.3.5 Effective Communication

Effective communication within organizations is essential. Fostering and developing effective cybersecurity threat or incident communication within an organization is crucial for the early detection, response, and mitigation of cyber hazards. To achieve this, the firm needs a communication structure, governance protocol, and policies that clearly articulate responsibilities and reporting guidelines, incident reporting channels, and risk awareness initiatives to enhance its cybersecurity posture. It must design a clear communication architecture that outlines roles and duties, assigning specific responsibilities for incident communication (e.g., CISO, Incident Response Team, Legal, IT, PR). Escalation pathways must determine who should be notified at various severity levels (e.g., low-risk versus major breach). The framework specifies internal and external stakeholders who must be informed (e.g., employees, management, regulators, customers, law enforcement).

Organizations must develop a robust cybersecurity communication strategy that enhances resilience and facilitates quick responses to emerging threats by adopting proactive communication, establishing clear protocols to prevent confusion during crises, and continuously training staff to keep them prepared.

7.3.6 Access Controls (Physical and Digital)

By implementing access controls that restrict access to sensitive data and systems, organizations can ensure that employees have access only to the information and systems necessary for their jobs, thereby reducing the likelihood of human error. To achieve this, organizations can utilize multi-factor authentication or role-based access controls (RBAC). To guarantee that employees access only the information and systems essential for their roles, organizations should implement RBAC and regularly review and adjust access permissions, particularly when employees leave or their job responsibilities change. As a result, companies can securely manage access rights during employee onboarding and ensure that access is promptly revoked upon offboarding. Additionally, they should conduct exit interviews to remind departing employees of their obligations regarding the confidentiality of sensitive information.

In addition to access restrictions, companies should protect sensitive data through encryption and secure storage. Depending on the industry, they must also ensure full compliance with data protection regulations, such as the General Data Protection Regulation (GDPR) or the Health Insurance Portability and Accountability Act (HIPAA).

7.3.7 Monitoring and Incident Reporting

Organizations should establish systems to monitor suspicious activities by deploying intrusion detection and prevention systems (IDS/IPS) and respond promptly when such activities are identified. In addition to implementing logging and tracking systems to maintain an audit record of HR-related operations, businesses should use monitoring technologies to detect anomalous activity in HR systems, such as unauthorized access attempts or data exfiltration. Identifying such attacks may also involve monitoring network traffic, reviewing system logs, and using threat intelligence to detect and mitigate potential threats. Utilizing big data analytics and AI applications can enhance the effectiveness of these measures. Furthermore, employees should be encouraged to report unusual or suspicious activities to strengthen the organization's security culture.

7.3.8 Culture of Security and Awareness

Enterprise Security Culture encompasses an organization's collaborative attitudes, behaviors, and procedures that prioritize and reinforce cybersecurity as a collective responsibility. It reflects how individuals at all levels of the organization—from leadership to frontline staff—understand, value, and actively engage in the protection of digital assets. Security awareness is a crucial element of security culture, aimed at educating employees about cyber threats, safe practices, and organizational policies and procedures to mitigate human-related risks (such as phishing, weak passwords, or data misuse).

A strong security culture is primarily composed of the following: documented security policies and procedures (risk control processes, password rules, incident reporting, and accountability); employee engagement and training (regular, role-specific training and clear communication about threats); leadership commitment (understanding human behaviors and allocating resources for cybersecurity initiatives); and continuous improvement (feedback chain). Furthermore, employees should be given incentives for secure behavior to reinforce a risk culture.

7.3.9 Testing and Simulations

Regular plan testing and simulations, including tabletop exercises, are essential for identifying gaps in readiness and mitigation procedures, as well as for assessing the clarity of roles and responsibilities assigned to all stakeholders. Consequently, the Board of Directors and C-suite executives must consistently ask about any improvements, adjustments, or changes made to the strategy to enhance the company's cybersecurity posture.

7.3.10 Stakeholders' Involvement

The success of the risk management strategy relies on the support of all parties involved, including the Board of Directors, senior management, and every department, such as IT, which must stay engaged. Furthermore, all stakeholders' tasks and responsibilities must be clearly defined and documented. Organizations can mitigate the risks of hostile behavior and human error, although it is impossible to eliminate human vulnerabilities to cybersecurity. This involves engaging all stakeholders in providing instruction and training, implementing strict regulations and processes, controlling access, monitoring suspicious activities, and promoting a culture of security awareness.

7.4 Technologies for Mitigating Human Threats

In addition to the strategies highlighted in Section "People's Role in Enhancing Cybersecurity", firms can utilize several technologies to mitigate the risks associated with human-technology interaction. We discuss some of these technologies here (Table 7.4), including Multi-Factor Authentication (MFA), Security Information and Event Management (SIEM), User Behavior Analytics (UBA), Data Loss Prevention (DLP), and Endpoint Detection and Response (EDR) systems, along with their implications for governance.

Technologies such as multi-factor authentication, SIEM, UBA, DLP, and EDR can help mitigate human threats to cybersecurity by identifying potential risks and adding additional layers of security to prevent data breaches and cyberattacks.

Table 7.4 Mitigation technologies for human threats

Multi-Factor Authentication (MFA)	To access a system or account, users must provide two or more forms of authentication, also known as multi-factor authentication (MFA). MFA can be something the person is (like a fingerprint), something they have (like a smartphone), or something they know (like a password). Using MFA can reduce the possibility of human error in password management
User Behavior Analytics (UBA)	UBA solutions utilize machine learning algorithms to detect unusual user behavior that may indicate a security risk. For instance, UBA can examine file access patterns to identify data exfiltration or user login patterns to identify potential account intrusions
Security Information and Event Management (SIEM)	Network devices, servers, and applications are just a few sources of security-related data that SIEM systems aim to gather and analyze. By analyzing this data, SIEM systems can identify possible security incidents and notify security teams to take action
Endpoint Detection and Response (EDR)	EDR solutions offer real-time monitoring and threat detection on endpoint devices, including laptops and mobile phones. This involves examining user behavior to detect potential malware infections or insider threats
Data Loss Prevention (DLP)	DLP solutions prevent sensitive information from being stolen or disclosed. This can involve implementing policies to prevent workers from exchanging private information via cloud services or email, or utilizing technology to identify and stop data exfiltration

7.5 Role of HR in E-CyG

Human Resources (HR) plays a crucial role in strategic cybersecurity governance by aligning employee policies with cybersecurity objectives (Sotira, 2018). HR serves as a strategic enabler of cybersecurity governance, bridging the gap between people and technology to mitigate risk. HR enhances an organization's overall cyber resilience by integrating security into its hiring, training, and policy enforcement. People play a vital role in managing cybersecurity risks. They can help identify and mitigate risks before they lead to significant harm and are often the first line of defense against cyberattacks. Here are some strategies organizations can implement to manage cybersecurity risks more effectively.

7.5.1 Security Awareness

Security awareness is a critical component of effective cybersecurity governance, ensuring that employees, management, and third parties recognize and mitigate threats (Li et al., 2019). Continuous training on simulated attacks, as well as role-specific content customized to different business units, such as executives, IT, HR, legal, third-party, and finance, are critical components of effective awareness programs. HR must ensure that employees are aware of the dangers and threats to help mitigate cybersecurity risks. This involves utilizing security features such as multi-factor authentication, creating robust passwords, and recognizing and responding to suspicious emails or other forms of communication. Strategic cybersecurity governance is directly supported by security awareness, which turns staff members from weakest points into first-line defenders.

7.5.2 Culture, Training, and Education

Beyond technical security, cybersecurity education and training are vital defensive strategies. One effective approach to managing cyber risk is to utilize customized training programs that shift employees' perceptions of cybersecurity threats. Employers can also provide education and training for their staff to help them understand the importance of cybersecurity and how to protect sensitive data. With ongoing mandatory cybersecurity training and awareness programs, including phishing simulations, secure coding, and compliance training, organizations can promote a culture of security and a security-first mindset across the organization, thereby reinforcing and enhancing their cybersecurity resilience. Ongoing education about new risks and vulnerabilities, along with training on identifying and mitigating cyber threats, is an essential component of this process.

7.5.3 Policy Compliance

Individuals can help mitigate cybersecurity risks by adhering to established policies and procedures. These include practices such as using strong passwords, updating software, and securely disposing of sensitive data. Greater compliance with implementing standards and regulations that align with risk management strategies, such as cybersecurity awareness and knowledge training, can reduce an organization's exposure to cyber threats through effective risk management processes (Swinton & Hedges, 2019).

7.5.4 Incident Response

Organizations need a comprehensive incident response plan that outlines HR-related actions for preventing and responding to cybersecurity incidents, including network or system disruptions, data breaches, and unauthorized access. Individuals can play a pivotal role in addressing cybersecurity incidents by reporting suspicious activity, following established incident response protocols, and determining the nature, source, and scope of the event. They should also ensure that HR staff are informed about how to promptly report issues and work together with IT and security teams to mitigate risks.

7.5.5 Risk-Based Approach

Individuals can contribute to cybersecurity by helping identify potential risks and weaknesses within an organization. This involves voicing security concerns, participating in risk analyses and drills, and offering suggestions for possible security improvements. People are essential to cybersecurity risk management because they can engage in incident response and risk assessments, recognize potential risks and threats, and adhere to established policies and procedures to protect sensitive data and reduce the impact of cyberattacks.

7.5.6 Performance

Tracking employee performance helps identify weaknesses and vulnerabilities related to cybersecurity risk management within the HR function. Organizations can evaluate HR's role in cybersecurity and enhance employee security practices by monitoring key performance indicators (KPIs). Here are some HR-specific cybersecurity metrics for assessing people-related performance (Table 7.5):

7.6 Cybersecurity HR Governance Framework

The HR cybersecurity governance framework (HR/CyG) employs a risk-based approach that ensures HR operations align with cybersecurity policies and best practices, thereby mitigating risks associated with insider threats, insufficient access control, and employee-related vulnerabilities. As part of the broader Enterprise Cybersecurity Governance Framework (E-CyG), the HR/CyG integrates HR practices and cybersecurity regulations to protect an organization's networks, systems, data, and personnel from cyber threats. Employees must understand their roles within the organization's 5-step E-CyG process, which encompasses risk identification, assessment, mitigation, detection, reporting, and incident risk response activities. The following illustrates the essential components of the HR/CyG framework.

Table 7.5 Performance metrics

KPI	Objective
Security training completion rate	The percentage of employees who finish the required cybersecurity training
Scores from the security culture survey	How important do employees think cybersecurity is?
Background check compliance	Percentage of checks on hires for security risks
Phishing test failure rate	The percentage of staff members who click on phishing email simulations
Policy acknowledgement rate	The percentage of workers who are aware of IT security policies
Training frequency	Measure the frequency of staff security training updates
Employee-reported incidents	The number of security concerns that employees have reported
Insider threat incidents	Incidents involving deliberate or unintentional breaches by staff members are known to occur
Privileged access reviews	The frequency of audits of access privileges
Confidential data handling	Incidents of misuse of employee data (PII, payroll information)
MFA adoption rate	The percentage of users who have multi-factor authentication activated
Password policy compliance	The percentage of staff members who use secure, current passwords
Role-based access compliance	The proportion of workers with the proper access levels
Offboarding efficiency	The amount of time it takes to deny access to departing employees
Multi-Factor Authentication (MFA) Adoption	Employee MFA adoption percentage
Shadow IT usage	The number of employees who use unapproved software or services
Third-party vendor security	Adherence to cybersecurity requirements by HR vendors

7.6.1 Governance Role Structure

In human resource cybersecurity governance, the Board of Directors is responsible for approving the human resource strategy, policies, and budgets. The CISO, as the cybersecurity leader, has leadership, oversight, and control over the human resource cybersecurity function.

The CISO develops HR cybersecurity policies and procedures, assesses HR threats, and ensures compliance with NIST CSF or ISO 27001 in collaboration with the C-suite, cybersecurity team, IT, and HR representatives. Operationally, the CISO

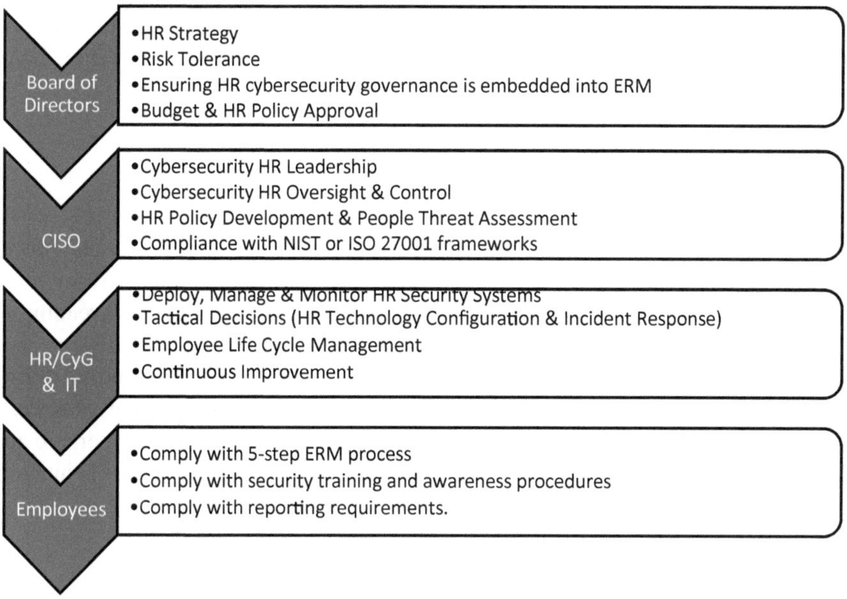

Fig. 7.1 HR cybersecurity governance structure

makes decisions regarding HR risk control within the board-approved HR cybersecurity strategy, policies, and procedures and oversees the HR cybersecurity processes. The CISO, IT, and cybersecurity teams are collectively responsible for deploying, managing, and monitoring HR security systems. The CISO is primarily accountable for reporting HR cybersecurity developments to the risk committee and the C-suite (Fig. 7.1).

7.6.2 HR Security Collaborations and Processes

In partnership with various departments, HR/CyG enforces policies by collaborating with the cybersecurity, IT security (technical), legal, and compliance teams. In contrast, cybersecurity provides expertise (i.e., CISO and the security team). The CISO works with HR to establish governance, HR security policies, and procedures. Based on these policies, HR identifies and mitigates insider threats while managing the employee life cycle, including pre-hire background checks, checks for IT/security positions, and evaluating third-party suppliers. Onboarding activities include cybersecurity training, awareness programs, and role-based access controls. During employment, HR/CyG ensures regular security training (social engineering simulations) and monitors for suspicious behavior (insider threats). HR promptly revokes access during offboarding and conducts exit interviews to recover company assets and ensure a seamless transition. At the line level, employees must observe and comply with security training, awareness, and reporting procedures (Fig. 7.1).

7.6.3 Policy Alignment

The HR policies must align with the organization's access control policy and procedures, acceptable use policy (AUP), incident response plan, and data privacy regulations (e.g., GDPR, HIPAA, CCPA). They include pre-employment screening to validate candidates' backgrounds, role-based permissions or least privilege access, and onboarding security training (e.g., password hygiene). HR risk controls during offboarding and role changes must ensure the timely deprovisioning of access, conduct exit interviews to remind departing employees of their data ownership and the restrictions on disclosing private information, and facilitate the return of company devices.

7.6.4 Compliance

In cybersecurity governance, human resources serve as a link between people and policy. Through training, effective communication, and enforcement, the HR department plays a crucial role in ensuring that staff members understand and comply with cybersecurity regulations. HR governance, HR/CyG, should ensure training is conducted to increase employee awareness of policy and regulatory compliance. Mandatory training for all employees, along with keeping records of training completion for audits, is essential.

7.6.5 Continuing Employee Monitoring and Third-Party Risk

Ongoing employee management is essential for monitoring and identifying internal threats and negligence. This is achieved through behavioral monitoring, annual security training, phishing simulations, and regular role-based reviews. Risks from third parties or the supply chain require constant monitoring to ensure compliance and timely evaluation of vendor credentials.

7.7 Conclusion

By integrating cybersecurity governance into human resource management (i.e., HR/CyG), organizations can enhance the protection of their networks, systems, and data, ensure compliance, and mitigate the risk of vulnerabilities related to human error in cybersecurity defenses. They can also lessen the impact of human mistakes on their security posture by providing training, implementing best practices, and increasing awareness of the risks associated with cyberattacks. Cybersecurity governance in HR ensures that staff, often the weakest link in security, are effectively managed, informed, and monitored. Organizations minimize risks by aligning HR processes with cybersecurity strategies while maintaining compliance and fostering a security-aware workforce.

References

Alghamdi, A. (2022). A systematic review on human factors in cybersecurity. *International Journal of Computer Science and Network Security, 22*(10), 282–290.

Corradini, I., & Nardelli, E. (2020). Social engineering and the value of data: The need of specific awareness programs. *Advances in Intelligent Systems and Computing*, 59–65.

Glaspie, H., & Karwowski, W. (2018). Human factors in information security culture: A literature review. *Advances in Intelligent Systems and Computing*, 269–280.

Hadlington, L. (2017). Human factors in cybersecurity: Examining the link between Internet addiction, impulsivity, attitudes towards cybersecurity, and risky cybersecurity behaviors. *Heliyon, 3*(7), e00346. https://doi.org/10.1016/j.heliyon.2017

Hadlington, L. (2018). The human factor in cybersecurity: Exploring the accidental insider. *Psychological and Behavioral Examinations in Cyber Security*, 46–63.

Li, L., He, W., Xu, L., Ash, I., Anwar, M., & Yuan, X. (2019). Investigating the impact of cybersecurity policy awareness on employees' cybersecurity behavior. *International Journal of Information Management, 45*, 13–24. https://doi.org/10.1016/j.ijinfomgt.2018.10.017

Obi, O., Akagha, O., Dawodu, S., Anyanwu, A., Onwusinkwue, S., & Ahmad, I. (2024). Comprehensive review on cybersecurity: Modern threats and advanced defense strategies. *Computer Science & IT Research Journal, 5*(2), 293–310.

Oh, K., & Ho, B. (2022). *Cybersecurity risk management: An enterprise risk management approach.* Nova Science Publishers.

Safa, N., Solms, R., & Futcher, L. (2016). Human aspects of information security in organizations. *Computer Fraud & Security* (2), 15–18.

Schneier, B. (2000). *Secrets and lies: Security in a digital world*. Wiley.

Sotira, N. (2018). The human factor in cybersecurity. *Cyber Security: A Peer-Reviewed Journal, 1*, 326–330.

Swinton, S., & Hedges, S. (2019). *Cybersecurity Governance, Part 1: 5 Fundamental Challenges (cmu.edu).* https://insights.sei.cmu.edu/blog/cybersecurity-governance-part-1-5-fundamental-challenges/#:~:text=Cybersecurity%20Governance%2C%20Part%201%3A%205%20Fundamental%20Challenges%201,Senior%20Leadership%20Oversight%20...%205%205.%20Resources%20. Accessed 29 September 2024.

Wang, L., Zhu, H., & Sun, L. (2021). Social engineering in cybersecurity: Effect mechanisms, human vulnerabilities and attack methods. *IEEE Access, 9*, 11895–11910.

Zwilling, M., Klien, G., Lesjak, D., Wiechetek, Ł, Cetin, F., & Basim, H. (2022). Cybersecurity awareness, knowledge and behavior: A comparative study. *Journal of Computer Information Systems*. https://doi.org/10.1080/08874417.2020.1712269

Chapter 8
Finance

Abstract This chapter addresses the financial governance of cybersecurity within the broader ERM framework. In the current business environment, corporate activities are becoming more digital. As a result, cyber hazards are more rampant as firms become common targets for cyberattacks, resulting in significant financial losses, reputational harm, and legal liability. The process of allocating economic resources and determining expenditure priorities to support the successful adoption and upkeep of cybersecurity measures within an organization entails figuring out the extent of the risk exposure and how much money is needed to safeguard the organization's networks, business systems, and data from online threats. Relevant governance factors addressed in cybersecurity financial management include valuation, investment, and budgeting. The presence of a well-designed cybersecurity financial governance as a tool underpinning the evaluation and ranking of cyber threats and prioritizing investments is crucial to taking cyber threats into account.

8.1 Introduction

The relationship between finance and cybersecurity is crucial in today's business climate, as organizations with a digital presence are becoming increasingly common targets for cyberattacks. Strong governance helps organizations avoid costly incidents by preventing breaches, ensuring compliance, maintaining confidence, maximizing security investments, and being better prepared to manage risks when they arise. Cybersecurity governance mitigates financial risk by implementing structured policies, controls, and monitoring procedures to protect an organization's digital assets.

Cybersecurity is crucial for organizational performance, as cyber risks can result in substantial financial losses, reputational damage, and legal liability. Here are some key cybersecurity implications for finance governance.

- To manage risk effectively, organizations must develop and implement strategies to address the ever-evolving cybersecurity threats. Therefore, risk management involves conducting regular risk assessments, applying appropriate security

K. B. Oh et al., *Cybersecurity Governance*,
https://doi.org/10.1007/978-981-95-3865-2_8

controls, and monitoring systems for potential threats that could lead to financial losses.

- To prevent cyber fraud, businesses must implement preventive measures by establishing strong access controls, authentication and verification processes, identifying, detecting, and investigating suspicious activities, and regularly educating staff about the risks associated with fraud.
- Compliance requires organizations to adhere to cybersecurity regulations and industry standards (e.g., HIPAA, PCI DSS, GDPR, SOX). Following these regulations and standards is essential for minimizing legal risks and safeguarding the organization's reputation and business.
- Data protection is crucial because organizations handle sensitive personal and financial information, making it a significant concern. Methods such as encryption, access controls, and monitoring are essential components of cybersecurity that safeguard against unauthorized access and data breaches.
- In the event of a cybersecurity attack, organizations must act quickly and effectively to minimize the impact on customers and the company. To achieve this, they need a well-defined incident response plan, regular training and testing, and close collaboration with law enforcement and other relevant parties to investigate and resolve the issue.

Many organizations still view cybersecurity as a technical concern exclusive to information technology specialists, which can lead to management failures. Management must acknowledge that the connection between cybersecurity and finance is vital in today's business environment. Organizations need to prioritize cybersecurity to develop and implement effective security solutions. Maintaining a strong cybersecurity framework requires that organizations proactively manage their financial resources for incident response, data security, risk management, compliance, and fraud prevention.

Policies and regulations for cybersecurity financial governance enhance the visibility of cybersecurity to the Board of Directors and management, reinforcing their incentives to take responsibility for it (Crisanto & Prenio, 2017). This chapter examines financial functions within the context of the cybersecurity governance value chain, providing the reader with a comprehensive, cybersecurity-focused perspective on the discipline. In today's business landscape, corporate activities are increasingly digital, leading to more prevalent cyber threats, with companies often targeted by cyberattacks. Consequently, cybersecurity governance is a vital risk management enabling factor, as risks can result in significant financial losses, reputational damage, and legal liability. Estimating potential losses due to a breach, allocating economic resources, and determining spending priorities to support the effective adoption and maintenance of cybersecurity measures involves evaluating the financial aspects of safeguarding the organization's networks, information systems, and data from online threats. Therefore, in this chapter, we discuss financial governance from the perspectives of risk assessment, risk management, investment, and budgeting for cybersecurity.

8.2 The Finance-Cybersecurity Nexus

Cybersecurity is closely linked to finance in various ways. Cybersecurity threats can significantly impact an organization's value, resulting in financial losses, reputational damage, and legal liabilities. As a result, when evaluating organizations, investors, analysts, and other stakeholders are increasingly taking into account the financial ramifications of cybersecurity risks. A well-crafted financial governance policy, which serves as a tool for evaluation, risk management, investment, risk assessment, and investment prioritization, is essential when addressing cybersecurity threats. By making informed choices regarding cybersecurity measures and investments, organizations can reduce their risk of financial loss, reputational harm, and data breaches.

8.2.1 Finance and E-CyG

Shareholders and investors are increasingly aware of companies' financial exposure to cybersecurity risks. They are demanding a greater commitment from companies to prioritize the development of robust governance infrastructures. The enterprise risk management/cybersecurity governance framework (E-CyG) provides a focused, structured, and comprehensive approach to addressing organizational cyber risks. Below are the key factors that connect finance and E-CyG:

Financial Impact: Cybersecurity incidents can lead to substantial economic losses for organizations. For example, a data breach may result in the loss of sensitive data, leading to fines from authorities, increased legal fees, and a decline in customer trust. Ransomware attacks and system failures can cause significant business disruptions and harm to reputation. The financial repercussions of these events can have a direct impact on the organization's value. E-CyG can identify and assess cybersecurity threats that impact financial stability. Finance plays a crucial role in evaluating the likelihood of these risks and their financial effects by considering factors such as revenue loss, regulatory fines, reputational harm, and remediation costs.

Cybersecurity Events: A breach can significantly affect an organization's reputation, potentially impacting its valuation. For example, a high-profile data breach could result in negative media coverage and a loss of customer trust, which may influence valuation and lead to a decline in sales. The probability of a breach is decreased by strong financial governance, which guarantees sufficient financing for cybersecurity solutions (such as firewalls, staff training, and incident response plans).

Compliance Risks: Companies that violate cybersecurity laws and standards may face civil and criminal penalties, which can adversely affect their stock price and reputation. E-CyG ensures that cybersecurity financial governance aligns with industry-specific regulations, including the GDPR, HIPAA, and CCPA, as well as other relevant laws and regulations. Furthermore, E-CyG facilitates the development of audit and reporting systems to demonstrate compliance and provide stakeholders with transparency.

Due Diligence: To better understand the risks associated with investing in companies, investors and analysts are increasingly conducting due diligence on their cybersecurity practices. This process involves assessing the organization's cybersecurity policies, practices, controls, and readiness to respond to cybersecurity incidents.

Budgeting and Investments: Organizations must implement robust cybersecurity safeguards, allocating resources for staff training and technology. Budgets for security tools, firewalls, antivirus software, and regular security audits are also essential. Long-term investments are needed to maintain an organization's cybersecurity posture, while short-term measures, such as training, patches, and updates, are crucial but can incur significant costs. Balancing security spending with growth opportunities is essential, as other strategic projects may compete for the funds allocated to cybersecurity. Therefore, evaluating and prioritizing cybersecurity investments by aligning them with risk reduction and business objectives is a key governance measure that effectively allocates financial resources to mitigate the most significant cybersecurity risks.

Policies and Procedures: By ensuring that cybersecurity is viewed as a strategic business risk with sufficient funding, supervision, and accountability, financial policies and procedures can enhance cybersecurity governance by aligning cybersecurity investments and expenditures with overall risk management strategies. E-CyG assists in creating clear policies and processes that govern these investments and spending.

Overall, both organizations and investors are placing greater importance on the financial implications of cybersecurity. When prioritizing cybersecurity, employees should recognize the financial aspects of risk mitigation, and investors should consider cybersecurity risks when evaluating companies, as these risks can directly impact the organization's value.

8.2.2 Financial Impacts of Cyberattacks

Failing to establish a robust cybersecurity governance framework can result in significant financial losses for the company. Some effects may be short-term or immediate (direct), such as decreases in revenue, damage to reputation, and increased operational costs. In contrast, others may be long-term (indirect), including the loss of competitive advantage and a downgrade in credit rating. We discuss some potential losses in the following sections.

8.2.2.1 Loss of Revenue

Cyberattacks can disrupt company operations and result in lost revenue. They can significantly impact business continuity, resulting in operational downtime, disturbances, decreased productivity, and missed opportunities. Downtime caused by system failures or compromised services has a direct impact on a company's financial performance.

8.2.2.2 Increase Expenses

The financial impact of cyberattacks encompasses expenses for incident response and system restoration, forensic investigations, legal fees, increased insurance premiums, and regulatory fines, as well as potential costs associated with ransomware payments, fraud, and theft of funds.

8.2.2.3 Reputational Loss and Shareholder/Investor Confidence

A cybersecurity breach can harm a business's reputation, weaken customer loyalty and trust, and result in lost revenue from lost contracts and sales. The long-term effects on the brand's value and competitive position worry shareholders. This loss is also associated with declining sales and customer loyalty, which can have extended financial repercussions.

Cybersecurity breaches can lead to stock price volatility and decrease stock prices, which lowers shareholder value. Investors closely monitor an organization's cybersecurity measures to ensure it has sufficient protection against cyberattacks. A cybersecurity breach can negatively affect shareholder and investor confidence, influencing stock prices, market capitalization, and shareholder value. Davey et al. (2021) highlight that, in the longer term, company share prices underperformed the stock market by an average of 15.6% three years after a data breach. Furthermore, cybersecurity risks can impact shareholder value during any merger or acquisition process.

Corporate cybersecurity information should be made publicly available to reassure investors that adequate governance frameworks and mechanisms are in place to mitigate cybersecurity threats as a systemic risk factor (Oh & Ho, 2022).

8.2.2.4 Non-compliance Penalties

Heavy fines can be imposed for violating data privacy laws, including the GDPR. Organizations must allocate resources to ensure compliance and avoid financial difficulties. Therefore, to prevent fines and penalties, the company needs assurance that it adheres to relevant cybersecurity legislation. Since violations may lead to lawsuits from authorities, clients, and business partners, they could result in significant legal fees and settlements.

8.2.2.5 Incident Response Costs

Organizations face costs associated with communication, containment, recovery, and investigation after a cyber incident. Public relations campaigns, forensic experts, and legal fees are just a few examples of these expenses.

8.2.2.6 Supply Chain Risks

Incidents involving cybersecurity within a company can impact its suppliers. A compromised partner or vendor may lead to operational disruptions and financial losses. Disruptions in the supply chain can significantly affect a business's ability to deliver goods or services, resulting in customer inconvenience or loss. Consequently, the cybersecurity posture of vendors and third parties with access to the company's digital infrastructure requires governance oversight.

8.2.2.7 Intellectual Property and Data Confidentiality

Safeguarding the information of private clients is vital, as breaches can lead to a decline in customer trust and loyalty, as well as penalties from authorities. The theft of trade secrets or intellectual property can harm a business's competitive advantage, revenue, reputation, and market value.

8.2.2.8 Insurance

To mitigate financial damages from cyber catastrophes, E-CyG assists organizations in assessing the need for cyber insurance and other risk transfer methods. Businesses that have experienced cybersecurity breaches may face higher premiums for cyber insurance. However, due to the rise in claims in recent years, insurers have increased their prices for cyber risk insurance. Many insurance providers limit their cyber risk coverage or may not offer it at all. Others, like Lloyd, have disclaimed responsibility for damages from state-sponsored cyberattacks (Lloyd, 2022). With numerous insurance companies restricting their coverage, organizations will need to absorb the costs of cyber breaches, putting additional strain on enterprise finances and cybersecurity investment expenses.

8.3 Enterprise Financial Cybersecurity Governance

Enterprise financial cybersecurity governance (FIN/CyG) is a sub-governance process within the E-CyG framework that focuses on financial activities and their cybersecurity implications for the entire enterprise. Given the increasing risks arising from a more digitized business landscape, a governance framework that effectively addresses the unique nature of financial cyber risk is essential. Enterprise FIN/CyG must consider several critical factors when designing the governance framework.

8.3.1 Board of Directors-Level Governance

The Board of Directors plays a critical role in financial cybersecurity governance by overseeing risk management (i.e., risk-based evaluations, budget approvals, and investments) and safeguarding sensitive financial data. The directors are increasingly held accountable for ensuring that the executive team takes appropriate steps to mitigate cyber threats. The BoD typically participates in financial cybersecurity governance by approving policies on resource allocation, demanding accountability, and staying informed about emerging threats. Boards are responsible for effectively addressing cyber risks and managing incidents. BoD members should be able to challenge management regarding cybersecurity, financial policies, regulations, and issues, and advise their shareholders on risk mitigation strategies, even if they lack expertise in monetary or cybersecurity matters. Therefore, BoD oversight must be integrated into governance frameworks.

The Board of Directors' responsibilities extend beyond merely approving frameworks and strategies; they also include monitoring their successful execution. Furthermore, it ensures that the BoD has authorized the organization's strategies, policies, and procedures, which are regularly assessed for execution and operational risk management.

8.3.2 Strategic Alignment and Integration

Instead of viewing cybersecurity merely as a technical issue, the Board of Directors should consider it a strategic risk. From a financial governance perspective, the cybersecurity plan must align with and integrate into the overall business plan and enterprise risk management by assessing its exposure to cyber threats that could affect its business model. This approach will clarify the financial implications for the firm regarding potential investments in protection and losses from breaches. Furthermore, it will help identify and highlight the types and sensitivity of data at risk from cyber threats, thus enabling informed decision-making about resource allocation.

8.3.3 Senior Management

The responsibilities of an organization's senior management or C-suite regarding financial cybersecurity governance include developing policies, procedures, regulations, and guidelines for the cyber risk management financial framework (e.g., PCI DSS Requirements 5) that align with business objectives and monitor their implementation. Senior management must ensure proper implementation and maintenance of the cyber risk program, which requires financial planning and oversight to guarantee adequate resource allocation. C-suite officers receive periodic reports on cyber threats. To respond appropriately, they must assess the risk exposure and economic implications and formulate a cyber defense policy along with its associated risk management framework.

8.3.4 Investor Relations

Given that investors now prioritize cybersecurity, it is crucial to keep them informed. Investors are typically the most concerned about cyberattacks. Therefore, businesses must demonstrate robust governance frameworks and provide transparent disclosures about their cybersecurity measures. There should be comprehensive and effective Board of Directors oversight of the cybersecurity function, with adequate resources allocated to cyber risk management to ensure proper implementation and maintenance of enterprise cybersecurity governance. The BoD should ensure that appropriate industry security standards are integrated into the governance frameworks and that metrics are utilized to assess strategic and tactical performance, which should be reported to relevant personnel for information and action as necessary. Information about structures and controls should be communicated to investors to alleviate any uncertainty that could cause undue alarm regarding the firm's preparedness.

8.3.5 Risk-Based Approach

Adopting the E-CyG as a risk-based approach prioritizes security initiatives according to the risk levels faced by an organization's networks, systems, and data. The benefits of the E-CyG (and thus FIN/CyG) include a flexible method that can adapt to evolving threats, effective resource allocation for addressing critical risks, and customization to safeguard the organization's most vital assets, thereby ensuring business continuity. This approach also aligns security efforts with business objectives. It highlights the importance of identifying, evaluating, and mitigating risks in alignment with the organization's risk appetite and business objectives, rather than imposing uniform security measures. In summary, a risk-based strategy ensures that cybersecurity initiatives are targeted, strategic, and aligned with the organization's broader risk management framework.

8.3.5.1 Risk Identification

The integrated FIN/CyG process effectively identifies and mitigates cyber threats within organizations that may impact financial assets, including ransomware attacks, phishing scams, and data breaches. FIN/CyG improves risk identification across all areas to ensure that cyber threats related to financial risks are not ignored.

8.3.5.2 Risk Assessment

FIN/CyG is a risk-based approach that assesses the likelihood of cyber threats and their potential financial implications. This enables businesses to allocate resources efficiently and prioritize risks based on their severity. Moreover, it encourages organizations to consider various cybersecurity scenarios, helping them understand how cyber threats could impact their financial stability.

8.3.5.3 Risk Mitigation

Organizations can safeguard financial data by integrating risk-mitigating administrative measures into their FIN/CyG and employing proactive tools such as encryption, multi-factor authentication, and regular security assessments. To develop cohesive strategies for minimizing cyber risks, FIN/CyG promotes collaboration across all departments to align cybersecurity with financial controls.

8.3.5.4 Risk Detection, Monitoring, and Reporting

The E-CyG framework allows businesses to swiftly identify and address threats with minimal financial impact by utilizing updated, real-time monitoring tools for ongoing cyber threats. Regular risk reporting through FIN/CyG ensures that the Board of Directors and senior management are aware of the organization's vulnerability to financial cyber threats, enabling informed decision-making by both the BoD and senior management.

8.3.6 Incident Response Plan

Creating incident response plans tailored explicitly to financial cyber threats is a crucial aspect of E-CyG and a primary focus of the FIN/CyG process. This approach

Table 8.1 Financial metrics

KPIs	Objectives
ROI of security tools	Evaluates the cost and efficacy of security measures
Budget allocation versus risk	The proportion of funds allocated to high-risk exposures
Downtime due to security incidents	Business disruption brought on by cyberattacks
Data breach cost	The monetary costs of breaches

enables the company to minimize financial impacts and recover quickly from attacks. The E-CyG strategy promotes resilience and rapid recovery by integrating cybersecurity into business continuity planning. FIN/CyG mitigates the financial effects of cybersecurity incidents by allocating resources for incident response and recovery efforts, as well as developing, testing, and implementing incident response and disaster recovery plans and innovations.

8.3.7 Performance Evaluation

Conducting a cybersecurity assessment involves gathering, reviewing, and utilizing information about an organization's cybersecurity practices and controls related to individual financial measures. This process helps evaluate performance, provide feedback, and identify areas for improvement, including necessary corrective actions. Table 8.1 outlines the performance metrics for finance used to assess the effectiveness of cybersecurity assessments, investments, controls, and their impacts.

8.4 Financial Governance Policies and Procedures

Cybersecurity governance standards for managing corporate financial risk are essential for protecting sensitive financial data, ensuring compliance with regulations, and mitigating cyber risks. This section examines the governance policies and procedures required to manage cybersecurity financial resources and address the various financial challenges associated with cybersecurity risk management. The following highlights the financial areas that need attention regarding cybersecurity policies and procedures.

8.4.1 Risk Management

In collaboration with the cybersecurity team, the finance department conducts assessments to evaluate cyber financial risks. Its policies and procedures must ensure regular cybersecurity risk assessments to identify vulnerabilities in financial systems. The department head is responsible for overseeing financial risk modeling to assess potential cyber threats (e.g., fraud, data breaches). It must align with frameworks and regulations, such as NIST CSF, ISO 27001, COBIT, GDPR, SOX, and PCI DSS, for structured risk management. The finance department manages and allocates budgets for cybersecurity investments in technology and human resources to mitigate risks.

8.4.2 Data Security

Ensure sensitive data is protected to prevent unauthorized access that could result in losses for both the company and its customers. End-to-end data encryption is essential for safeguarding and encrypting sensitive financial information. Data classification (e.g., PII, bank details, public, internal, confidential, restricted) necessitates strict access controls.

8.4.3 Fraud Prevention

To detect and prevent fraud, the department uses AI-driven anomaly detection to identify suspicious transactions. It can also utilize blockchain or secure ledgers to establish tamper-resistant financial records.

Education and training are essential for enhancing cybersecurity awareness among employees and third parties regarding potential fraudulent cyber exploits. Additionally, implementing whistleblower policies for reporting fraudulent activities can help in identifying fraud.

8.4.4 Compliance

Investing in compliance enhances protection and helps avoid penalties and reputational damage. Therefore, finance policies must align with frameworks such as NIST CSF, ISO 27001, ISO 31000, or COBIT and comply with regulations like GDPR, SOX, and PCI DSS for financial data security and structured risk management.

8.4.5 Incident Response

For incident response and recovery, the organization should develop a cyber incident response plan (IRP) tailored to its financial systems, ensuring that backup and disaster recovery protocols are in place for financial or economic data. It must conduct regular breach simulations (e.g., ransomware, malware, phishing) to enhance awareness and familiarity with the policies and procedures. Additionally, it should allocate resources to maintain the incident response plan and ensure that business operations are not disrupted, thereby minimizing the financial impact of a breach.

8.5 Financial Governance Tools—Valuation Methods

One critical area of finance's involvement in cybersecurity governance is the use of valuation for risk assessment. Valuation, also known as asset pricing, determines the intrinsic value or worth of an asset, investment, business, or financial instrument. Asset pricing is employed in the second step of "Evaluation" or "Assessment" in the ERM risk control process for cybersecurity governance. Valuation provides insights into the probability of a cyber risk event and its financial impact on the organization. The information about likelihood and impact helps evaluate the costs and benefits of a mitigation policy or investment aimed at controlling a threat. This type of analysis can employ a cost-benefit analysis approach.

Financial governance, especially valuation, is intricately linked to cybersecurity in several ways. Cybersecurity threats can significantly impact an organization's value, resulting in financial losses, reputational harm, and legal liabilities. Valuation is akin to asset pricing, which determines the intrinsic value or worth of an asset, investment, business, or financial instrument. A well-designed cybersecurity governance policy serves as a tool to evaluate and prioritize cyber threats, making it essential for effective risk management. It plays a key role in decision-making and financial analysis, as cybersecurity decisions—such as feasibility, risk assessment, risk prioritization, returns on investment, and a firm's value—are common applications of valuation.

The valuation techniques employed to assess assets or investments differ based on the nature of the assets or investments being evaluated. Here are a few commonly used methods of valuation:

8.5.1 Cost–Benefit Analysis

FIN/CyG enables cost-effective risk management by allowing organizations to measure the potential financial impact of cyber risks and compare it to the cost of implementing controls. Cost-benefit analysis (CBA) is a systematic approach to evaluating the operational and economic trade-offs of cybersecurity efforts. It ensures effective resource allocation by helping organizations determine if the benefits of a security solution outweigh its costs. The calculation is as follows:

$$\text{Net Benefit(NB)} = \text{Total Benefits} - \text{Total Costs}$$

If NB > 0, the investment is justified, and

If NB ≤ 0, reconsider or seek cost-effective alternatives.

Cost-benefit analysis is a crucial tool for making informed, business-driven decisions in cybersecurity. As it compares anticipated expenses to prospective profits, it helps businesses assess cybersecurity investments, optimize resource allocation, ensure that security expenditures align with corporate goals, and support risk reduction techniques.

8.5.2 Market-Based Valuation

Market-based valuation compares an asset's worth to similar assets in the market. It assesses current transactions, market values, and financial ratios of comparable assets or businesses to establish its value. This approach evaluates the worth of cybersecurity products, services, or businesses by comparing them to similar companies within the industry. Unlike relying solely on internal financial data, this method also considers investor perspectives, competitive pricing, and real-world interactions.

Another approach involves using market-based valuation, which compares the cost-effectiveness of security controls such as firewalls, EDR, and employee training with market alternatives, industry standards, and actual ROI. This method establishes the financial value of cybersecurity mitigation measures by relying on market data to inform investments in specific security solutions. Market-based valuation examines actual costs, effectiveness, and alternatives to help prioritize cybersecurity spending. By utilizing industry data, organizations can allocate funds to the most cost-effective mitigations.

8.5.3 Income-Based Valuation

Income-based valuation (IBV) helps firms assess cybersecurity expenditures by quantifying the financial impact on revenue, profitability, and business continuity. IBV examines how cybersecurity impacts cash flows, valuation, and long-term financial health. The financial value of cybersecurity controls is estimated through income-based valuation, which assesses their effectiveness in reducing costs, preventing losses, or enhancing operational efficiency over time. This approach emphasizes the cash flow impact, or the amount of money a security measure saves or protects, rather than market-based techniques that rely on comparables. This method determines the asset's value based on projected future income or cash flows. It involves forecasting future cash flows, applying a discount rate to account for the time value of money, and calculating the present value of those cash flows. The formula using the Discounted Cash Flow (DCF) approach for cybersecurity investments to estimate the present value of future savings generated by a security control is as follows:

$$\text{Present Value} = \sum(\text{Annual Cost Savings})_t/(1+r)^t$$

Annual Cost Savings/Gains = Breach costs avoided + efficiency gains;
Discount rate (r) = Company's cost of capital, and
Time (t) = Lifespan of the control (e.g., 1…t years).

Income-based valuation enables strategic cybersecurity decision-making by linking cyber threats to financial performance and justifying security expenditures in terms of revenue protection.

8.5.4 Asset-Based Valuation

Asset-based assessment evaluates a company's underlying assets and liabilities to determine the value of an asset or business. To calculate net asset value, you must first assess the worth of both tangible and intangible assets, including digital infrastructure, inventory, real estate, and goodwill. Next, subtract the liabilities. Unlike methods that focus solely on the direct costs or income impacts of cybersecurity controls, this approach examines the tangible and intangible assets that these controls protect. It considers the economic value or replacement cost of these assets. However, the valuation can vary based on the assumptions and inputs used in the analysis. This requires a thorough understanding of the organization's digital landscape, business operations, technology systems, networks, and the specifics of the item being appraised.

Asset-based valuation focuses cybersecurity expenditures on what they truly protect. By linking controls to asset values, CISOs can justify spending based on the value protected rather than the risk reduced. Prioritizing investment in high-value targets is beneficial.

8.5.5 Risk Exposure Analysis

Evaluating a firm's financial cybersecurity exposure requires both quantitative and qualitative risk assessment methodologies. These methodologies enable organizations to estimate potential financial losses from cyberattacks and prioritize mitigation strategies. Ultimately, it is essential to assign a quantitative estimate of the firm's risk exposure, whether it concerns a single asset or a group of assets. Qualitative risk assessment strategies include the Delphi method, attack trees (also known as decision trees), risk matrices (also referred to as heat maps), and threat modeling.

Techniques for estimating quantitative risk utilize statistical models and historical data to assign monetary values to cyber risks. These techniques include Monte Carlo Simulation, Annualized Loss Expectancy (ALE), Value at Risk (VaR), Factor Analysis of Information Risk (FAIR), and financial-specific metrics such as downtime costs, regulatory fines, insurance premiums, or unit costs per breach of PII or healthcare records. To accurately assess their financial cybersecurity exposure, enterprises should combine qualitative methods—such as expert judgment and heat maps—with quantitative approaches like ALE, Monte Carlo, and FAIR.

8.6 Budget Considerations for Cybersecurity Resources

Organizations investing in cybersecurity resources must utilize effective decision-making techniques; implementing a probabilistic risk analysis methodology may be crucial. Cybersecurity budgeting and management allocate financial resources and establish expenditure priorities to support an organization's successful adoption and maintenance of cybersecurity measures aligned with its corporate cyber defense policy. This involves determining the funds necessary to safeguard the organization's networks, information systems, and data from online threats and cyberattacks. The main factors to consider while budgeting for cybersecurity risk management are outlined below:

Risk Evaluation: Conducting a thorough risk assessment is essential for identifying potential threats and vulnerabilities that may impact an organization's cybersecurity. This evaluation will help in determining the financial resources required to mitigate these risks effectively.

Resource Allocation: Estimate the costs associated with all cybersecurity activities, including the purchase of hardware and software, staff training, hiring external security services, and ongoing maintenance and updates. To create a practical budget, consider both one-time expenses and recurring costs.

Prioritization: Based on the identified threats and the organization's specific needs, rank cybersecurity initiatives by their importance. Focus on investing in measures that mitigate significant risks and potential consequences, such as protecting sensitive information, securing critical infrastructure, or complying with regulations and laws.

Investments: Companies should allocate funds to acquire and implement security tools and technologies, including firewalls, intrusion detection systems, antivirus software, vulnerability scanners, encryption programs, and security analytics platforms. They should also consider operating (maintenance and upgrades) and capital (purchase and installation) expenses.

HR Budgets: Allocate funds for cybersecurity personnel and training by hiring and retaining qualified experts such as security analysts, incident response teams, and security architects. Invest in ongoing education and certifications to ensure that security staff remain current on the latest threats, innovations, and best practices.

Auxiliary Services: Consider utilizing managed security service providers (MSSPs) or outsourcing cybersecurity tasks to external entities. Services such as penetration testing, security monitoring, threat intelligence, and incident response may fall within this category. Organizations should plan and allocate budget for these services.

Fund Allocation: Allocating funds for investigation, containment, remediation, and recovery efforts as part of incident response can assist in planning for future security issues. For instance, funds can be dedicated to hiring forensic professionals or purchasing incident response tools.

Compliance and Regulatory Requirements: A company operating in a regulated sector should allocate funds to ensure adherence to all applicable cybersecurity laws and standards. The compliance process may involve conducting audits, performing security assessments, and implementing necessary controls.

Monitoring and Assessment: Allocate funds for ongoing security measures, monitoring, and reviews. Identifying and addressing emerging risks requires investment in Security Information and Event Management (SIEM) systems, security analytics tools, and regular security audits.

Contingency Preparation: Allocate funds for contingencies, such as creating a cybersecurity incident response fund, and ensure that emergency preparedness measures are implemented. This strategy will empower the organization to address unforeseen security challenges and effectively reduce their financial impact.

In summary, it is essential to regularly review and adjust a firm's cybersecurity budget to ensure it remains aligned with the development of new technologies, evolving threats, and organizational changes. Maintaining a balance between security requirements and available resources is crucial for creating a robust, effective, and optimal cybersecurity management framework.

8.7 Other Cybersecurity Financial Governance Tools

As cyber infrastructure expands, cyber hazards are evolving rapidly. More complex attacks, such as those targeting financial gain and high network traffic infrastructures, may not be adequately addressed by traditional cybersecurity governance methods that focus solely on known risks. Supporting applications and technologies like artificial intelligence, machine learning, game theory, and blockchain may be better suited to address cybersecurity issues more effectively than conventional methods.

8.7.1 Artificial Intelligence

Artificial intelligence (AI) plays a significant role in preventing or reducing financial losses in cybersecurity governance by enhancing detection, response, and mitigation capabilities. It has had a profound impact on cybersecurity by transforming both technological and tactical aspects of risk mitigation, and it is poised to be crucial in cybersecurity data analytics (Sarker et al., 2020).

According to Forbes (2023),[1] fifty-one percent of companies interviewed currently use or plan to use AI in cybersecurity and fraud management. AI is a broad field of computer science focused on machines capable of performing tasks that typically require human intelligence. In cybersecurity governance, AI is used to predict, identify, assess, analyze, and mitigate financial threats in cyberspace. As a cybersecurity tool, AI can gather intelligence to protect the firm against evolving and emerging cyber threats (Kaur et al., 2023; Sarker et al., 2020; Wirkuttis & Klein, 2017). Among these tasks are pattern recognition, reasoning, problem-solving, and decision-making.

From a financial cybersecurity context, AI can help to manage threats in the following ways:

Transaction Monitoring: AI evaluates financial transactions in real time to identify instances of fraud, such as unauthorized transfers and unusual spending patterns.
Anomaly Detection: AI programs analyze user activity, network traffic, and system operations to identify unusual patterns that may indicate malware, ransomware, or phishing attacks.
Predictive Analytics: AI enables businesses to proactively tackle weaknesses by forecasting potential vulnerabilities or attack vectors using historical data and machine learning.
Real-Time Monitoring: Unlike traditional methods, AI continuously scans systems for signs of compromise, enabling quicker threat detection.
Behavioral Biometrics: AI monitors user actions, such as mouse clicks and typing patterns, to detect and prevent unauthorized access to financial systems.

However, considering the benefits that AI is expected to bring to cybersecurity, further research is necessary to assess the relevance and effectiveness of AI capabilities for cybersecurity tasks (Zhang et al., 2022).

8.7.2 Machine Learning

As a branch of artificial intelligence, machine learning (ML) focuses on creating statistical models and algorithms that enable computers to learn from data and make predictions or decisions. By automating threat detection, enhancing risk management, and enabling proactive defense measures, machine learning (ML) greatly improves financial cybersecurity governance. By facilitating data-driven, real-time decision-making, minimizing human error, and staying ahead of emerging threats, machine learning revolutionizes financial cybersecurity governance.

Machine learning systems utilize data to progressively enhance their performance rather than being explicitly taught to perform a task. Machine learning (ML) primarily

[1] Forbes 2023, "How Businesses Are Using Artificial Intelligence." https://www.forbes.com/advisor/business/software/ai-in-business/.

focuses on the development of algorithms that enable computers to learn from data. Although machine learning is a crucial component of many AI applications, not all AI systems incorporate it.

8.7.3 Game Theory

Game theory, the study of strategic interactions among rational decision-makers, is an effective method for solving cybersecurity governance problems that require logical decision-making. It is a field of applied mathematics that employs mathematical models to determine the optimal strategy (Patil et al., 2018; Schneider, 2013). Each player can win the game by leveraging the perceptions of rational decision-makers. Game theory aids management in better predicting hackers' actions based on "Adversarial Thinking" or "think like a hacker" (Dark & Mirkovic, 2015; Schneider, 2013), which focuses on understanding how hackers plan their attacks. For game theory to serve as a viable approach to addressing cybersecurity concerns, hacker tactics should be limited and predictable. However, game theory faces a drawback when the defender has only limited information about the opponent's tactics and choices; therefore, applying game theory to cybersecurity requires further study.

Hence, game theory provides effective frameworks for financial cybersecurity governance by simulating adversarial behaviors, optimizing defense measures, and enhancing risk management. It improves financial cybersecurity governance by simulating adversary behaviors and forecasting attack surface targets.

8.7.4 Blockchain

Blockchain technology can help a company manage its cybersecurity risks by enhancing data integrity, ensuring authentication, and increasing its resilience to attacks. Here's how blockchain can strengthen cybersecurity:

- The blockchain's decentralized ledger ensures that once data is recorded, it cannot be altered without consensus. This secures audit trails, maintains logs, and detects unauthorized changes to financial records or system logs.
- It protects against DDoS attacks by using a blockchain-based Domain Name System (DNS) to distribute records across nodes, making it more difficult for attackers to disrupt services through DDoS.
- It employs AI-driven anomaly detection connected to blockchain technology to provide real-time fraud alerts. Moreover, it can exchange threat intelligence data among companies on a blockchain network while maintaining the confidentiality of sensitive information.

- Blockchain can enable dependable backup and data recovery through a peer-to-peer network, such as the Interplanetary File System (IPFS), ensuring that data remains accessible even when primary systems are compromised.
- It offers transparency and monitoring to protect the supply chain from cyber threats and to prevent counterfeit software or hardware by tracking blockchain components. Furthermore, it ensures that only verified vendors and updates are incorporated into IT systems.

8.8 The Financial Cybersecurity Governance Framework

Cybersecurity governance is crucial in enterprise finance for safeguarding digital assets, ensuring regulatory compliance, and upholding stakeholder trust amid an increasingly complex digital threat landscape. This specialized governance framework integrates cybersecurity measures with financial operations to mitigate risks that could result in financial losses, damage to reputation, or regulatory penalties.

Financial cybersecurity governance (FIN/CyG) serves as the foundation for recognizing, assessing, and prioritizing cyber risks that could affect financial operations. Organizations face vulnerabilities to cyber threats, including phishing, ransomware attacks, malware, and advanced persistent threats (APTs), which compromise the security of their networks, systems, and data. Governance processes within the E-CyG framework enable organizations to evaluate these risks and adopt appropriate controls systematically. Regular risk assessments help organizations stay proactive against emerging risks.

A robust FIN/CyG framework integrates strategic business alignment, technology, compliance, best practices, innovation, and employee awareness to protect against cyber risks and ensure business continuity. Companies must enhance their practices and capabilities in response to the increasing number of cyber threats and regulatory changes. Key considerations and factors for developing an effective and resilient FIN/CyG framework are outlined below.

8.8.1 Governance Role Structure

FIN/CyG requires participation from senior executives in cybersecurity discussions, engagement from Board of Directors leadership, and clear accountability at this level. The BoD sets the tone for the cybersecurity strategy, approves policies, establishes priorities, and allocates resources. BoDs are increasingly expected to monitor cyber risk policies closely and ensure they align with business objectives. The Chief Information Security Officer (CISO) acts as the primary executive overseeing the business cybersecurity program. CISOs frequently report directly to the BoD, risk committee, or CEO, and collaborate with other C-suite executives to embed security into all business processes. Finance, IT, and security teams work together across functions

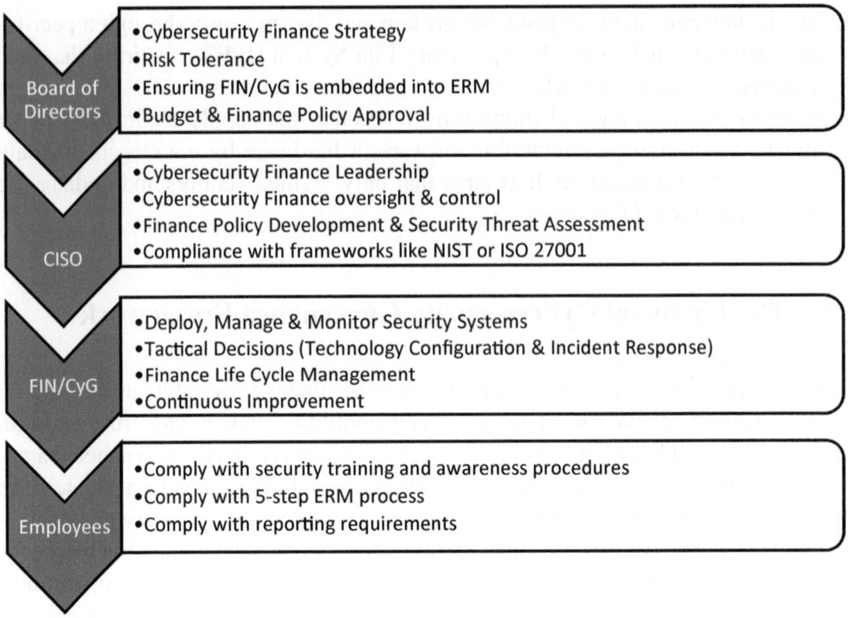

Fig. 8.1 FIN/CyG role structure

to implement, maintain, and monitor systems efficiently. Employees must recognize and stay informed about security risks at the line level and report any unusual or suspicious activities. They are also expected to understand their roles in the FIN/CyG framework concerning the ERM process and to partake in regular refresher training to enhance their knowledge (see Fig. 8.1).

8.8.2 Strategic Alignment

Aligning security plans with business objectives is crucial for effective cybersecurity governance, ensuring the company's continuity and security. FIN/CyG should sync with business goals regarding risk appetite by establishing an acceptable level of cybersecurity risk for the organization based on its risk tolerance and objectives (such as growth). To understand cyber threats and their impact on business goals, as well as how to manage them, it is crucial to analyze the financial impact of each risk category by evaluating and ranking the potential financial losses from breaches (e.g., human errors, malware, fraud, reputational damage) and allocating investments accordingly. Additionally, to link business objectives with industry-specific threats and their security measures, the FIN/CyG policy should also consider the industry's threat landscape.

8.8.3 Finance Cybersecurity Governance/ERM Integration

The Board of Directors must integrate FIN/CyG with enterprise risk management to achieve a comprehensive view of cybersecurity risk, treating cyber risk in finance as just another operational cyber risk within the ERM framework. The ERM approach would evaluate and address third-party risks to mitigate any vulnerabilities in the supply chain.

8.8.4 Technology Investment

FIN/CyG prioritizes technological applications by focusing on security investments. A cost-benefit analysis would evaluate security spending against return-on-investment (ROI) metrics, including network/system availability, ransomware protection, fraud detection, or revenue protection. Given the sophistication of modern technology, investing in automation, machine learning, and AI-driven detection systems to monitor anomalies and enable automated incident response, thereby mitigating financial risks, is a viable option. Implementing a Zero-Trust Architecture (ZTA) would be prudent for access controls related to economic data and the protection of transaction systems.

8.8.5 Compliance

Guidelines for the structured FIN/CyG are essential for establishing a resilient framework that adheres to industry standards such as NIST CSF, ISO 27001, or COBIT 5. To meet regulatory requirements, the organization must ensure compliance with regulatory frameworks (e.g., SOX financial reporting, PCI DSS payment security, and GDPR data privacy).

8.8.6 Incident Response

FIN/CyG's IRP policy outlines a simple process for reporting breaches within the hierarchy to prevent confusion and ensure a prompt response. Obtaining cyber insurance is part of incident response to mitigate financial damage, but determining the insurance coverage requires assessing potential monetary losses from breaches (e.g., expert consulting, legal liability, ransomware payouts). A crisis communication plan with customer and PR notification strategies must be prepared to reduce reputational harm. The IRP should include a strategy for maintaining audit trails to ensure regulatory compliance and support financial fraud investigations.

8.8.7 *Risk Culture and Awareness*

FIN/CyG ensures that a robust risk culture and awareness are vital for mitigating threats and ensuring compliance in cybersecurity finance governance. Leadership should consider key factors, such as executive commitment and prioritizing cybersecurity risk as a strategic business issue, which must be demonstrated. Specific roles for the Board of Directors, Risk Committees, C-suite, and CISO should be both defined and enforced, with established governance accountability. The organization's cybersecurity risk appetite ought to align with its overall risk tolerance. At the operational level, the organization provides employee awareness and training, as well as role-specific education (e.g., finance and cybersecurity) and compliance training.

8.8.8 *Performance and Continual Improvement*

FIN/CyG performance management involves the ongoing assessment and tracking of key performance indicators (KPIs). It is essential to monitor performance metrics related to various cybersecurity functions or activities in the finance sector, such as training, simulations, response time, security awareness, and stress testing.

8.8.9 *Risk Assessment Capabilities*

The finance department, through FIN/CyG, offers risk assessment services to the cybersecurity function within the organization. The aim is to quantify the likelihood and potential financial impact of a cyber threat, thereby prioritizing each risk for effective mitigation. To achieve this, the finance department must be knowledgeable about the organization's risk environment, digital infrastructure, and processes, and possess the necessary resources and capabilities to conduct the required analyses and determine risk exposures.

8.9 Conclusion

In conclusion, an organization's size, industry, and risk tolerance significantly impact the financial implications of cybersecurity governance. E-CyG offers a holistic and systematic approach, while FIN/CyG, a finance-centric component of the E-CyG framework, promotes collaborative enterprise governance with other enablers, focusing on managing cybersecurity threats within the finance function. By integrating FIN/CyG into the comprehensive E-CyG, businesses can protect their digital assets, comply with legal requirements, and achieve their strategic objectives. Additionally, incorporating cybersecurity awareness into daily operations enables the finance function to better safeguard itself against evolving cyber threats while maintaining stakeholder trust.

References

Crisanto, J., & Prenio, J. (2017). *Regulatory approaches to enhance banks' cybersecurity frameworks*. FSI Insights on policy implementation No 2. Financial Stability Institute, Bank of International Settlements. https://www.readkong.com/page/regulatory-approaches-to-enhance-banks-cyber-security-bis-2047412#:~:text=At%20the%20international%20level,%20the%20G7

Dark, M., & Mirkovic, J. (2015). Evaluation theory and practice applied to cybersecurity education. *IEEE Security & Privacy, 13*(2), 75–80.

Davey, J., Baudry, A., Lakhani, F., & Tyler, A. (2021). *Age of cybersecurity: Spend to defend*. HSBC Global Research. https://www.research.hsbc.com/C/1/1/320/xbKjPvd#:~:text=This%20chapter%20outlines%20ten%20key%20examples%20of%20cyber,price%2C%20with%20comparison%20to%20local%20stock%20market%20indices

Kaur, R., Gabrijelcic, D., & Klobucar, T. (2023). Artificial intelligence for cybersecurity: Literature review and future research directions. *Information Fusion, 97*.

Lloyd. (2022). *Market Bulletin*, Ref: Y5381. https://assets.lloyds.com/media/eb6de9ce-293b-4213-80f8-9dc69c45b1a9/Y5381%20Market%20Bulletin%20-%20Cyber-attack%20exclusions.pdf

Oh, K., & Ho, B. (2022). *Cybersecurity risk management: An enterprise risk management approach*. Nova Science Publishers.

Patil, A., Bharath, S., & Annigeri, N. (2018). Applications of game theory for cybersecurity system: A survey. *International Journal of Applied Engineering Research, 13*(17), 12987–12990.

Sarker, I., Kayes, A., Badsha, S., Alqahtani, H., Watters, P., & Ng, A. (2020). Cybersecurity data science: An overview from machine learning perspective. *Journal of Big Data, 7*(1), 1–29. https://doi.org/10.1186/s40537-020-00318-5

Schneider, F. (2013). Cybersecurity education in universities. *IEEE Security & Privacy, 11*(4), 3–4.

Wirkuttis, N., & Klein, H. (2017). Artificial intelligence in cybersecurity. *Cyber, Intelligence and Security, 1*(1), 103–119.

Zhang, Z., Ning, H., Shi, F., Farha, Y., Xu, J., Zhang, F., & Choo, K. (2022). Artificial intelligence in cybersecurity: Research advances, challenges, and opportunities. *Artificial Intelligence Review, 55*(2), 1029–1053. https://doi.org/10.1007/s10462-021-09976-0

Chapter 9
Cybersecurity Governance Value Chain

Abstract The value chain is essential in cybersecurity management because it enables organizations to comprehend and optimize the various processes involved in controlling cyber threats. Managers can use the value chain as a framework to help them decide on strategic options. By understanding where value is added, companies can focus on strengthening those areas to enhance their cybersecurity posture. Businesses may find cybersecurity flaws, inefficiencies, and possible threat hotspots by analyzing every stage of the supply chain. Therefore, the value chain analysis in this chapter provides a structured process that highlights the critical components of cybersecurity governance that are essential for improving the effectiveness of cybersecurity policies and frameworks. This approach facilitates strategic understanding and operational clarity that enhance cybersecurity governance. The organizational cybersecurity value chain also includes continuous improvement, which entails evaluating the efficiency of the organization's governance procedures and making adjustments to strengthen the security posture. This value chain component is also essential for the business to keep ahead of emerging cyber risks.

9.1 Introduction

A value chain approach can significantly enhance cybersecurity governance by integrating security measures with business processes and incorporating risk management at all operational stages. The governance value chain is crucial in cybersecurity management because it allows organizations to understand and optimize the processes and components involved in mitigating cyber threats. This value chain employs a structured and systematic approach to addressing cyber threats, ensuring that the organization's cybersecurity posture is robust and aligned with its business objectives. Managers can leverage the governance value chain (GVC) to identify where threats pose a risk to the organization and determine strategic options for addressing them by formally establishing cybersecurity-related systems, roles, responsibilities, and tools in a firm's cybersecurity plan. By understanding when, how, where, and why threats arise, companies can identify opportunities to improve

K. B. Oh et al., *Cybersecurity Governance*,
https://doi.org/10.1007/978-981-95-3865-2_9

their digital landscape, clarify responsibilities, and focus on managing exposures while reinforcing those areas to enhance their cybersecurity posture. Businesses can uncover cybersecurity vulnerabilities, inefficiencies, and potential threat hotspots by analyzing every aspect of their supply chain, from strategy development to cybersecurity operation maintenance. Therefore, the GVC provides the Board of Directors and senior management with oversight of cybersecurity strategies, threats, policies, processes, budgets, and communications through a structured and systematic approach that boosts effectiveness. Additionally, this approach encourages leadership initiatives, understanding, collaboration, and operational clarity that fortify digital security.

Our cybersecurity governance value chain consists of strategic and tactical support activities.[1] Strategic activities contribute to oversight and direction, helping to establish policies and regulations for the cybersecurity function. Tactical support activities involve implementing and maintaining the organization's day-to-day cybersecurity tasks. Each element is essential: the Board of Directors, Senior Management, Information Technology, Human Resources, and Finance. This chapter outlines the functions of each component and explains the governance process.

9.2 The Value Chain Components

The enterprise cybersecurity value chain organizes operations into key activities, allowing cybersecurity controls to be customized for each stage and providing protection where risks are greatest. The value chain aims to mitigate the risk of cyberattacks that could result in financial loss, damage to the company's reputation, and legal liability. It also protects the availability of its digital assets and information.

The cybersecurity value chain can be presented at different functional levels and divided into various components. These levels encompass several essential components—leadership, strategic and operational functions, policies and procedures, systems, rules, technology, human resources, and finance—that form the corporate cybersecurity value chain, which protects a company's digital assets and information from cyber threats. By analyzing each component of their value chain, organizations can identify cyber hazards. This process enables risk-based prioritization, ensuring that critical assets are better safeguarded. The primary components of the corporate cybersecurity value chain at these levels include the following:

[1] These activities are what Michael Porter considers the primary and support activities of a value chain.

9.2.1 Governance Oversight

Complete involvement and focus from management leadership are essential for effective cybersecurity governance, which extends throughout the organization (Swinton & Hedges, 2019). Executive-level governance leadership typically includes a security team led by the CISO, who oversees and directs a virtual team through a dispersed cybersecurity function that utilizes resources from various teams within the company. The teams responsible for managing and monitoring the cybersecurity governance function include the Board of Directors, C-suite, and departmental levels, such as IT, finance, legal, human resources, physical security, and infrastructure management, all of which collaborate closely to oversee and monitor the cybersecurity function (Table 9.1). They must consistently demonstrate their commitment to the cybersecurity program by ensuring it meets its objectives.

Table 9.1 outlines the key leadership elements of the cybersecurity governance value chain. It illustrates the cybersecurity hierarchical framework, emphasizing the essential components of roles and responsibilities for protecting a company's digital assets and information from online threats. With leadership oversight and decision-making authority, the Board of Directors and management can implement some of the best cybersecurity governance policies and practices to secure the organization's networks, systems, and data, ensuring effective governance at the highest level.

Table 9.1 Governance leadership and the value chain

Board of Directors	• Define cybersecurity strategy and objective. • Cyber risk evaluation & strategic alignment. • Allocate resources for implementation. • Create a cyber risk committee. • Oversight & review of cybersecurity governance.
Risk committee	• Advise the Board of Directors on cybersecurity issues. • Assess cybersecurity threats and their impact. • Examine issues raised in audit reports to ensure compliance. • Communicate with the Board of Directors regularly on leading cybersecurity threats and the countermeasures taken by the company.
Senior management/C-suite	• The C-suite has oversight of cybersecurity operational governance. • Create the cybersecurity architecture. • Develop governance policies and procedures. • CISO is responsible for the cybersecurity value chain. • CISO is responsible for implementing, monitoring, reporting, and reviewing cybersecurity risk governance.
Departmental heads	• Heads have line oversight of cybersecurity compliance. • Monitor & report threats. • Upstream and downstream communication on security matters.
Cybersecurity & IT teams	• Operational cybersecurity oversight. • Maintain cybersecurity systems to ensure efficiency.

9.2.1.1 Board of Directors

The Board of Directors ensures that cybersecurity governance (E-CyG) is integrated into the organization's broader risk management framework (i.e., ERM) and provides strategic oversight. It allocates resources, approves cybersecurity policies, and holds senior management accountable for cybersecurity performance. The BoD establishes the cybersecurity mission and goals to align with the company's business objectives and growth strategy.

Its role involves reviewing risk evaluations to pinpoint potential dangers and risk exposure to its digital assets and information. The assessment uncovers weaknesses in the firm's cybersecurity that could jeopardize its digital infrastructure and assesses the likelihood of these vulnerabilities materializing. The firm's cybersecurity strategy is built on risk assessment and alignment with business objectives. This strategy must encompass all facets of the organization's digital infrastructure, including hardware, software, networks, and other components, while ensuring compliance with relevant laws and regulations.

After assessing the firm's risk exposure, the Board of Directors will allocate resources and budgets for the various phases and levels detailed in the cybersecurity strategic plan, which includes development, implementation, and maintenance. This process will also involve reviewing and approving cybersecurity expenditures and investments.

The Board of Directors' role requires the appointment of a risk committee comprising members with cyber expertise to oversee the cybersecurity function. This committee will report to the BoD for ongoing oversight and monitoring of cybersecurity threats and incidents, as well as recommending improvements. Therefore, BoD governance ensures continuous oversight and review of the cybersecurity function, enabling the implementation of appropriate adjustments and new measures to address emerging threats.

9.2.1.2 Senior Management

Senior management is responsible for implementing the cybersecurity plan approved by the Board of Directors. They ensure that cybersecurity measures align with operational needs and business objectives. The CEO sets the "tone at the top" for a security culture, integrates cybersecurity into the corporate strategy, and allocates funding based on organizational priorities to uphold a cohesive cybersecurity strategy.

The C-suite oversees cybersecurity governance and establishes, implements, maintains, and reviews the cybersecurity architecture, policies, and procedures. It is collectively and functionally responsible for the ongoing oversight, monitoring, and assessment of the firm's cybersecurity governance and posture. C-suite executives are charged with developing the firm's cybersecurity architecture and strategy. A business's cybersecurity architecture provides the framework for executing its strategy. It includes governance standards, policies, practices, and the technological safeguards needed to protect the business's data and digital assets. It ensures that governance policies and procedures are documented, outlining the steps, controls, and technologies necessary to mitigate identified risks. This information is communicated to all relevant parties for implementation and risk management. Such a policy reduces the vulnerabilities of the company's digital infrastructure and information systems. The organization's cybersecurity architecture can effectively decrease potential threats through a policy for periodic cybersecurity evaluations, which includes penetration testing, vulnerability assessments, simulations, and other security checks.

The CISO oversees the security operations aspect of the value chain. This encompasses monitoring potential threats to the company's digital infrastructure, identifying and responding to cybersecurity events or incidents, and managing the organization's overall cybersecurity posture. Senior management works with other stakeholders to develop and implement cybersecurity guidelines and protocols. In the event of a security incident, the CISO leads the incident response team, which is responsible for determining the root cause of the issue, minimizing damage, and rapidly recovering from the incident. This component of the value chain necessitates a well-developed and tested incident response plan.

9.2.1.3 Departmental Heads

Department heads oversee cyber risk governance and are responsible for the daily operations of cyber risk control within their respective departments. They assign key personnel to work with the cybersecurity team, ensure compliance with E-CyG policies and procedures, and monitor and report any cyber threats to the incident response team.

In summary, effective management leadership promotes proper conduct by holding individuals accountable for the effective management of information security. It encompasses the processes, roles, guidelines, standards, and metrics that ensure the efficient and effective use of information to help an organization achieve its objectives. Additionally, it informs the B&SM and security teams about incidents and performance updates.

9.2.1.4 Cybersecurity and IT Teams

The cybersecurity team plays a crucial role in risk governance by ensuring cyber risks are identified, assessed, mitigated, and monitored in alignment with organizational goals and regulatory requirements. Their responsibilities encompass the entire E-CyG process, which includes overseeing risk identification, assessment, mitigation, monitoring, and reporting to assist senior leadership and the Board of Directors in making informed decisions and responding to incidents to minimize financial losses. Thus, the cybersecurity team ensures effective management of cyber risks and that security measures are aligned with business objectives, strategies, and policies. They serve as advisers, monitors, and enforcers, supporting leadership in operationalizing and making risk-informed decisions that protect the organization's assets and reputation.

The IT team, a component of the IT/CyG process, implements the IT cybersecurity detail by translating high-level policies into practical security solutions, thus bridging the gap between risk management and IT operations. It is essential to risk governance as it implements and manages technological controls, monitors threats, and ensures IT systems align with organizational risk management strategies. Consequently, the cybersecurity IT team acts as the tactical enforcer of risk governance, ensuring that technical risks are managed proactively. Their responsibilities encompass making sure that technological solutions, execution, and risk oversight are compliant and effective, thereby minimizing cyber risks at the operational level.

The cybersecurity and IT teams work together to execute the enterprise cybersecurity governance task. Their collaboration, along with that of the business units, is essential for effectively implementing enterprise cyber risk strategies. They bring complementary skills, with IT concentrating on system functionality and operations, while cybersecurity focuses on risk mitigation and defense.

9.2.2 Strategy and Direction

The initial phase of the E-CyG framework requires a clear understanding and articulation of the goals and objectives related to the business model. Incorporating cybersecurity risk factors significantly alters the strategic decision-making landscape. The inextricable link between achieving organizational objectives and digital resilience is recognized by integrating cybersecurity risk management into strategic management processes. We define strategic risk management as an organization's strategic decisions and actions to mitigate risks associated with uncertainty, focusing on how its written strategic plan, policies, procedures, and execution impact its value (Oh & Ho, 2022).

It is impossible to overlook the potential impact of cyber threats on a business's growth, innovation, and market positioning strategies. By integrating cybersecurity risk governance with strategic management processes, potential weaknesses are proactively identified and addressed, enabling the company to advance efficiently without being hindered by unnecessary setbacks.

The following actions are crucial for establishing a strong governance framework.

Aligning Cybersecurity with Business Vision, Goals, and Objectives: The first step in the cybersecurity governance value chain is establishing a clear alignment between the organization's cybersecurity vision and its business goals. A company's business objectives outline the digital engagement and opportunities it chooses to pursue, which should be closely integrated with its cybersecurity strategy.

Security Objectives: Establish cybersecurity goals, objectives, and scope that align with business needs and legal requirements by identifying all relevant networks, systems, and data essential for protecting the business while upholding the "confidentiality, integrity, and availability" of information. These objectives may pertain to the organization, a strategic business unit, a specific process or project, function, activity, event, or a reporting and compliance requirement.

Cybersecurity Architecture: The architecture serves as the foundation and framework for the business's cybersecurity hierarchy, encompassing both strategic and operational activities. It can be customized or adopted from industry standards and regulations. However, there is no one-size-fits-all approach; organizations must tailor their architecture by developing or integrating specific features from relevant standards and regulations that align with their business model, size, industry, and market.

Governance Standards, Regulations, and Policies: To ensure ongoing maintenance and improvement, all policies must align with current industry standards and regulations, including the NIST CSF, ISO/IEC 27001, COBIT, GDPR, and the Information Security Management System (ISMS) guidelines. These standards outline the requirements for compliance, data protection, permissible usage, access controls, and incident response, detailing the security measures for company networks, systems, and data, as well as the methods by which employees may access them. Therefore, policies and procedures should reflect these standards and incorporate the guidelines, practices, processes, and technological safeguards necessary to protect the business's data and digital assets.

E-CyG strategies and policies must be regularly reviewed and updated to reflect changes in the digital landscape, organizational structures, emerging threats, and technological advancements. The Chief Information Security Officer (CISO) oversees and manages the organizational and departmental cybersecurity strategies and policies by assigning tasks to various systems and data stewards. This exemplifies the necessity for policies to clearly delegate accountability for implementing and maintaining cybersecurity measures throughout the company.

Roles and Responsibilities: The policy must define the structure, roles, and accountability of all participants involved in cybersecurity governance, in line with the five lines of accountability. In cybersecurity governance, clearly defined roles and responsibilities are crucial as they ensure accountability, transparency, and effectiveness in safeguarding an organization's digital assets. By explicitly assigning duties to stakeholders, an effective E-CyG system mitigates risks and ensures legal compliance. Without well-defined roles and responsibilities, cybersecurity activities can become fragmented, leading to vulnerabilities, non-compliance, and inadequate incident response. Strong governance ensures that everyone understands their role in defending the organization against online threats (see Table 9.2).

Risk-Based Approach: Since cyber risks can potentially jeopardize the achievement of company objectives, identifying and mitigating these risks is essential for aligning objectives with strategy. In risk assessment, the business identifies potential threats to its data and digital assets. This evaluation involves recognizing vulnerabilities and threats to the business's digital infrastructure and assessing the likelihood of these risks materializing. Identifying and evaluating assets, weaknesses, and potential threats informs the development of targeted policies.

Table 9.2 Key responsibilities

Role	Key Responsibilities
Board of Directors	Oversee cyber risk vision, goals, strategy, and budget approval.
Risk committee	Support and inform the Board of Directors on E-CyG operations.
C-suite	Establish strategies, security policies, and procedures.
CISO	Implement security policies, manage risks, and report to leadership.
IT team	Implement & deploy technological systems and patch vulnerabilities.
Security team	Monitor threats and enforce controls.
Employees & vendors	Follow security policies, report incidents.
Auditors & compliance	Ensure adherence to regulations and conduct assessments.

In E-CyG, a risk-based approach is essential because it ensures that security initiatives align with an organization's most significant threats and vulnerabilities, maximizing resource allocation and enhancing overall resilience. It aligns security with business objectives by providing proportionate security measures, prioritizes security efforts by ranking risks, adapts to evolving threats through continuous monitoring, improves ROI by reducing waste, fosters regulatory compliance, and enhances decision-making.

Cybersecurity Plan: A business establishes a security plan that is essential to enhancing its Enterprise Risk Management (ERM) program. This plan outlines the measures and controls necessary to address threats identified through risk assessment results. It should encompass the business's digital infrastructure, including networks, software, hardware, and environmental factors that impact its operations. A cybersecurity plan is a crucial component of E-CyG, as it provides a roadmap and systematic approach for managing cyber risks, ensuring compliance, and safeguarding an organization's digital assets. It is vital because it serves as a proactive risk management tool that aligns cybersecurity with business objectives, defines clear roles and responsibilities, ensures regulatory compliance, promotes best practices, provides guidelines for incident response preparedness, adapts to evolving threats, and encourages continuous improvement.

9.2.3 Implementation and Operations

The operations component of the cybersecurity value chain is tasked with executing and maintaining the cybersecurity plan in alignment with specific goals, objectives, and the architectural framework, ensuring its relevance and effectiveness. At the operational level, the following activities are underway:

Cybersecurity Operations: Implement administrative, policies and technical safeguards, such as encryption, firewalls, and access management systems, to mitigate identified risks. This process involves identifying potential threats to the company's digital infrastructure, addressing these threats, responding to cybersecurity incidents, and maintaining the organization's overall cybersecurity posture.

Assessment, Mitigation, and Reporting: The E-CyG provides a comprehensive overview of the organization's cybersecurity operational framework. It establishes procedures for ongoing risk assessment, security control monitoring, mitigation, and reporting that comply with relevant standards, regulations, policies, and best practices, along with a consistent need for reviews and audits. To identify gaps or weaknesses in the company's information systems and digital infrastructure, penetration testing, vulnerability assessments, and various security evaluations are conducted, addressing and mitigating the identified vulnerabilities. Consequently, regular security reviews and audits are essential for effectively minimizing potential threats.

Incident response: In this process, the company develops a comprehensive incident response strategy that outlines procedures for identifying, reporting, and recovering from cybersecurity incidents. Establishing a response team with clear responsibilities to manage data breaches and setting standards for stakeholder communication are key components of the Incident Response Plan (IRP). Following a cybersecurity incident, a company's incident response team is tasked with determining the cause, minimizing damage, and ensuring a swift recovery. This value chain link demands a thoroughly developed and tested incident response strategy.

9.2.4 Performance and Continuity

Performance management in the cybersecurity value chain is a systematic process for measuring, monitoring, and optimizing security controls, procedures, and outcomes at every phase of the corporate value chain. In this context, organizations can enhance business performance, reduce risks, and strengthen defenses by evaluating efficiency at each level. Performance management transforms security from a cost center into a strategic enabler, ensuring that safeguards evolve in tandem with business needs. It aligns cybersecurity activities with corporate objectives, effectively manages risks, and delivers measurable value. This process includes key performance indicators (e.g., awareness training rate), security posture metrics (e.g., mean time to detect), compliance metrics (e.g., GDPR compliance), and business impact metrics (e.g., incident-related financial losses and downtime costs).

The corporate cybersecurity value chain also incorporates continuous improvement, which involves assessing the effectiveness of the organization's cybersecurity governance policies and procedures and making adjustments to enhance its cybersecurity posture. This aspect of the value chain is crucial for the business to stay ahead of emerging cyber risks and to ensure that the cybersecurity plan's policies and procedures are executed accurately and maintained in alignment with the strategic plan. Continuous improvement is a vital component of the corporate cybersecurity value chain. It encompasses systems thinking (Senge, 2006), evaluating the organization's security performance measures, and making necessary adjustments to bolster its

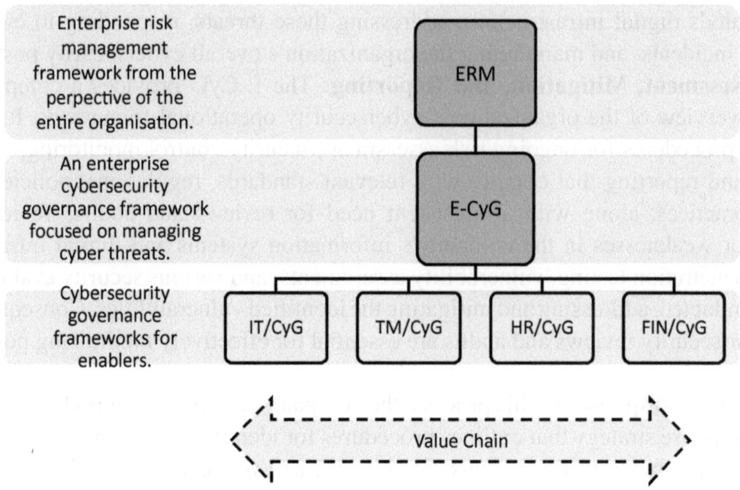

Fig. 9.1 Cybersecurity enabler value chain

cybersecurity posture. This connection in the value chain is essential for keeping the business proactive against evolving cyber threats. Continuous improvement through feedback loops enhances security performance. Monitoring throughout the value chain enables adaptive governance, permitting the updating of controls in response to new threats in the digital infrastructure. Furthermore, cybersecurity incidents can inform governance policies.

The above highlights the actions needed to establish a robust governance framework. To complete the value chain picture, it is essential to incorporate the key components (Fig. 9.1). The following sections discuss the four enablers within the context of the enterprise cybersecurity value chain, examining their roles and contributions to the overall framework.

9.3 Technology Governance Value Chain

Technology management (TM/CyG) and systems technologies (IT/CyG), collectively referred to as technology, work together to enable the E-CyG value chain. In the technology governance process for security, the primary role of TM/CyG is to ensure that the organization's technology infrastructure and systems (as configured by IT/CyG selection) are secure, reliable, and effective in protecting the company's digital assets and information from online threats. Firewalls, antivirus software, endpoint detection and response, and intrusion detection systems represent traditional system technologies; however, they only address specific threats. The inherent weaknesses of these traditional systems technologies, including their reactive rather than proactive nature, siloed security measures, reliance on manual updates and static rules, limited behavioral analysis, dependence on human intervention, and slow response times due to the lack of automated response capabilities, restrict their ability to mitigate cybersecurity risks. The limitations of these conventional methods include a lack of quantitative analysis and decision-making capabilities; modern tools such as quantum computing, artificial intelligence, and machine learning can help address these shortcomings.

As the operational arm of cybersecurity, the IT department implements and maintains technical measures to safeguard the company's digital assets. Its primary responsibilities include offering technical assistance and cybersecurity support to other departments, such as deploying and managing cybersecurity tools (e.g., firewalls, EDR, encryption, and intrusion detection systems), monitoring networks and systems for threats and vulnerabilities, and responding to and recovering from cybersecurity incidents.

9.3.1 Technology Management

Technology management is crucial to the corporate cybersecurity value chain, as the IT department manages the technology infrastructure and systems supporting the business's cybersecurity efforts. The cybersecurity technology management function oversees and administers the company's cyber risk technical infrastructure, which safeguards servers, business systems, networks, and other essential technologies critical to business operations. Technology management ensures these cyber protection systems remain compliant, effective, updated, patched, and secure, thereby reducing the risk of cyberattacks.

The following important responsibilities of the technology management function are vital to maintaining the company's cybersecurity posture:

- Implementing Security Technologies: The technology management function assesses, recommends, implements, and maintains cybersecurity systems, including intrusion detection and prevention systems, antivirus software, and other related security solutions.
- Implementing Access Controls: The technology management function establishes access controls to ensure that only authorized individuals can access the company's digital assets and data. To guarantee that users have the appropriate level of access based on their roles and responsibilities, it is essential to adopt user authentication and authorization procedures, such as multi-factor authentication.
- Monitoring and Reporting: The technology management function assigns monitoring roles for security incidents and potential risks to the company's digital infrastructure and systems. In this effort, security monitoring tools and technologies are used to identify possible security gaps and generate reports that provide an overview of the organization's security posture.

- Incident Response: In the event of a security incident, the technology management function organizes the company's response efforts by coordinating with the business's incident response team to minimize damage and accelerate recovery.
- Performance, review, improvement, and innovation: TM/CyG ensures that regular performance measurements are conducted to review the efficacy of systems technologies for improvement. It encourages innovation to enhance the organization's cybersecurity posture further.

9.3.2 Security or Systems Technology

Systems technology is vital to cybersecurity because it provides the essential tools, processes, and infrastructure needed to safeguard digital assets from attacks. It acts as the backbone of cybersecurity, allowing for real-time monitoring, proactive defense, and quick response to threats. In the realm of cybersecurity, systems and technology are interconnected concepts that work together to achieve specific goals. Technology is crucial for improving the capabilities and performance of systems, which in turn establish the framework for managing and implementing technology. Developing a strong cybersecurity infrastructure in today's rapidly evolving digital threat landscape requires the effective integration of security systems and technologies.

By integrating system security technology at every level—networks, cloud, software, and hardware—businesses can establish strong defenses against evolving cyber threats. Systems technology supports IT/CyG in auditing and compliance reporting by facilitating policy enforcement, ensuring regulatory compliance, providing insights into potential risks, automating responses, and gathering logs from various sources to monitor suspicious activity. System technology can reinforce the controls mandated by NIST CSF and GDPR as part of IT/CyG, including Security Information and Event Management (SIEM) and Security Orchestration, Automation, and Response (SOAR), which align with the continuous monitoring governance requirement of NIST CSF. Another aspect of governance involves enforcing access policies through firewalls. Data security is improved by encryption, which is essential for compliance with regulations such as GDPR.

9.4 HR Governance Value Chain

Human resource management (HRM) in the corporate cybersecurity value chain ensures that the organization has the right human resources to support its cybersecurity program (Pham et al., 2017) and to build resilience against threats. The four main components of cybersecurity resilience are culture, behavior, usability, and safety (Fairburn et al., 2021). Cybersecurity education and training can help close the gap and improve overall resilience by increasing individual knowledge and awareness to better manage threats. HRM makes sure that staff members are trained to follow best practices and are aware of cybersecurity threats. It also helps mitigate insider threats and ensures compliance with cybersecurity policies.

Some techniques aimed at the facilities and human resources applied to mitigate cybersecurity risks arising from human factors include frequent evaluations and approvals of individuals granted access to secure areas, stringent physical access controls for the property and infrastructure, prohibiting photography in restricted zones, and providing constant escorts for visitors to sensitive locations. Other essential strategies involve routinely screening new hires, requiring them to sign a confidentiality oath, creating long, complex, and secure passwords, and regularly updating their physical access rights. The human factors to consider for establishing a robust HR/CyG process within the E-CyG value chain include:

Leadership: Effective leadership in strategic cybersecurity governance is crucial for aligning security initiatives with organizational objectives, mitigating risks, and maintaining resilience against evolving threats. In cybersecurity governance, appointing individuals with leadership qualities enables efficient management that encompasses strategy, decision-making, and execution, ensuring that security is integrated into the business culture while promoting trust and resilience.

Hiring and Staffing: HR/CyG is responsible for identifying and hiring cybersecurity experts who have the necessary knowledge and experience to support the business's cybersecurity program. This process involves creating job descriptions, reviewing resumes, conducting interviews, and extending employment offers.

Policy and Procedure Development, Implementation, and Maintenance: HR/CyG policies involve establishing guidelines, protocols, and best practices to manage cybersecurity risks related to employees. To mitigate insider threats and human errors that could result in breaches, these policies ensure that personnel—often the weakest link in security—are thoroughly screened, trained, and monitored. They cover operational responsibilities, accountabilities, access control, data protection, and the proper use of business systems and equipment.

Employee Education: HR/CyG is responsible for educating staff members about cybersecurity threats and best practices. Training programs and awareness campaigns should be implemented to educate staff about cybersecurity risks and provide guidance on how to mitigate them.

Training and Development: HR/CyG is responsible for ensuring that cybersecurity experts possess the essential knowledge and skills to manage the company's cybersecurity risks effectively. This encompasses providing them with ongoing training on current security threats and technologies, as well as exploring opportunities for professional growth.

Performance Management: HR/CyG oversees the performance of cybersecurity experts, ensuring they meet the company's standards and expectations. This includes setting performance goals, providing regular feedback, and conducting performance evaluations.

Overall, HR/CyG's role in the enterprise cybersecurity governance value chain is to ensure that the organization has the necessary human resources to support its cybersecurity program and that staff members understand their responsibilities in mitigating cybersecurity risks. HR/CyG is vital in protecting the organization's digital assets and information from cyber threats through recruiting, educating, and developing cybersecurity specialists, creating and implementing policies and procedures, enhancing employee knowledge, and ensuring compliance.

9.5 Finance Governance Value Chain

The responsibility of financial cybersecurity governance (FIN/CyG) within the E-CyG value chain is to ensure that finance-related cyber threats and their implications are recognized, properly identified, and assessed, and that the business possesses the necessary financial resources to launch and sustain a successful cybersecurity program. To make a significant contribution to the E-CyG value chain, FIN/CyG must:

- Assist the firm in evaluating risks through various risk-based strategies, including valuation, cost-benefit analysis, sensitivity analysis, and value at risk.
- Facilitate and justify funding sources while managing the distribution of funds to support the company's cybersecurity program. Budgeting should encompass cybersecurity experts, firewalls, antivirus software, and security monitoring tools, as these are vital components that bolster the organization's security posture.
- Prioritize investments in cybersecurity according to the organization's risk profile, risk tolerance, and corporate objectives. This process involves evaluating the potential impact of cyber threats on business operations and determining the appropriate level of investment necessary to mitigate those risks.
- Perform a return-on-investment (ROI) analysis to evaluate the effectiveness and viability of the cybersecurity program. This analysis examines the cost-effectiveness and impact of the company's cybersecurity measures in mitigating potential risks.
- FIN/CyG ensures that the company's cybersecurity program adheres to all applicable standards, laws, and requirements. This includes planning a budget for compliance activities, such as audits and assessments, to guarantee effective management.
- Manage the firm's insurance plans by assessing the potential financial effects of cyber threats and securing suitable, cost-effective insurance options to mitigate these risks.

Financial management plays a crucial role in the corporate cybersecurity value chain by ensuring that the organization has the necessary funds to establish and maintain an effective cybersecurity program, and that its investments in cybersecurity are justified and aligned with the risk profile and corporate objectives.

9.6 Enterprise Cybersecurity Governance Value Chain

With each component playing a unique yet interconnected role in safeguarding the value chain, the Enterprise Cyber Governance (E-CyG) process ensures that cybersecurity is a collective responsibility throughout the organization. This section outlines the roles and responsibilities at various levels within the value chain, as illustrated in Fig. 9.2.

9.6.1 The Board of Directors

The Board of Directors prioritizes, authorizes, and integrates cybersecurity policies into the ERM and E-CyG through advocacy, strategic oversight, guidance, and monitoring. The BoD emphasizes leadership and oversight in the E-CyG value chain by treating cybersecurity as a business enabler rather than just an IT issue, ensuring it aligns with organizational objectives. As the primary leader, it seeks executive support and involvement to advocate for cybersecurity at the highest levels. The BoD oversees cybersecurity risks and ensures that its strategy aligns with the company's overarching business goals.

Regarding responsibilities, the Board of Directors confirms that the cybersecurity plan aligns with the company's objectives. It assesses risk exposure and significant cyber incidents, evaluates and approves cybersecurity policies and governance frameworks, and ensures that cybersecurity efforts are adequately funded and supported. The BoD holds senior management accountable for cybersecurity performance. A risk committee supports the BoD's strategic initiatives and serves as a liaison between the BoD and senior management.

The Board of Directors advocates for a risk-based approach that prioritizes threats based on their business impact rather than their technical severity. This method is widely used in cybersecurity governance, as it enables organizations to allocate resources effectively and align security measures with business objectives from a risk exposure perspective. By ranking risks, it secures the cybersecurity budget and ensures compliance with relevant frameworks and regulations, striking a balance between security and business prudence. This approach guarantees that security efforts are proportional to actual threats, optimizing protection while maintaining operational efficiency.

The Board of Directors promotes a corporate risk culture that fosters awareness and accountability at all levels. Roles from the BoD down are clearly outlined through governance structures and responsibilities that ensure interdepartmental collaboration and coordination. Effective BoD leadership translates strategies and policies into actionable practices throughout the organization, reducing risk and fostering growth.

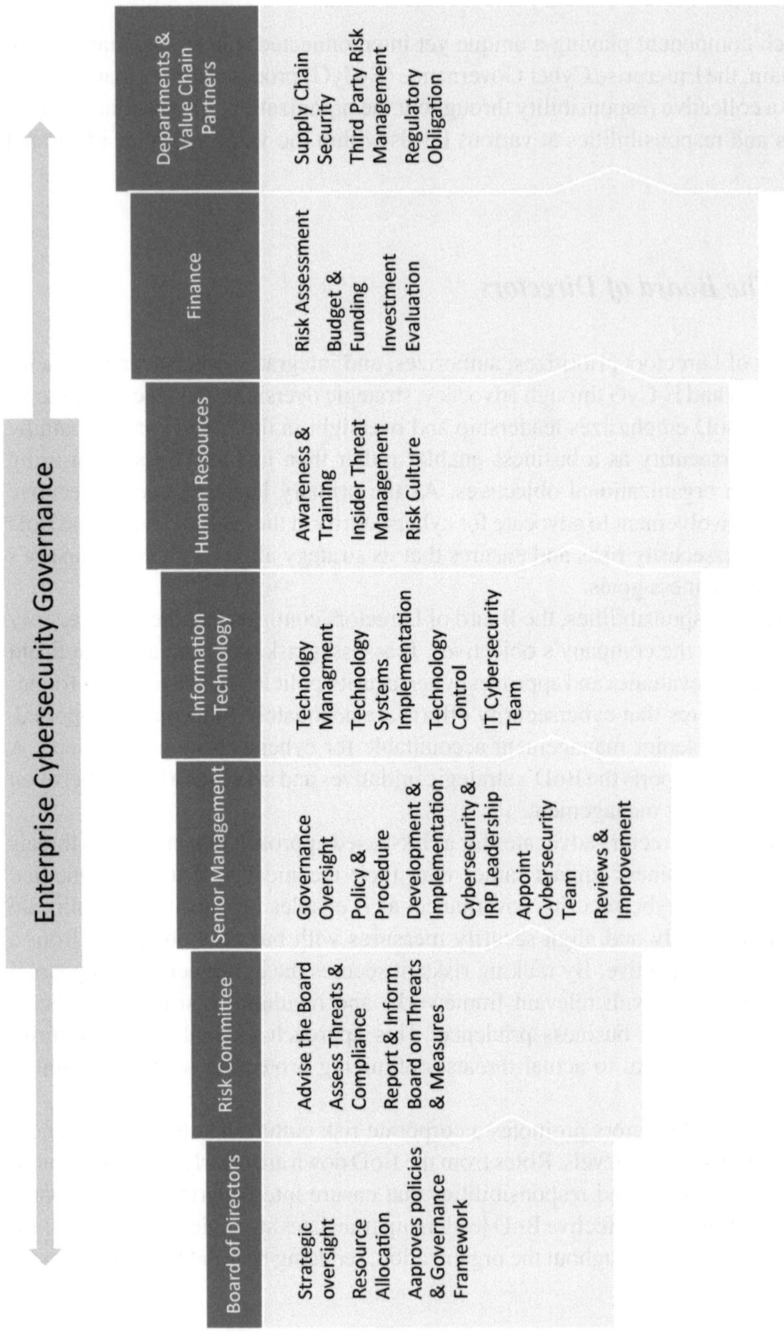

Fig. 9.2 Strategic Cybersecurity Governance Roles

9.6.2 Risk Committee

The risk committee's role is to advise the Board of Directors on matters of compliance and cybersecurity. One of the committee's responsibilities is to assess cybersecurity threats and their impact on company operations. The committee reviews cybersecurity-related issues in internal and external audit reports to ensure compliance with the company's cybersecurity strategy, framework, and regulatory obligations (such as NIST, ISO 27001, GDPR, and CCPA). It regularly informs the BoD of the main cybersecurity threats and the countermeasures implemented by the company.

9.6.3 Senior Management (C-Suite)

In addition to assisting the Board of Directors in developing the cybersecurity strategy, senior management's primary role is to implement and ensure the operational execution of that strategy. Their activities span multiple levels, including the BoD, the risk committee, and various departments. They coordinate departmental efforts and translate the BoD's strategy into actionable policies by creating and executing procedures while overseeing their implementation. To achieve this, the E-CyG must be established based on relevant standards and regulations, ensuring alignment with business objectives and best practices. While the Chief Information Security Officer (CISO) is designated as the primary executive responsible for the E-CyG, senior management is collectively accountable for its oversight. They provide leadership and ensure that cybersecurity remains one of their top priorities, regularly including it on their agenda.

Senior management should adopt emerging technologies creatively and swiftly to manage new risks, integrating AI, automation, and enhanced threat detection. They must make informed decisions that leverage risk assessments and threat intelligence to guide security actions and investments. Senior management maintains oversight and coordination of cyber risk for operational procedures and third-party management by requiring vendors and partners to comply with stringent security standards. They embrace a crisis leadership approach to anticipate and respond effectively to breaches, implementing well-defined incident response procedures (Ho et al., 2009).

It is responsible for continuously improving the company's cybersecurity posture by utilizing resilience planning to ensure business continuity through strong support, recovery, and cyber resilience strategies. In reporting to the Board of Directors and the risk committee, senior management plays a vital role in communication and transparency. This is achieved by translating technical hazards into business terms for informed decision-making. Senior management openly addresses disclosures after a breach to maintain the trust of stakeholders, the general public, and customers. Additionally, it collaborates with business and government partners on regulatory and threat-sharing initiatives.

The CISO serves as the chief cybersecurity executive, tasked with developing and implementing cybersecurity policies, standards, and procedures. This role includes overseeing incident response and disaster recovery planning, as well as managing staff security awareness training. Additionally, the CISO reports on cybersecurity developments, incidents, and hazards to the Board of Directors and the Risk Committee. Furthermore, the CISO manages interactions with authorities and cybersecurity vendors.

In summary, the CEO prioritizes cybersecurity in business decisions. At the same time, the CISO integrates Enterprise Cybersecurity Governance (E-CyG) into Enterprise Risk Management (ERM) by aligning TM/CyG, IT/CyG, HR/CyG, and FIN/CyG processes with the enterprise's security requirements. Additionally, the CISO supports cybersecurity budgets and investments. The following sections provide a detailed discussion of the supporting governance roles of the three enablers—technology, people, and finance, which are the primary focus of this book.

9.6.4 IT Department

The IT department safeguards the company's digital assets by implementing technical controls and managing incidents. In addition to deploying and maintaining security systems such as firewalls, EDR, and SIEM, the department is also responsible for the technical oversight, management, and review of cybersecurity processes. In this role, the Technology Management (TM) function evaluates and reviews cybersecurity technologies to ensure they remain suitable for the company's digital environment and align with its business objectives, while effectively protecting the company from all cyber threats through vulnerability assessments and penetration tests. Together with HR, TM oversees identity management and access controls.

9.6.5 Human Resource Department

Employee awareness, training, and insider threat management are top priorities for the HR department. HR must ensure that appropriate security measures are implemented to address risks posed by employees and former employees who may, due to lack of knowledge, carelessness, human error, or emotional distress, harm the company's systems. Similarly, they may pose a threat because they possess insider knowledge about the company's computer systems, data, and security protocols that they can exploit. Thus, HR primarily oversees staff cybersecurity compliance training and insider threat programs, as well as enforces background checks for new hires.

9.6.6 Finance

The finance department plays a crucial role in supporting cybersecurity governance by ensuring that cybersecurity efforts are sufficiently funded, aligned with business objectives, and effectively integrated into financial risk management. It guarantees that security projects are financially viable, risks are assessed, and compliance is maintained. The FIN/CyG adopts a risk-based approach, evaluating the financial implications of threats and ranking them according to their severity. It ensures that cybersecurity programs receive adequate funding to acquire security technologies and support personnel, thereby sustaining the process. Additionally, it manages cybersecurity insurance policies to ensure they are suitable and sufficient for the firm's security exposure, aligning with its risk tolerance and posture. By incorporating cybersecurity into financial planning and risk management, the FIN/CyG safeguards the organization's assets and reputation while supporting strategic decision-making.

9.6.7 Other Departments

Department heads and business unit leaders (e.g., finance, IT, marketing, HR, and legal) are tasked with implementing cybersecurity controls within their respective departments. Each department will appoint a security team to oversee its respective governance program and cooperate with the E-CyG and IT security teams. They must manage policies, procedures, and data in line with cybersecurity policies and procedures and notify the IT and security teams of any suspicious activity. Department heads should ensure that line employees adhere to cybersecurity policies and procedures in their daily operations by following best practices and promptly reporting any suspicious activities.

9.6.8 Supply Chain Partners

Supply chain partners or third-party vendors in cybersecurity are external organizations that provide products, services, or support to maintain an organization's business or enhance its security posture. Supply chain risks in cybersecurity governance are typically viewed as vulnerabilities resulting from third-party vendors, contractors, suppliers, or logistics partners that can compromise an enterprise's security systems. They arise from external entities as these third parties are granted access to or influence over an enterprise's systems, data, or operations as part of their involvement in the supply chain process. There is a broad spectrum of supply chain risks that can include but are not limited to weak security practices by vendors (unpatched systems, poor access controls), software attacks (compromised software updates or open-source vulnerability), physical supply chain risks, insider threats as a result of malicious or negligent actions by vendor staff or geopolitical risks due to political instability or civil unrest. Supply chain risks can lead to severe consequences, including data breaches, operational disruptions, financial losses, reputational damage, and erosion of customer confidence.

Supply chain partners are also subject to the governance process, which ensures that customers, outside suppliers, and vendors who have access to, possess, or can exploit insider knowledge about the company's computer systems, data, and security procedures comply with the company's cybersecurity guidelines. Senior management is also responsible for ensuring that third-party vendors adhere to company standards, regulations, and policies and procedures to prevent process weaknesses, non-compliance, and associated penalties.

As a result, apart from internal risk management to mitigate supply chain risks for safe and sound cybersecurity governance, enterprises should develop a vendor risk management framework to provide guidelines on vendor selection, due diligence, and contractual safeguards. Continuous monitoring should be in place to minimize supply chain risks. It is recommended that companies utilize various tools for real-time tracking of vendor security posture, such as security rating platforms like BitSight or SecurityScorecard, to quantify and assess their vendors' cybersecurity risk scores. Third parties should also be required to report incidents promptly and share threat intelligence. As we mentioned in Chapters 5 and 6, enterprises should limit vendors' access by applying the principle of least privilege and use zero-trust architecture to verify all third-party interactions. To summarize, firms can adopt many best practices associated with vendor risk management, which might include (1) developing supply chain security policies to specify vendor cybersecurity requirements and compliance obligations, (2) encouraging vendors to use Software Bill of Materials (SBOM) to track software components and vulnerabilities, (3) ensuring vendors are included in incident response plans and tabletop exercises, (4) educating procurement and IT teams on supply chain risks and secure vendor management, and (5) considering the use of cyber insurance for supply chain-related incidents.

Avoidance of Over-reliance on Cybersecurity Vendors and Sufficient Coverage of Cyber Insurance

Another aspect of supply chain cybersecurity governance we want to analyze is the use of cybersecurity vendors, which has become a popular trend among many medium to large-sized organizations worldwide. According to industry reports, the cybersecurity market is dominated by a few players. The top 10 cybersecurity vendors control approximately 62% of the market, indicating a substantial level of concentration (Gartner, n.d.). CrowdStrike and Microsoft Defender, in particular, dominate the endpoint protection market due to their scalability and integration with enterprise ecosystems. However, these vendors can also be exposed to malicious attacks and/or non-malicious errors.

The CrowdStrike incident, which caused 8.5 million Microsoft Windows devices to crash, was attributed to a faulty update to CrowdStrike's Falcon Sensor. Known as the most significant IT outage in history, it disrupted airlines (Delta's estimated loss was $500 million), healthcare, banking, and government services, resulting in an approximate global financial loss of $10 billion (Milmo et al., 2024). This incident highlighted the risks of over-reliance on a few cybersecurity vendors, as disruptions in a single vendor's service can negatively affect global supply chains and multiple sectors (Franceschi-Bicchierai & Lorenzo, 2024).

Cybersecurity governance implications are twofold. First, organizations should avoid excessive reliance on these dominant vendors to mitigate systemic risks and seek to expand vendor diversification, conducting regular supply chain risk assessments. Policies like the EU's Digital Operational Resilience Act (DORA), effective from early 2025, focus on stringent third-party risk assessments to enhance operational resilience and can serve as a valuable source of reference. Second, when things go beyond the control of enterprises and their vendors, utilizing cyber insurance might help them minimize the cost. It has been observed that most cyber insurance products are specialized and designed to protect organizations from financial losses and liabilities resulting from malicious cyber incidents, such as data breaches, ransomware attacks, and system disruptions. However, the CrowdStrike outage, which was caused by a human error, not a malicious attack, reveals gaps in coverage for system failures. These gaps in many insurance policies leave organizations exposed to losses from unintentional disruptions. Therefore, enterprises must ensure that their cyber insurance policies provide adequate coverage.

Equifax Incident: The Role of Board of Directors Oversight

Equifax has been one of the three biggest US credit reporting agencies. On September 7, 2017, it announced a massive data breach affecting more than 140 million consumers, sparking a public backlash across the USA. Subsequent investigations revealed that Equifax had been aware of critical faults in its cybersecurity infrastructure, policies, and procedures for years but had failed to address them (Srinivasan et al., 2017). The incident has garnered attention not only from the public, authorities, affected entities, and consumers but also from researchers and practitioners. MIT's Kabanov and Madnick (2021) conducted their independent research. They concluded that the root causes of the Equifax cybersecurity incident were the absence of multiple protection mechanisms and systematic failures of the existing safety control elements at all levels of the company's hierarchical safety control structure. The designs of most control elements in Equifax's safety structure were found to be subpar. Specifically, they were based on invalid assumptions and lacked support from controls at higher levels of the hierarchy. These authors also claimed that most parts of the safety control structure contributed in some way to the propagation of the cybersecurity incident. Miyashiro (2021) also pointed out that IT and Security's inability to locate and patch Apache Struts can be attributed to existing flaws in their cybersecurity policy, namely a lack of comprehensive IT asset inventory, failure to follow patch management policies, inadequate IT and security management, and failure to maintain cybersecurity technologies. Equifax was also late in delivering public disclosure, prioritizing reputation management over consumer protection. This incident resulted in a total financial cost of US$700 million, including Equifax's settlement costs with relevant authorities and 50 US states, as well as consumer compensation (Federal Trade Commission 2024). It also forced the company to spend $1.4 billion on security upgrades. Lessons from the Equifax event are varied, ranging from proactive security measures to avoid exploitation of vulnerabilities to consumer-centered responses and transparency. However, most importantly, it highlighted the role of Board of Directors' oversight in cybersecurity governance. It must be a board-level priority.

9.7 Conclusion

A strategic framework that integrates enterprise cybersecurity governance (E-CyG) into every aspect of an organization's risk operations (ERM) acknowledges their interdependence and ensures that security is embedded in partnerships, processes, efficiency, and value delivery. The value chain approach to E-CyG reduces risks while enhancing resilience by aligning cybersecurity with business objectives. This approach guarantees that E-CyG serves as a business enabler. By systematically addressing risks throughout the operational cycle, organizations can strengthen resilience, compliance, and trust while maintaining operational agility. This strategy is becoming increasingly crucial in a world where cyber threats exploit interdependencies between digital and physical supply chains. As a vital part of risk management and value creation, cybersecurity must be integrated into an organization's core business plan, rather than being treated as a standalone or afterthought. Organizations that do so will gain a competitive edge in market reputation, security, and compliance. To highlight the E-CyG as a dynamic and adaptive tool for protection and value creation, the next chapter will explore the strategic aspects of the E-CyG.

References

Fairburn, N., Shelton, A., Ackroyd, F., & Selfe, R. (2021). Beyond murphy's law: Applying wider human factors behavioural science approaches in cybersecurity resilience. *Lecture Notes in Computer Science, 12788*. https://doi.org/10.1007/978-3-030-77392-2_9

Federal Trade Commission. (2024). *Equifax Data Breach Settlement*. Federal Trade Commission. https://www.ftc.gov/enforcement/refunds/equifax-data-breach-settlement

Franceschi-Bicchierai, Z. W., Lorenzo. (2024). *What we know about CrowdStrike's update fail that's causing global outages and travel chaos*. TechCrunch. https://techcrunch.com/2024/07/19/what-we-know-about-crowdstrikes-update-fail-thats-causing-global-outages-and-travel-chaos/

Gartner. (n.d.). *Product—Gartner Special Reports*. Gartner. https://www.gartner.com/en/products/special-reports

Ho, B., Oh, K., Durden, G., & Slade, B. (2009). *Crisis decision making*. Nova Science Publishing.

Kabanov, I., & Madnick, S. (2021). Applying the lessons from the Equifax cybersecurity incident to build a better Defense. *MIS Quarterly Executive*, 109–125. https://doi.org/10.17705/2msqe.00044

Milmo, D., Kollewe, J., Quinn, B., Taylor, J., & Ibrahim, M. (2024). Slow recovery from IT outage begins as experts warn of future risks. *The Guardian*. https://www.theguardian.com/australia-news/article/2024/jul/19/microsoft-windows-pcs-outage-blue-screen-of-death

Miyashiro, I. K. (2021). *Case study: Equifax Data Breach*. Seven Pillars Institute. https://sevenpillarsinstitute.org/case-study-equifax-data-breach/

Oh, K., & Ho, B. (2022). *Cybersecurity risk management: An enterprise risk management approach*. Nova Science Publishers.

Pham, H., Pham, D., Brennan, L., & Richardson, J. (2017). Information security and people: A conundrum for compliance. *Australasian Journal of Information Systems, 21*. https://journal.acs.org.au/index.php/ajis/article/view/1321/751

Senge, P. (2006). *The fifth discipline*. Random House.

Srinivasan, S., Pitcher, Q., & Goldberg, J. S. (2017). Data breach at Equifax. *Harvard Business School Case*, 118–131. https://www.hbs.edu/faculty/Pages/item.aspx?num=53509&ref=breached.company

Swinton, S., Hedges, S. (2019). *Cybersecurity governance, Part 1: 5 Fundamental Challenges*. Retrieved September 29, 2024, from https://insights.sei.cmu.edu/blog/cybersecurity-governance-part-1-5-fundamental-challenges/#:~:text=Cybersecurity%20Governance%2C%20Part%201%3A%205%20Fundamental%20Challenges%201,Senior%20Leadership%20Oversight%20...%205%205.%20Resources%20

Chapter 10
Strategic Cybersecurity Governance

Abstract This chapter consolidates all the relevant literature, guidelines, concepts, standards, best practices, and material we have covered in the preceding nine chapters to propose a comprehensive and practical enterprise cybersecurity governance framework. The purpose is to offer a model, the "Strategic Enterprise Cybersecurity Governance Model" (ECyG-M), that incorporates the significant strategies, policies, systems, procedures, and preventative and corrective measures that firms can take to safeguard the CIA attributes of information system assets. A business's strategies, policies, procedures, and actions to manage and protect its digital assets and customer data from cyber threats form part of the cybersecurity value chain. We incorporate the critical governance elements and capabilities presented in the preceding chapter into the strategic cybersecurity model. The ECyG-M approach can help reduce cyber risk exposure through a robust and comprehensive governance regime. The ECyG-M and its inherent value chain, created by adopting an ERM approach, offer a thorough and integrated method for cybersecurity risk management across the organization. Organizations can use the ECyG-M structured processes to identify, evaluate, prioritize, and manage cyber risks to accomplish their strategic goals.

10.1 Introduction

In today's rapidly evolving cyber threat landscape, traditional, static, compliance-driven cybersecurity governance proves ineffective. Organizations require a dynamic, flexible, and value-creating governance architecture that aligns security with business objectives while continuously enhancing resilience. A significant shift in the digital landscape today is the increasing recognition of the necessity to align cybersecurity risk governance with broader organizational goals, objectives, and strategies. Cybersecurity risk management, no longer confined to IT departments, now demands a more adaptable strategic approach to addressing what is regarded as a significant challenge. This book acknowledges and emphasizes the dynamic role of "governance as a vital element of enterprise risk management" (Oh & Ho, 2022) in coordinating enterprise cybersecurity goals, objectives, strategies, and tactics.

K. B. Oh et al., *Cybersecurity Governance*,
https://doi.org/10.1007/978-981-95-3865-2_10

This chapter consolidates all relevant literature, guidelines, concepts, standards, practices, and materials examined in the previous nine chapters to discuss and reinforce the E-CyG as a comprehensive, structured, systematic, and practical strategic framework process. Based on this premise, we propose a strategic governance model called the "Strategic Enterprise Cybersecurity Governance Model" (ECyG-M), which exemplifies the constructs, attributes, and benefits of the E-CyG from a strategic perspective. The ECyG-M is presented in Sect. 10.4, highlighting and demonstrating its key components, which illustrate how businesses can seamlessly integrate protection against cyberattacks with the achievement of broader strategic goals. The aim is to present an integrated framework that is both strategic and pragmatic, linking enterprise-wide cybersecurity risk governance with strategic management. It examines how businesses integrate cybersecurity risk governance into their overarching risk control strategy to protect digital infrastructure and assets amid constantly evolving cyber threats.

A robust ECyG-M framework provides a clear and practical governance structure for managing cyber risks, ensuring accountability and oversight across all organizational levels and functions. Its purpose is to establish a best practice, standards-oriented, and risk-based governance model that incorporates all significant risk governance attributes, including leadership, structure, roles, accountabilities, policies, procedures, systems, compliance, and preventive and corrective measures to protect the "CIA triad" (Anderson, 1972) of information assets. A strategic and operational governance model enhances management's ability to implement governance and strengthens the Board of Directors' oversight capabilities (Deloitte, 2013). The ECyG-M supports and informs management and the BoD regarding their governance responsibilities. It provides governance structures, policies, and procedures for cybersecurity governance to the BoD and C-suite leadership. An effectively structured operational model for cybersecurity governance enables the BoD to promote clarity and understanding of the tasks executed by individuals in governance and security management roles. We argue that these attributes are essential for the organization's adopted framework, whether it is a standard-based model or the outcome of the firm's organic development. This chapter aims to illustrate the imperatives and inclusions for a best-practice cybersecurity governance framework in the ECyG-M, designed to enhance the strategic and tactical effectiveness and awareness of BoDs, management, and policymakers.

Cyber threats are dynamic and constantly evolving, making it challenging to predict the intentions and behaviors of hostile actors. Traditional risk governance models for digital, human, financial, and physical assets may prove ineffective in managing cyber risk. The approach to cybersecurity governance architecture is not a one-size-fits-all solution. To manage cyber risks effectively, the Board of Directors must understand the organization's threat landscape through various oversight mechanisms and dedicated resources, including specialized committees, risk management standards (e.g., NIST CSF and ISO 27001), regulations (e.g., GDPR and HIPAA), technologies (software and hardware), stakeholders, budgets, and external experts. A cybersecurity strategy outlines an organization's comprehensive plan to protect its most critical digital assets, personnel, and processes. The set of policies, procedures, and actions a business undertakes to manage and protect its digital assets and customer data from cyber threats forms part of the cybersecurity value chain. In this chapter, we summarize and address some crucial governance elements or capabilities in the cybersecurity value chain that are essential for developing the ECyG-M that is dynamic, adaptive, and value-creating, which include the following:

- Establish the ERM-oriented Cybersecurity Governance Plan (CGP)[1] or the Enterprise Information Security Policy (EISP)[2] to define planning, allocate budgets, and set risk tolerances for implementing strategic and operational risk policies and procedures. This is conducted at the Board of Directors, C-suite, and risk committee levels (Fig. 10.1).
- This is a risk-based decision-making model that prioritizes security investments according to their business impact.
- It uses a cost-benefit and ROI-focused security investment strategy to assess cybersecurity success in business terms to create value.
- The CGP is based on a risk assessment of the organization's digital environment. These plans involve aligning cybersecurity goals and objectives with those of the business, establishing strategies and tactics, adopting relevant standards and regulations, documenting policies and procedures, and recommending controls and security technologies essential for mitigating identified risks. The CGP must encompass all components of the organization's digital infrastructure, including risk, architecture, personnel, budget, and networks, systems, and data (both hardware and software).
- Cybersecurity governance architecture enables a business to establish the framework for implementing its cybersecurity strategy (Fig. 10.1). It encompasses the structures, policies, procedures, responsibilities, guidelines, practices, personnel, financial resources, and technological safeguards necessary for protecting the business's data and digital assets.
- It enables a flexible security architecture that uses "Zero Trust" through continuous verification rather than perimeter-based security.
- The cybersecurity operations component of the value chain implements and maintains the security architecture. This process involves monitoring potential threats to the organization's digital infrastructure, identifying and responding to security incidents, and sustaining the overall security posture of the organization.
- It is cross-functional collaboration that embeds and involves cybersecurity in business operations, technology, human resources, legal, and finance, and their participation in cyber risk discussions.

[1] A Cybersecurity Governance Plan is a structured framework that outlines how an organization maintains and oversees its cybersecurity strategy, policies, and controls to secure digital assets, comply with legislation, and mitigate risks. It ensures that cybersecurity aligns with business objectives and is considered at all levels of decision-making.

[2] Organizations use the Enterprise Information Security Program (EISP), a structured framework, to protect their information assets from online attacks. The CIA triad—confidentiality, integrity, and availability—of data is ensured by defining rules, processes, controls, and governance systems.

- Assessing risks during the initial stage enables an organization to scope, identify, and scale potential threats to its digital assets and information throughout this phase of the cybersecurity value chain. This assessment uncovers weaknesses and threats to the company's digital infrastructure and evaluates the likelihood of their occurrence. This process aims to highlight the organization's risk exposure by identifying security gaps and vulnerabilities, thereby determining its security posture in relation to its current cybersecurity maturity.
- An agile policy framework, which includes ongoing adjustments based on regular policy reviews or significant incidents, would utilize NIST CSF, ISO 27001, or COBIT as adaptable baselines instead of rigid checklists, resulting in a dynamic governance approach to address emerging threats.
- Support the integration of real-time threat intelligence to guide governance decisions and adapt policies in response to emerging attack vectors.
- Ensure that ongoing risk management actions and measures are considered and remain accessible (Fig. 10.1—Risk Awareness, Risk Reduction) to keep up with the evolving threat landscape.
- Perform cybersecurity assessments and reviews to ensure the organization's security architecture effectively mitigates potential threats; regular security evaluations are crucial. This includes carrying out penetration testing, vulnerability assessments, and other security checks to identify weaknesses in the company's digital infrastructure and information systems.
- In a security incident, an organization's incident response team is responsible for determining the root cause of the problem, minimizing damage, and swiftly recovering from the incident. This value chain link requires a well-developed and tested incident response plan.
- It adds value by leveraging cyber resilience and a robust security posture in marketing to build client trust (e.g., Security Organisation Control 2—SOC 2 compliant).
- It fosters innovation through security by enabling AI and ML-driven security automation, which reduces human tasks and supports secure digital transformations like safe cloud migration and IoT deployment to create value.

The ECyG-M in Fig. 10.1 represents the strategic cybersecurity governance taxonomy, highlighting three vertical dimensions: goals, processes, and frameworks, along with two levels of control for strategic cybersecurity risk management (SCRM) and tactical cybersecurity risk management (TCRM). The organizational cybersecurity value chain also entails continuous improvement, which involves assessing the organization's governance procedures and making adjustments to enhance its security posture. This aspect of the value chain is essential for the business to stay ahead of emerging cyber risks.

The ECyG-M approach discussed in this chapter emphasizes its cybersecurity value chain and crucial elements for digital risk management within a broader Enterprise Risk Management (ERM) framework, and assists organizations in mitigating cyber risk. It provides a strategic, structured, comprehensive, and practical method for addressing cybersecurity challenges. Organizations can leverage the ECyG-M

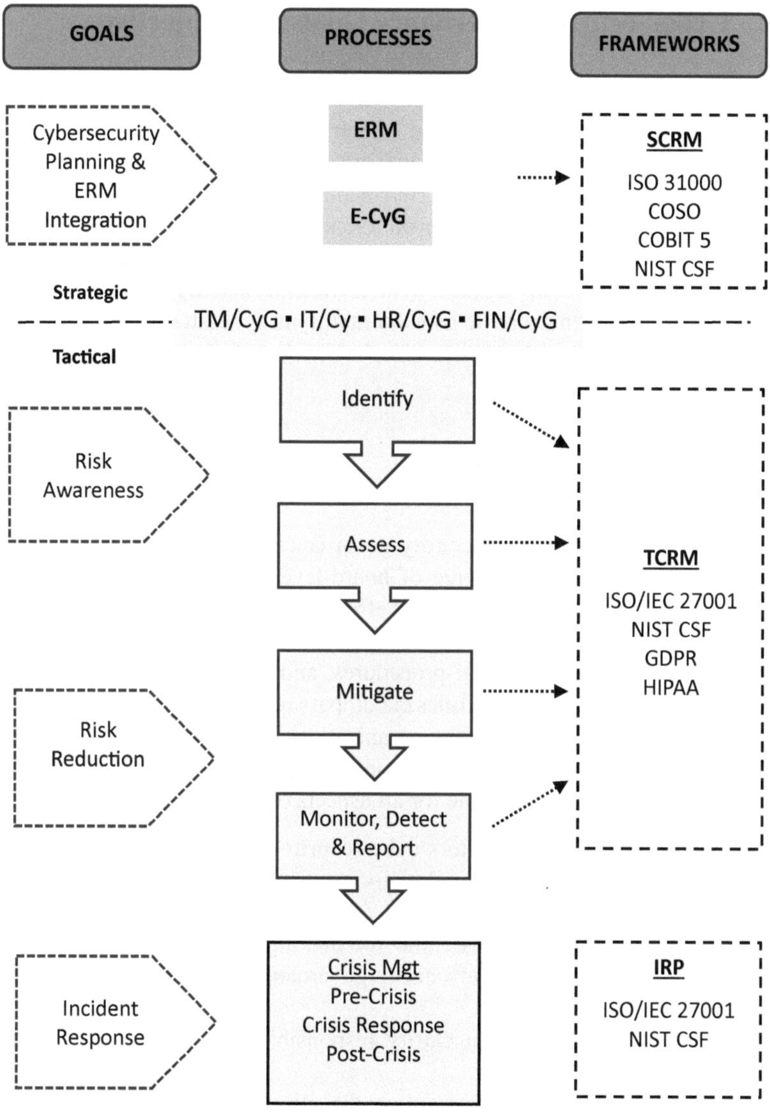

Fig. 10.1 ECyG-M cybersecurity governance taxonomy

processes to achieve their goals by identifying, assessing, prioritizing, and monitoring risks, thereby managing cyber threats that could negatively impact their business objectives and value.

10.2 Cybersecurity Governance Goals and Objectives

Strategic and tactical steps are taken as part of cybersecurity governance to protect digital assets, ensure compliance, and effectively manage risks. It is essential to emphasize that enterprise-wide risk management is a central component of cybersecurity governance (Anderson, 2022; Herrmann & Pridöhl, 2020; Oh & Ho, 2022). All related decisions and actions rely on a risk-based approach. Organizations can utilize various standard cybersecurity strategies and tactics to protect their networks, systems, and data at both strategic and tactical levels. By implementing these measures, a business can decrease its vulnerability to cyberattacks and strengthen its cybersecurity posture.

10.2.1 Strategic Governance

The primary authority of cybersecurity governance at the strategic level lies with the Board of Directors. The degree of board-level involvement in the enterprise cybersecurity function is essential for its effectiveness. For the BoD to comprehend the risks that management takes and manages, it must possess sufficient insight into corporate operations, oversight of procedures, and awareness of potential threats. The BoD's governance responsibilities encompass reviewing corporate plans, setting the tone at the top, establishing the organizational structure, shaping the culture, approving budgets, and promoting the organization's vision, values, and fundamental principles. The BoD is accountable for all aspects of governance, such as:

- The Board of Directors monitors cybersecurity risks within the organization's overall risk profile framework, and senior management must oversee the ECyG-M processes.
- A cyber risk committee is essential for making key decisions, such as overseeing and ensuring that cybersecurity governance aligns with ERM principles and policies.
- Organizational structures that clarify responsibilities for oversight, strategies, tactics, control, and reporting.
- Establishing and promoting a risk culture that aligns with the organization's vision, values, and core principles while ensuring awareness and tolerance.
- Management, staff, and external stakeholders must comprehend the organization's cybersecurity governance plan, design, and strategy.
- The organization must ensure that the risk committee regularly updates the Board of Directors on cybersecurity developments and that this topic is consistently discussed during BoD meetings. Senior leadership must also be adequately informed about cybersecurity risks and strategies.

Strategic measures for cybersecurity governance encompass high-level activities that align security initiatives with company objectives, ensure adherence to standards and regulatory compliance, and enhance resilience against cyber threats. Based on industry best practices and guidelines, Table 10.1 below outlines the primary strategic measures adopted at this level, which are included in cybersecurity governance strategies and translated into policies and procedures during implementation.

The evolving nature of cyber threats presents a challenge for developing effective cybersecurity mitigation strategies. Organizations must stay ahead by establishing a practical strategic framework that addresses the current risk landscape and remains agile enough to adapt to changing threat environments. By integrating these strategic measures, organizations can create a dynamic cybersecurity governance program that responds to threats while supporting business objectives.

10.2.2 Tactical Governance

Integrating cybersecurity strategies with operational procedures is crucial for effective cyber risk management at the tactical level. This is where businesses can deploy security controls to mitigate risks after establishing a risk management strategy. Technical controls, such as antivirus software and firewalls, along with administrative controls like access restrictions and security policies, serve as tactical measures for implementation. To reduce risks, promote compliance, and maintain resilience against evolving threats, these tactical methods enable organizations to enforce effective cybersecurity governance. These approaches require a blend of personnel, processes, and technology to establish a robust security posture. Table 10.2 presents various examples of these security measures, including technical controls and administrative processes.

10.2.3 Establishing Governance Policies and Procedures

A structured approach is essential for developing comprehensive cybersecurity policies and procedures that foster a security-conscious culture and align with corporate objectives. This systematic process of crafting effective cybersecurity policies and procedures ensures that an organization's networks, systems, and data remain safeguarded against attacks. A step-by-step process is detailed below.

- After evaluating the organization's critical assets and risks, the next stage involves identifying goals (commonly articulated in the objectives and strategies) and determining whether the policy scope is organization wide, department specific, or system specific.
- The policies should align with business goals, comply with standards and regulations, be articulated, and emphasize the cybersecurity strategies intended for enforcement.

Table 10.1 Governance strategies and outcomes

Strategy	Outcome
Align cybersecurity with business goals	Prioritize resources and accountability by involving the board and C-suite in cybersecurity supervision. Integration to guarantee that cybersecurity initiatives support operational priorities and organizational missions. A risk culture and tolerance should be established to educate staff and stakeholders about cybersecurity hazards and acceptable practices, thereby reducing human error and carelessness. Specify explicit risk tolerance limits that leadership has agreed upon, which are consistent with the organization's risk appetite, to balance security spending and business expansion.
ERM-oriented cybersecurity risk management	Establish a proactive cybersecurity risk governance framework with processes and procedures that align with the organization's Enterprise risk management (ERM) framework and principles. The framework enables continuous risk identification, assessment, mitigation, and detection and provides measures for incident response in the event of a security breach.
Board-approved budgets	To set aside funds for continuing cybersecurity projects, such as state-of-the-art threat detection systems to address high-impact risks, personnel development courses, and incident response tools.
Policies & procedures	Develop comprehensive policies and procedures for network, system, data protection, incident response, and access control that are regularly updated to address emerging threats.
Roles & Accountability	Assign cybersecurity leaders and specify their roles and accountability within the IT, HR, finance, legal, compliance departments, and security teams.
Risk committee and C-level responsibilities	The Board of Directors is responsible for establishing a risk committee to enhance its role in cybersecurity management. The committee ensures the C-suite's individual and collective responsibility for risk management and regulatory compliance is clear.
Role of the chief information security officer (CISO)	The CISO is responsible for spearheading the organization's ongoing cybersecurity education, raising awareness of cyber threats, and educating all company members—Including the Board of Directors, senior management, staff, suppliers, customers, and partners—About threats and mitigation techniques. In this educational role, the CISO must also initiate and conduct cyber exercises, such as drills and war games (see Sect. 9.6.3.1).
Ratify Cybersecurity Standards & Robust Governance Framework	Appropriate cybersecurity frameworks, such as NIST, ISO/IEC 27001, or COBIT 5, should guide the organization's security frameworks, policies, and procedures, or a professionally tailored one, to standardize risk management and controls.
Layered architecture	Computer networks with a layered architecture split a network's operation across several layers to prevent potential attacks from spreading.

(continued)

Table 10.1 (continued)

Strategy	Outcome
Leveraging technology	Utilizing cutting-edge security technologies (e.g., AI, machine learning, quantum computing) for automated monitoring, threat intelligence systems for real-time detection, and the design of secure cloud data storage is critical.
Regulatory compliance	GDPR, HIPAA, or industry-specific regulations must be followed. Maintaining audit trails and creating a mandatory incident disclosure plan for reporting are also crucial for ensuring accountability and mitigating liability.
Network security and access control compliance	These policies outline the security procedures established to protect the company's networks, business systems, and data infrastructures from unauthorized access, intrusions, attacks, and other security threats. Implement robust network security protocols and manage access to sensitive data. Strengthen permission management and access controls by adopting strong, unique passwords and encouraging frequent password changes. The policy should address password complexity, length, expiration, and restrictions on sharing.
Adopt acceptable use (AUP) policies	These policies reflect the organization's vision, values, and fundamental principles. The AUP outlines how workers, contractors, and other stakeholders should utilize corporate resources and technology. This strategy helps define boundaries for acceptable behavior and deters the compromise of corporate assets.
Regular software updates and patch management	Update and install all systems and applications, including the most recent security patches.
Data security and compliance	Data security policies outline the methods employed by the organization to protect confidential data, encompassing data storage, encryption, classification, transmission, and destruction. For instance, firms should encrypt corporate sensitive data both in transit and at rest to prevent unauthorized access.
Data backup and recovery	Data backup and recovery policies establish guidelines and procedures for backing up sensitive data and restoring it in the event of a disaster or other data loss incidents.
Multi-factor authentication (MFA)	Use multi-factor authentication (MFA) to enhance security beyond passwords.
Third-party management security	Third-party security guidelines are necessary for suppliers to access the company's network and data. Check for security flaws with partners and suppliers and enforce contract security provisions.
Remote access	Outline the security requirements for remote connections to the organization's network and resources: Virtual private networks (VPNs) and other technologies for remote access fall under this category.

(continued)

Table 10.1 (continued)

Strategy	Outcome
Regular security reviews and assessments	Identify and address any vulnerabilities through routine security audits, penetration testing, and vulnerability assessments.
Incident response plan	Develop and maintain a well-defined incident response process with clearly defined roles that outlines how to contain, investigate promptly, define escalation paths, and implement recovery steps to mitigate security breaches and minimize their effects.
Cybersecurity insurance	Cybersecurity insurance is a solution to minimize financial losses in the event of a cyber incident.

- Once the policies are ready, the procedures and controls outline how the policies will be implemented, highlighting the roles, responsibilities, actions, and activities associated with each policy.
- The Board of Directors reviews, revises (if necessary), and approves the policies once the stakeholders—namely, the risk committee, C-suite, IT, HR, and Finance—reach an agreement.
- When the policies are implemented, they are communicated clearly and made easily accessible to employees, who subsequently receive training on the policies and procedures.
- When policies and procedures are implemented, the organization must monitor, ensure, and enforce compliance to remain operationally effective. Regular reviews and updates are essential to maintain relevance and effectiveness.

10.2.4 Effective Communication

Cybersecurity affects the entire organization, and its governance should encompass all aspects and be integrated into the overall business strategy. Cybersecurity-related information must permeate and be shared with every layer of the organization to ensure success. The Board of Directors can gain a clearer understanding and manage cyber threats more effectively by collaborating with the C-suite, particularly the CISO, who has the primary responsibility for overseeing cybersecurity governance. The governance framework must establish that the CISO is the main executive responsible for communicating cyber threats and mitigation strategies to the BoD and C-level executives.

Policies governing communication and reporting should be established and implemented at all levels of hierarchy and across departments to prevent confusion, promote cooperation, and facilitate the sharing of information. Furthermore, investors concerned about the impact of cybersecurity on companies are demanding more detailed disclosures regarding existing risks, incidents, and mitigation strategies.

Table 10.2 Governance tactics and outcomes

Tactic	Outcome
Maintain network perimeter security	Install intrusion detection and prevention systems, such as next-generation firewalls (NGFWs), to filter malicious traffic. Implement network segmentation to isolate critical systems and limit the impact of breaches. Additionally, utilize zero-trust architecture (ZTA) to verify every access request, thereby securing the network perimeter and protecting the company's IT infrastructure.
Identity management and access control	To enforce stringent access restrictions to restrict access to sensitive data and systems by only authorized personnel.
Compliance and policy enforcement	Align governance practices with standards (ISO 31000, NIST, ISO 27001, COBIT 5) and legal and regulatory requirements (GDPR, HIPAA). Ensure compliance with the organization's cybersecurity policies and procedures by tracking user activities and conducting regular audits.
Cyber Risk & Policy Awareness	Conduct regular training sessions to educate staff members on security policies, best practices, and the latest cybersecurity threats. A lack of cybersecurity knowledge and employees' failure to adhere to their organization's information security policies can result in an underestimation of risks (Li et al., 2019).
Security controls—threat monitoring and detection	Intrusion detection and prevention systems (IDS/IPS) monitor systems and block malicious activities. SIEM aggregates and analyzes logs for anomalies. Endpoint security measures, including endpoint protection and intrusion detection and response (IDR) systems, can safeguard a company's devices and IT infrastructure.
Vulnerability and patch management	Firms should identify system weaknesses, promptly install software patches, and regularly update their systems to protect against known vulnerabilities.
Data protection	Data loss prevention (DLP) preventive measures include encryption for data in transit and at rest, as well as backup and recovery, to enhance data resilience against attacks.
Supply chain or third-party risk	This necessitates contractual security clauses to enforce security obligations with partners and supply chain vendor security evaluations to assess third-party cybersecurity posture.
Employee Training & Awareness	This includes teaching staff members about best practices, testing and training them against social engineering, and conducting drills to simulate incident response and prepare teams for actual cyberattacks.

(continued)

Table 10.2 (continued)

Tactic	Outcome
Incident response	Define a process and practice incident response to familiarize employees with promptly handling and mitigating the effects of cybersecurity incidents. Contain breaches and investigate them to prevent them from happening again. Plan for business continuity to ensure operations even in the event of disruptions.
Performance and continuous improvement	Regular performance evaluation is necessary to gauge security efficacy and continuous improvement using security metrics, key risk indicators (KRIs), and key performance indicators (KPIs). In addition, security defenses are assessed through penetration testing and adversarial simulations to identify gaps and vulnerabilities.

10.2.5 Budget

At the strategic level, management must allocate funds to establish and implement effective cybersecurity risk management strategies, ensuring successful execution (Lerbinger, 1997; Quarantelli, 1988). Adequate budget allocations for resources and a suitable organizational structure, supported by specific policies and procedures, are essential for comprehensive cyber threat protection and disaster preparedness. The ISO 31000 standard provides high-level guidelines for risk management and designates resources for implementing cybersecurity strategies and procedures.

10.3 The ERM Cybersecurity Governance Framework (E-CyG)

We define cybersecurity governance leadership as the system that effectively directs and controls companies to shield them from cyber threats. To manage security projects successfully, cybersecurity leadership must possess particular skills to navigate the complexities of cybersecurity. Some of these qualities include strategic vision and alignment, change management expertise, strong networking and communication skills, commitment, and adaptability to the rapidly changing digital landscape. Therefore, cybersecurity governance involves a combination of dedicated leadership, technologies, human resources, financial practices, and policies to detect, mitigate, and respond to cyberattacks.

Our definition emphasizes that all stakeholders share the responsibility for effectively aligning cybersecurity goals with business objectives. Therefore, establishing a cybersecurity governance mechanism protects the interests of the organization and all its stakeholders. It outlines the leadership roles, responsibilities, and duties of an organization's Board of Directors and C-suite officers in successfully guiding its cyber risk control program. In partnership with senior management, the BoD is responsible for implementing and maintaining effective cybersecurity governance. The engagement of shareholders and other investors in cybersecurity governance serves as a counterbalance, ensuring that directors, risk committees, and senior management effectively manage governance processes.

The cybersecurity governance value chain outlines the vision, mission, goals, objectives, strategies, policies, procedures, and actions that a business undertakes to manage and protect its digital assets and customer data from cyber threats. A practical approach to cyber risk governance requires a multi-layered strategy, emphasizing strong leadership, both hierarchical and matrix communications, proactive stakeholder engagement, financial investment, employee training, technology solutions, and compliance with relevant standards, regulations, and best practices. It also requires ongoing vigilance and adaptation to emerging threats as they arise.

In this chapter, we compile and integrate cybersecurity governance concepts and constructs to develop a mechanism that supports the E-CyG from both strategic and functional risk governance perspectives. The goal is to create a comprehensive management tool that incorporates essential elements of an effective and practical cybersecurity governance framework. The E-CyG structure defines roles and responsibilities within the ERM, ensuring diverse representation from across the organization in the ERM process and promoting strategic alignment throughout the company's infrastructure. Figure 10.2 illustrates the E-CyG governance framework structure, enabling senior management and operational personnel to understand and monitor each other's expectations, goals, performance, risk tolerance, and reporting requirements. It establishes goals, policies, procedures, culture, values, accountability, communication, and performance standards. Thus, the E-CyG governance framework and its structure serve as a foundational and guiding system, comprising standard management practices tailored to fit the organization. This framework also serves as the foundation for our proposed "Strategic Enterprise Cybersecurity Governance Model" (i.e., ECyG-M), which is presented in the latter part of this chapter.

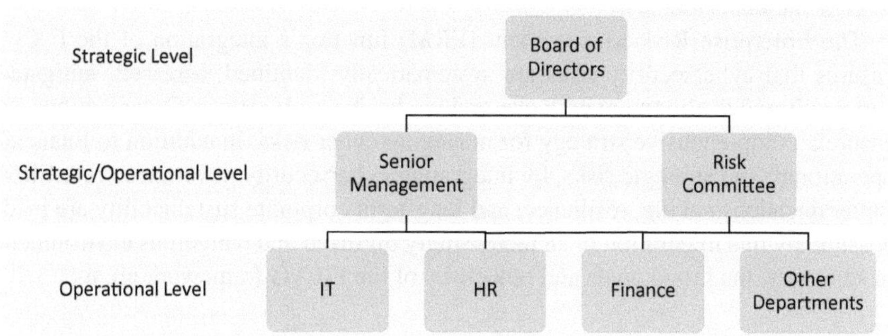

Fig. 10.2 E-CyG hierarchy

At the strategic level, the Board of Directors supports the ERM-embedded cybersecurity governance (E-CyG) program by approving resources and providing oversight, direction, and guidance to ensure effective implementation.

The risk committee comprises representatives from the Board of Directors, senior management, and various departments, who validate risks, prioritize them, and confirm risk mitigation strategies. The E-CyG is governance-oriented and aligns with the broader corporate governance process. At this level, the risk committee regularly reports to the BoD on the progress of E-CyG activities.

The "strategic and operational level" overlaps strategic and operational responsibilities. The senior management group provides input, direction, oversight, and guidance to the program by establishing strategies, policies, and procedures, and overseeing their implementation and maintenance. As the designated C-suite executive for cybersecurity, the CISO is primarily responsible for identifying and assessing cyber risks, as well as developing and implementing mitigation strategies. The digital environment in which businesses operate is ever-changing. Consequently, E-CyG implementation is an ongoing process, much like the organization's strategy that E-CyG supports. C-suite executives must consistently focus on maintaining E-CyG, and integrating it into ongoing management activities underscores its significance to employees at all levels. As prescribed, the CISO regularly reports on the cybersecurity function to the Board of Directors, risk committee, and senior management. During cyber incidents, a process should be in place for the CISO and the IRP team to brief the BoD, risk committee, and senior leadership on response strategies and developments.

Day-to-day risk management is carried out at the operational level, led by IT and involving representatives from various departments across the organization. The E-CyG cybersecurity team implements strategies for the risk control process, which includes identification, assessment, mitigation, monitoring, review, reporting, incident response, and recovery. Department heads and those responsible for daily departmental operations of E-CyG teams must regularly report department-level risk activities to the CISO and enterprise-level security E-CyG teams, as well as any new risks or incidents that arise.

The Enterprise Risk Management (ERM) function's integration of the E-CyG ensures that cybersecurity risks are systematically identified, assessed, mitigated, and monitored in alignment with overarching business objectives. Organizations can ensure a comprehensive strategy for managing cyber risks, in addition to financial, operational, and strategic risks, by integrating cybersecurity governance into ERM. Better decision-making, resilience, and long-term corporate sustainability are made possible by this integration in an increasingly digitized and dangerous environment. In summary, the broad goals and objectives of the E-CyG framework are to:

10.3.1 Identify and Evaluate Potential Risks

Ideally, a firm should conduct comprehensive and ongoing risk assessments to identify critical cyber assets, threats, and weaknesses (Hoffmann et al., 2020). Effective enterprise risk management assessments maximize resource utilization and ensure that cybersecurity protocols align with corporate objectives. To align the firm's cybersecurity with its business goals, it must identify and evaluate potential threats to its information systems and digital infrastructure. To effectively assess and manage risk, it is essential to stay informed about emerging trends in cyber technologies, cyber actors, threats, vulnerabilities, and the nature of cyberattack processes. Conduct thorough risk assessments to identify the threats and weaknesses that could impact these critical assets. This assessment facilitates the coordination of security initiatives with essential mission components.

10.3.2 Create a Comprehensive Cybersecurity Governance Plan

The Cybersecurity Governance Plan (CGP) serves as a comprehensive roadmap for developing a cybersecurity risk strategy that aligns with the business's operational objectives and risk profile. Formulating an effective enterprise CGP with the relevant strategy requires a systematic approach to protecting critical assets, mitigating risks, and ensuring compliance while supporting business goals. It entails creating a methodical framework for managing, supervising, and coordinating cybersecurity initiatives aligned with business goals, while ensuring risk reduction and compliance. The following outlines the step-by-step method for constructing one.

- Identify corporate objectives and legal requirements (e.g., GDPR, HIPAA, NIST CSF, ISO 27001) before establishing the goals and scope, which can include the entire organization, specific departments, or third-party providers.
- Define cybersecurity goals, objectives, and strategies that align with business objectives.
- Establish a governance structure that assigns roles and responsibilities, including the Board of Directors—oversight and accountability; the Risk Committee—oversight, review, strategic decisions, and reporting to the BoD; the CEO (Chief Executive Officer) and CISO (Chief Information Security Officer)—leadership, oversight, and execution; the IT Security Team—implementation and monitoring; the Cybersecurity Team—operational monitoring, compliance, and response; and Department or Business Unit Leaders—compliance within their domains.
- Assess the organization's current security posture and identify all IT assets (hardware, software, cloud services, data) to create a comprehensive inventory of assets that may require protection.
- A risk assessment of internal and external threats is conducted to evaluate vulnerabilities, identify gaps, and assess potential impacts.

- A compliance review ensures alignment with relevant standards and regulations such as NIST, ISO 27001, GDPR, and HIPAA.
- Conduct a gap analysis to assess the organization's cybersecurity posture in comparison with industry best practices, a specific standard, framework, or ideal state.
- Assess the tolerance for security risks and set risk priorities.
- Develop policies and procedures that align with frameworks such as the NIST CSF, ISO 27001, and CIS Controls, encompassing access control, acceptable use, operational risk management, technology investment, data protection, and incident response.
- Put in place administrative controls (training, simulations, policies, audits), technical controls (SIEM, firewalls, EDR, MFA, encryption, AI, ML), and physical controls (biometric access, surveillance).

The key components of the Cybersecurity Governance Plan to focus on are as follows.

- The Board of Directors and executive management must engage to prioritize and enhance the visibility of cybersecurity. Leadership roles, responsibilities, and accountability must be clearly defined for the BoD, risk committee, C-suite, CISO, IT, and cybersecurity teams;
- Security policies and procedures must be documented for all risk control and mitigation activities, including identity management and access control, network and endpoint security, data handling, incident response, data security and privacy, as well as recovery;
- A risk management framework that encompasses vulnerability management for regular scanning, patching, and penetration testing; third-party risk management to evaluate supply chain and vendor risk exposures; and threat modeling to pinpoint potential attack vectors such as phishing, ransomware, and insider threats;
- Performance metrics, ongoing monitoring processes, and measures to enhance cybersecurity risk control are clearly defined and documented to inform and guide employees;
- Employee risk awareness and training programs are detailed, along with the frequency of these events; and.
- The CGP's implementation and maintenance procedures have been documented and clarified.

The ultimate deliverables of this process include the "Cybersecurity Governance Plan" document, the Risk Register (which contains risk profile information, owners, and mitigation strategies), Incident Response and Crisis Management strategies, Compliance Reports, and Audit Logs. This methodical approach enables businesses to develop a robust CGP that minimizes risks and supports safe business operations.

10.3.3 Designing the Governance Architecture

The firm must provide an organizational cybersecurity architecture within an operational governance model that outlines the leadership, roles, responsibilities, practices, policies, procedures, technological measures, personnel, and financial measures necessary to protect the organization's digital assets and data. The first step in designing the framework is to define the business objectives and identify the cyber threats that may impact the fulfillment of these objectives, taking into account the firm's digital environment and assets. Designing hierarchical cybersecurity frameworks requires consideration of cultural traits, such as high versus low power distance and uncertainty avoidance (Hofstede, 1980), to ensure effective oversight, alignment, and enforcement of policies.

To ensure effective management of cybersecurity governance risks, ERM promotes cross-functional collaboration between the cybersecurity team and other business units. It is crucial to assess and define the firm's technological, human, legal, operational, and financial factors, along with their risk implications, both as sources of threats (such as cyber risks, legal issues, operational challenges, compliance matters, finance, and HR) and as drivers of risk mitigation. This will facilitate a comprehensive overview of the organization's cyber risk exposure and security posture. This definition will clarify the design of the components of the governance framework.

Establishing a cybersecurity governance architecture requires a systematic approach that ensures compliance, effectively manages risks, and aligns security procedures with business objectives. Below are the key structures and components of a cybersecurity governance framework.

- Identify the objectives and scope of the framework by defining business goals, regulatory requirements, risk tolerance, and the included organizational structure;
- Establish a governance structure by assigning roles to the Board of Directors, C-suite leaders, CISO, IT, security team, and department heads. This structure also involves defining decision-making authority and accountability;
- Prioritize risks according to their likelihood and business impact by conducting risk assessments to identify assets, threats, vulnerabilities, and potential consequences;
- Develop policies and processes that align with industry best practices, such as COBIT, NIST CSF, and ISO 27001;
- Ensure adherence to all relevant laws and regulations (GDPR, HIPAA, etc.);
- Implement controls and procedures by using physical controls, security technologies, and offering administrative training in addition to awareness programs;
- Regular audits, penetration tests, and continuous monitoring are essential for maintaining system integrity and assessing effectiveness;
- By conducting regular exercises and revising recovery plans to ensure that incident response and recovery protocols align with best practices;
- Regular training and awareness campaigns are essential for educating staff members about corporate risk culture and security best practices; and.

- Policies are updated based on lessons learned from past incidents and industry trends, and regular evaluations are conducted to adapt to emerging risks and technologies.

10.3.4 Establishing the Cybersecurity Defense Policies

A policy is a clear and concise statement that outlines how to achieve an organization's objectives. Organizations must implement robust cybersecurity policies to safeguard their resources, maintain stakeholder trust, and comply with applicable legal requirements. Developing policies involves creating recommendations and directives to support information security and ensure the safe operation of systems. These policies should align with the organization's strategic plans, risk landscape, security-related factors, technology, and funding. Unlike procedures, a policy serves as the guiding goal statement that leads to the achievement of the objective.

A well-structured policy must clearly define goals that align with business objectives, legal requirements, and all relevant networks, systems, and data. The organization's human factors and technical aspects must be considered and integrated into the policies. Firms must ensure proactive leadership (Nolan et al., 2019), awareness, training, and the allocation of sufficient resources to make cybersecurity policies effective. Therefore, leadership, inclusion, understanding, support, and a relevant framework that encourages actions to safeguard the confidentiality, integrity, and accessibility of data, networks, and systems are prerequisites for exercising policy authority.

The following sections outline the essential policies necessary for effective strategic enterprise cybersecurity governance, organized by chapter in the book.

Governance

Governance plays a critical role in managing cyber threats and ensuring compliance with relevant regulations. Therefore, an enterprise cybersecurity risk governance policy must clearly define the cybersecurity objectives, strategies, and alignment with relevant frameworks or standards. It should also require regular enterprise-wide cyber risk assessments for review by the Board of Directors. Additionally, the policy assigns authority to the risk committee and senior management to implement and oversee the risk mitigation process, as well as its progress. A compliance and regulatory policy is essential to ensure adherence to industry-specific laws, such as the General Data Protection Regulation (GDPR) or the Health Insurance Portability and Accountability Act (HIPAA). Under this policy, third-party compliance audits must be planned, specified, and scheduled in advance.

The governance, roles, and accountability policy delineates the responsibilities and oversight of the Board of Directors, risk committee, and senior management. It specifies the formation, appointment, and authority of committees and responsible personnel to implement and operationalize the Cybersecurity Risk Management Policy. Additionally, it requires the CEO's support and oversight, with the CISO primarily leading the operational cybersecurity program and being accountable for reporting metrics and performance.

Enterprise Risk Management

A strategic approach that enhances organizational resilience, aligns security with business objectives, and ensures a comprehensive risk management plan involves integrating the cybersecurity governance framework into the Enterprise Risk Management (ERM) function. When cybersecurity governance is integrated into Enterprise Risk Management (ERM), cyber hazards are treated as strategic business risks rather than as technical issues. This integration results in improved decision-making, cost savings, enhanced regulatory compliance, and increased organizational resilience.

Technology

Through automation, integration, and intelligence-driven methodologies, the application of systems technology in cybersecurity governance enhances the efficacy, efficiency, and adaptability of security frameworks. Employing systems technology in cybersecurity governance transitions security from a reactive to a proactive, intelligent, and scalable discipline. Advantages include a more holistic and comprehensive approach, improved alignment with company objectives, quicker threat detection and response, automated compliance and risk management, cost savings from increased efficiency, and adaptability to emerging cyber threats.

The integration of technology management into cybersecurity governance ensures that security tools, processes, and systems align strategically with business goals, are efficiently maintained, and undergo continual improvement. This structured approach enhances cyber resilience while optimizing resource allocation. Technology management in cybersecurity governance refines security operations by overseeing the entire lifecycle of security technologies, ensuring proper deployment, maintenance, and retirement, and improving resource efficiency by reducing tool sprawl and eliminating redundant or obsolete technologies. This enables cost-effective, scalable security operations; quicker, automated threat response; ongoing compliance and risk reduction; and adaptability to new threats and technologies.

Human Resources

The cybersecurity human resource governance policy addresses employees regarding risk culture, education, training, awareness, and cybersecurity performance. It outlines the requirements for personnel cybersecurity education and performance evaluation, as well as the training, which includes simulation drills. Additionally, the cultural norms of individualism versus collectivism, as defined by Hofstede's cultural dimensions (Hofstede, 1980; Hofstede et al., 2010), must be considered when designing awareness programs. By recognizing the differences between individualism and collectivism, cybersecurity policy, training, and communication can be better tailored to fit cultural norms, thereby increasing compliance and engagement. A one-size-fits-all strategy may not be effective; cultural perspectives must be acknowledged for cybersecurity education to succeed. For instance, employees in collectivistic cultures (e.g., China, Japan) may hesitate to report errors due to concerns about embarrassing the group or disrupting workplace harmony, which could lead to underreporting incidents. In contrast, employees in individualistic cultures (e.g., Australia, the UK, the USA) might be more likely to report breaches if they feel accountable or fear personal repercussions.

Finance

The cybersecurity financial governance policy outlines the budget allocation for technologies that mitigate cybersecurity threats and support technology management. A budget is also designated for the CISO and any necessary supporting staff. Insurance policies addressing cybersecurity threats, such as ransomware, data breaches, and business interruptions, are maintained and reviewed at least once a year. The finance department supports cybersecurity risk assessment by quantifying, prioritizing, and mitigating threats within budgetary constraints. It justifies investments and builds business cases by calculating potential financial losses from breaches and prioritizing risks based on their financial exposure. Additionally, it examines cyber insurance coverage to address potential losses, as well as incident response and recovery funding. The incident response and resilience policy outlines a current and relevant incident response plan, along with clear escalation procedures. Breach simulations require regular awareness and training, including tabletop exercises.

Supply Chain

The supply chain risk management policy mandates cybersecurity provisions in contracts and requires security evaluations of the security practices of key suppliers and service providers. It outlines the procedures and controls that an organization employs to detect, assess, manage, and monitor cybersecurity risks posed by third-party vendors, suppliers, and service providers. The Board of Directors and the risk committee establish governance and hold executives accountable. The Chief Information Security Officer (CISO) oversees the enterprise's cybersecurity strategy, which includes addressing supply chain threats. A professional third-party risk management team assesses vendor risks while the procurement and legal teams ensure that contracts include security criteria.

10.3.5 Implementing Cybersecurity Operations and Procedures

A procedure is a systematic series of actions designed to fulfill the organization's goals and objectives. Cybersecurity procedures outline actions intended to achieve a specific policy purpose, thereby managing the organization's overall cybersecurity posture. This includes conducting cybersecurity operations that monitor potential threats to the company's digital infrastructure and identify and address security incidents. Additionally, this process involves evaluating the effectiveness of the cyber defense and collaborating with both internal and external risk governance entities.

10.3.6 Security Assessments, Reviews, and Upgrades

Organizations need to conduct regular security assessments and reviews to identify gaps and weaknesses in their digital infrastructure and information systems. This process involves discussing the operational implications of cyber risks, receiving consistent reports on relevant internal and external cyber incidents and their consequences, and providing guidance and oversight for implementing necessary adjustments. Therefore, senior management should receive routine reports on cyber risks and incidents to establish or improve a practical cyber risk management framework and cyber defense policy. The Board of Directors must also receive this information to understand and endorse such a framework and policy, and to oversee its efficient implementation by senior management.

10.3.7 IRP: Drills and War Games

Organizations test their Incident Response Plans (IRPs) through simulated exercises to ensure they are ready. An IRP should outline and assess the necessary actions to be taken in the event of a security breach. Companies should regularly review and test the IRP, conducting trials or practice runs to evaluate its effectiveness. This includes:

- Conduct tabletop exercises (TTX) to brainstorm hypothetical situations in a discussion-based format, involving key stakeholders such as management, IT, HR, finance, legal, security teams, and PR, to explore potential solutions in response to an attack.
- War Games are strategic simulations of cyber warfare or significant breaches affecting numerous companies, such as a supply chain attack, where executives, government agencies, and others participate in multi-team exercises.

There are other variations of drills and wargames, such as "functional drills" for testing a specific component of the IRP and "full-scale simulations" to simulate a realistic attack to test detection and response. A well-tested Incident Response Plan helps organizations remain prepared for evolving threats and fosters cybersecurity resilience.

10.3.8 Compliance

Maintaining compliance is crucial for an effective cybersecurity plan. A robust cybersecurity strategy, combined with compliance, defends against attacks, fosters confidence, promotes transparency, mitigates penalties, and ensures long-term resilience. Cybersecurity compliance is a shared responsibility that involves various roles across different hierarchical levels and departments. It requires collaboration across functions; the CISO, legal team, audit teams, and data protection officer (DPO) all have vital roles. Additionally, every employee is responsible for adhering to security policies. The breakdown of key stakeholders responsible for maintaining compliance (Table 10.3) is as follows[3]:

10.3.9 Performance Review and Training

The firm should continuously improve its security posture by regularly assessing the effectiveness of its current security measures and implementing enhancements to mitigate risks and tackle emerging cyber threats. To achieve this, it is essential to establish specific metrics to evaluate the performance of cybersecurity policies and keep management informed about developments. Ensure that staff members understand and adhere to cybersecurity policies by consistently communicating their importance and providing training.

Additionally, it is crucial to establish KPIs that align with and balance the cultural motivations and traits of specific countries, such as Hofstede's (1980) dimensions of individualism, uncertainty avoidance, collectivism, and power distance. For example, performance measures should reconcile high-power distance with individualism and collectivism to enhance oversight, promote feedback, and foster collaboration.

10.4 ECyG-M as a Strategic Framework

The "Strategic Enterprise Cybersecurity Governance Model" (ECyG-M) is the proposed framework based on the concepts and constructs covered in this book thus far. Since cybersecurity risks are a significant part of an organization's overall risk landscape, Enterprise Risk Management (ERM) and cybersecurity governance are closely connected. Enterprise risk management serves as the foundation for a strong and effective cybersecurity strategy and efficient corporate operations. A strategic cybersecurity governance value chain within the ERM framework provides an integrated and balanced approach for managing risks across the organization. Organizations can collectively leverage the ERM process to identify, evaluate, prioritize, mitigate, monitor, detect, report, and manage risk events, ultimately achieving

[3] The DPO is required by GDPR.

Table 10.3 Cybersecurity compliance

Strategic Leadership	
Board of Directors	They are ultimately responsible for cybersecurity governance and risk management.
Risk committee	It oversees the cybersecurity function and reports to the Board of Directors on compliance.
C-suite & chief information security officer	The C-suite, headed by the CEO, has collective and functional responsibility for overseeing cybersecurity operations. The CISO is directly responsible for overseeing the cybersecurity strategy, ensuring adherence to operational procedures and regulatory compliance, and reporting to the Board of Directors, risk committee, and C-suite.
Chief legal officer	The CLO manages regulatory compliance (e.g., GDPR, HIPAA) and collaborates with other departments to oversee compliance.
Operational leadership	
Senior management	It ensures cybersecurity procedures are implemented and enforced in compliance with policies.
Enterprise risk management team	It conducts audits, evaluates third-party risks, and closes compliance gaps.
Cybersecurity team	It implements the strategic plan and security safeguards (firewalls, encryption, SIEM) in conjunction with the IT department's security safeguards, monitoring, and reporting threats.
IT department	The department ensures systems are patched, set up securely, and fulfill compliance criteria.
HRM Department	It enforces security policies, such as background checks and access controls, and investigates employee-related breaches. It also conducts security awareness training to educate staff on compliance requirements, password hygiene, and cyber risks.
Legal department	It interprets laws and regulations, ensuring that policies align with them.
Department heads (including IT, HR, and finance)	They ensure their units comply with security policies and procedures and report any non-compliance or breaches to the CISO and cybersecurity team.
Internal and external auditors	They conduct compliance audits, such as those based on NIST, SOX, GDPR, PCI DSS, and ISO 27001, and identify areas for improvement.
Data protection officer	The DPO oversees data protection and compliance reporting.

their overall strategic objectives. These actions include developing and implementing cybersecurity policies and procedures, training employees on security awareness, and routinely monitoring and assessing the effectiveness of these measures.

To create integrated strategies for reducing cyber risks by incorporating cybersecurity governance into ERM, the resulting ECyG-M framework fosters hierarchical oversight and supervision, along with operational collaboration among IT, HR, finance, and other departments (see Fig. 10.1). Within this comprehensive risk management framework, oversight and cooperation ensure that cybersecurity controls are implemented effectively and efficiently across all enterprise layers and functions, enabling the organization to identify, assess, mitigate, and track cyber risks that align with corporate objectives.

The ECyG-M is founded on a comprehensive and ongoing strategy to identify, assess, mitigate, detect, and manage risks to an organization's IT systems, data, and operations. This approach necessitates optimizing risk governance policies across the entire cybersecurity value chain. The need to enhance risk governance as a going concern arises because hackers are continually developing new methods to breach an organization's network as technology advances.

In summary, ERM helps organizations manage cybersecurity by integrating governance to establish effective controls and reduce cyber risks. It serves as a broad strategic value chain framework, whose principles are consistent with the cybersecurity standards and regulations, for enterprise cybersecurity governance in the following ways:

- Risk Identification: ERM helps businesses identify and understand the various internal and external cybersecurity risks they face. This process involves evaluating potential risks to networks, systems, and data, identifying vulnerabilities, and assessing their impact on the organization's operations and resources, which include information, software, hardware, and intellectual property.
- Risk Evaluation and Prioritization: ERM allows organizations to assess potential risks, vulnerabilities, and cybersecurity gaps, as well as their impacts on operations, financial performance, reputation, and other strategic objectives across the organization. This step involves evaluating existing controls and identifying situations that necessitate additional measures. By conducting a comprehensive evaluation of cyber risks, organizations can adopt the ERM approach to prioritize risks based on their potential effect on strategic goals. This prioritization is essential for assessing the level of risk exposure for each risk based on its likelihood and impact vis-à-vis other risks.
- Risk Mitigation: The business can reduce risks by implementing suitable security procedures. These measures consist of technical controls, such as firewalls, SIEM, and antivirus software, along with administrative controls, including access limits, security policies, insurance, and physical controls.
- Risk Monitoring, Detection, and Reporting: ERM enables organizations to continuously monitor and detect cybersecurity risks, allowing them to adjust their risk management strategies as needed. Tracking and evaluating the effectiveness of this step is essential to ensure that the risk management approach functions as

intended. Security teams may conduct regular security audits, tests, and assessments. These actions involve consistently tracking and reporting cybersecurity threats while actively developing procedures and controls to mitigate those risks. Consequently, this process ensures that measures remain relevant and effective, aligning with the company's evolving risk profile. This may involve enhancing security controls, introducing new technologies, and revising security protocols.

Adopting ERM as a foundational framework for enterprise cybersecurity governance can help organizations manage cybersecurity risks more comprehensively and effectively. The success of the cybersecurity governance strategy depends on the support of all parties involved. Therefore, the Board of Directors, risk committee, C-suite management, IT, HR, and finance departments must all participate. Additionally, clearly defining the roles and responsibilities of each stakeholder is critical. This clarity allows companies to manage cybersecurity risks efficiently, prioritize their cybersecurity investments, and align their cybersecurity programs with strategic objectives. Consequently, ERM ensures that investments in cybersecurity initiatives and technologies align with the organization's strategic goals, risk appetite, and cultural dimension, particularly the long-term versus short-term security orientation (Hofstede, 1980; Hofstede et al., 2010; Onumo et al., 2017).

10.4.1 Strategic Cyber Risk Control

Strategic cybersecurity governance within the ERM can help reduce cyber risk by providing a structured, visible, definitive, and integrated approach to managing risks that may affect an organization's strategic objectives. ERM can manage strategic risks efficiently in alignment with its company objectives, and the following are ways that strategic risk management in ERM contributes to reducing cyber risk:

- Integrated Strategy: ERM provides a comprehensive approach to risk management by identifying and evaluating risks across the entire organization, including cybersecurity threats. By integrating cybersecurity risk governance into the ERM framework, organizations can ensure they consistently address cyber risks in alignment with their overall strategic objectives.
- Risk Assessment: ERM enables businesses to evaluate the potential impacts of cyber threats on their strategic objectives, including financial performance, public image, and consumer trust. By analyzing these possible impacts, organizations can prioritize their investments in cybersecurity and develop effective risk mitigation plans.
- Risk Reduction: ERM enables businesses to create and implement appropriate safeguards against online threats. By integrating cybersecurity controls into the overall risk management framework, organizations can ensure they are using a risk-based approach to managing cyber risks.

- Risk Monitoring: ERM offers a framework for tracking and reporting cyber risks, including evaluating the effectiveness of cybersecurity safeguards. By continuously monitoring these risks, organizations can swiftly respond to new threats and adjust their risk management policies accordingly.
- ERM offers a structured approach to the Board of Directors oversight of cyber risk management. By integrating cyber risk management initiatives into the ERM framework, the BoD can more effectively understand, monitor, and ensure that the organization's initiatives align with its overall strategic objectives.

Organizations can manage cyber risks more comprehensively and proactively by utilizing Enterprise Risk Management (ERM) to address strategic risks. ERM can assist companies in prioritizing their investments in cybersecurity, effectively managing cyber risks across the organization, and aligning cyber risk management activities with overall business objectives.

10.4.2 Operational Risk Governance

ERM's operational risk governance supports cybersecurity risk management by providing a structured approach for identifying, assessing, and mitigating risks that could impact an organization's daily operations. By incorporating operational risk governance into the ERM framework, organizations can better understand and manage cybersecurity risks that may compromise their business processes, impact customer satisfaction, or result in financial losses. The operational risk governance's role in cybersecurity risk management and its significance are:

- ERM assists organizations in recognizing and understanding the various operational risks they encounter in cybersecurity management. This approach entails identifying risks associated with data breaches, system failures, employee errors or misconduct, and threats from third parties. By identifying and prioritizing these operational hazards, organizations can allocate resources more efficiently to address the most significant risks.
- Risk Assessment: ERM helps organizations identify how operational risks may impact their daily business activities. This evaluation offers insights into the likelihood and severity of cybersecurity incidents and their potential consequences for the organization's reputation, clientele, and financial performance. By assessing the effects of operational hazards, organizations can prioritize their cybersecurity efforts and develop effective risk mitigation strategies.
- Risk Reduction: ERM helps businesses develop and implement necessary controls to mitigate operational risks in cybersecurity management. These controls include establishing security policies and procedures, training staff in security awareness, and implementing technical measures such as firewalls, intrusion detection systems, and encryption. By establishing proper safeguards, organizations can reduce the likelihood and impact of cybersecurity incidents.

- Risk Monitoring: In cybersecurity management, ERM offers a methodology for tracking and reporting operational risks. This process continuously monitors cybersecurity safeguards, reports issues, and conducts root cause investigations to create corrective action plans. Organizations can quickly identify and address emerging threats through ongoing monitoring of operational risks.
- Continuous Improvement: ERM helps organizations consistently enhance their cybersecurity management programs by conducting regular risk assessments, updating security policies and processes, and investing in new cybersecurity technologies. By continuously refining their cybersecurity programs, organizations can stay ahead of emerging threats and lower their overall risk exposure.

Overall, operational risk governance within ERM is essential for cybersecurity management, as it provides a structured and integrated approach to addressing operational risks that may impact an organization's regular operations. By incorporating operational risk governance into the broader ERM framework, organizations can more effectively manage cybersecurity threats and reduce their overall risk exposure.

10.5 The ECyG-M Design

Careful planning and a commitment to an informed, cautious, step-by-step approach along the cybersecurity governance value chain are crucial for creating a holistic and comprehensive cybersecurity governance program (Fig. 10.3). This process begins at the strategic level by defining the scope, goals, objectives, and strategies while assessing the organization's cybersecurity risk exposure and maturity. Next, it involves establishing the governance operating model, which includes documenting policies and procedures that incorporate relevant standards and best practices. The policies and procedures must clearly outline the cybersecurity governance plan, including a formal chain of command and communication, as well as specifying responsibilities and accountabilities. Once the business goals and objectives align with the cybersecurity strategies, policies, and procedures, it is time to implement the governance model. Implementation requires that procedures comply with the cybersecurity plan to maintain oversight, management, monitoring, compliance, and review of systems throughout the entire governance value chain. Additionally, the Board of Directors should ensure the allocation of budgets for the complete implementation of the ECyG-M.

Top management should emphasize the importance of risk mitigation in fostering organizational resilience and the benefits that businesses can achieve through an effective risk governance strategy. This section presents the Strategic Enterprise Cybersecurity Governance Model (ECyG-M), which integrates key factors discussed in previous chapters to establish an optimal cybersecurity governance model within the broader enterprise risk management framework. As noted in Chap. 3, incorporating ERM into the cybersecurity governance framework enables management

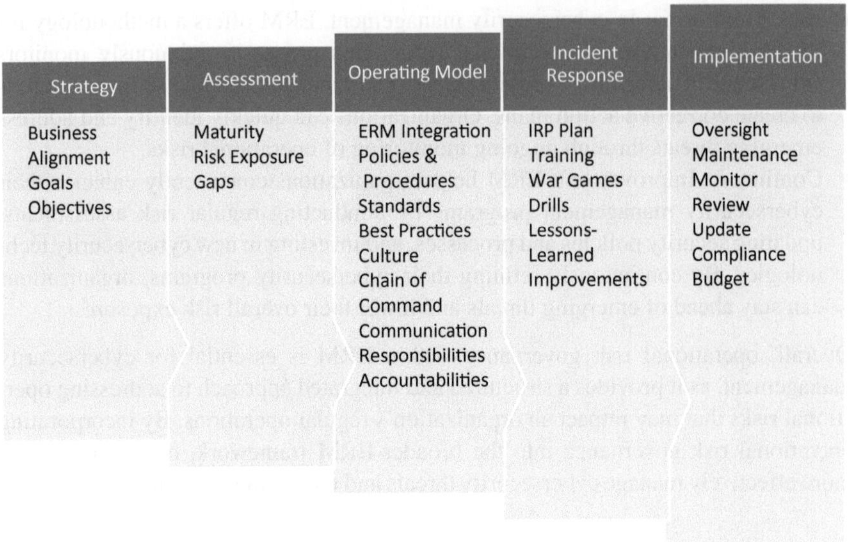

Fig. 10.3 Process for designing the ECyG-M

to conduct thorough and systematic enterprise-wide cyber risk assessments, identifying and prioritizing cyber risks that align with the organization's risk appetite and business objectives. This alignment facilitates the development of the organization's cyber risk governance strategy and tactical response. Therefore, risk leadership must ensure the identification, understanding, management, and communication of cyber threats and their various elements to all stakeholders. Furthermore, ERM serves as an effective tool for cybersecurity governance, as its principles align with the common elements of cyber risk control standards, including NIST CSF, ISO, and COBIT.

In addition to the enterprise risk management model, the constructs and attributes of the theoretical models (Fig. 10.4) presented in Chapter Two support the design architecture of the ECyG-M. They are implicitly integrated into the ECyG-M's governance structures, policies, and procedures. In other words, the ECyG-M adopts a hierarchical cybersecurity organizational structure, goal-driven decision-making, a risk-based decision-making process, a five-line accountability framework, and a learning organization that also considers the organization's cyber risk maturity. Figure 10.3 illustrates the relationships between the relevant base models and the ECyG-M.

Cybersecurity governance encompasses both strategic and tactical levels of management. The ECyG-M establishes the structures, processes, and guidelines necessary for cybersecurity governance, managing the risks associated with the safe use of technology, and ensuring the CIA triad security of interconnected information systems. Governance, risk management, and compliance form the foundation of cybersecurity (Mitchell, 2007), as illustrated in Fig. 10.5. In this context, ECyG-M adopts a policy-oriented approach at the strategic level, while the tactical level focuses on procedural administration. Additionally, the ECyG-M emphasizes

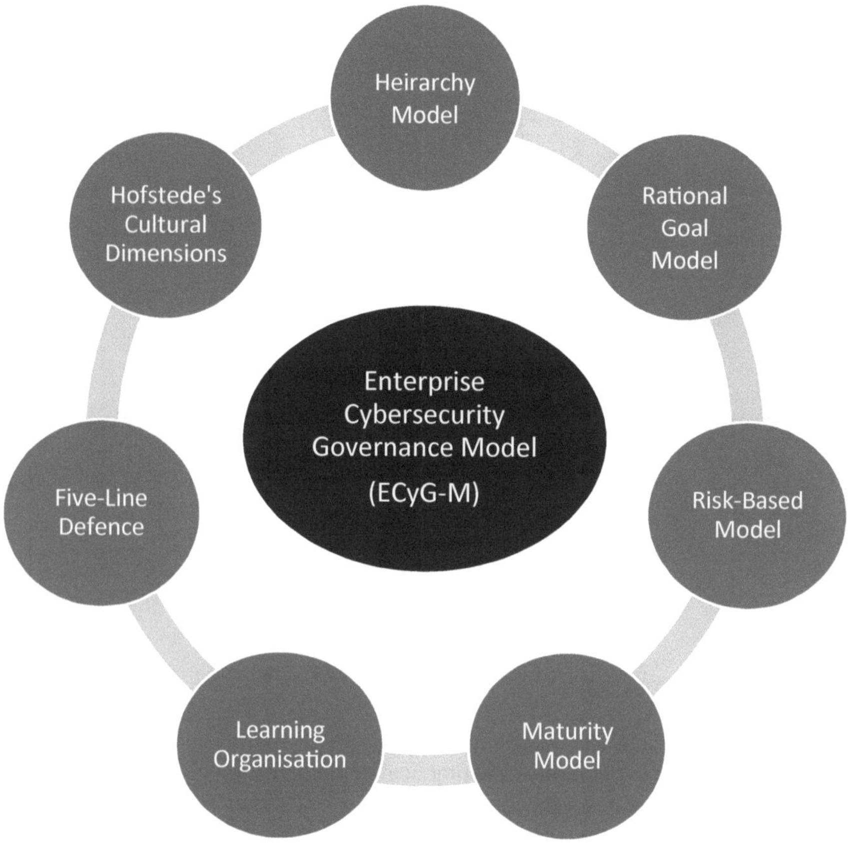

Fig. 10.4 Foundational models of ECyG-M

three enablers—technology, people, and finance—and their significance for optimal control of the cybersecurity function.

The central tenets of the hierarchy model are predictability, control, and responsibility (Simon, 1962), whereas the collaborative approach (Mihm et al., 2010) is essential for enhancing decision-making and the quality of solutions (Mihm et al., 2010; Rivkin & Siggelkow, 2003) in modern cybersecurity governance. The Rational Goal Model (Taylor, 1911) asserts that senior management establishes goals and targets, with performance thoroughly examined and reviewed. The fundamental characteristic of the model is change, which occurs through modifying incentives and achieving objectives and policy goals, a crucial aspect of cybersecurity due to its rapidly evolving threat landscape. The maturity-based and risk-based methods represent the other two leading risk governance solutions available to enterprises. The maturity-based approach (Hillson, 1997) is the conventional technique for managing cyber risk, in which companies implement specific risk management controls and capabilities to reach a desired level of maturity. The "risk-based" approach aims to

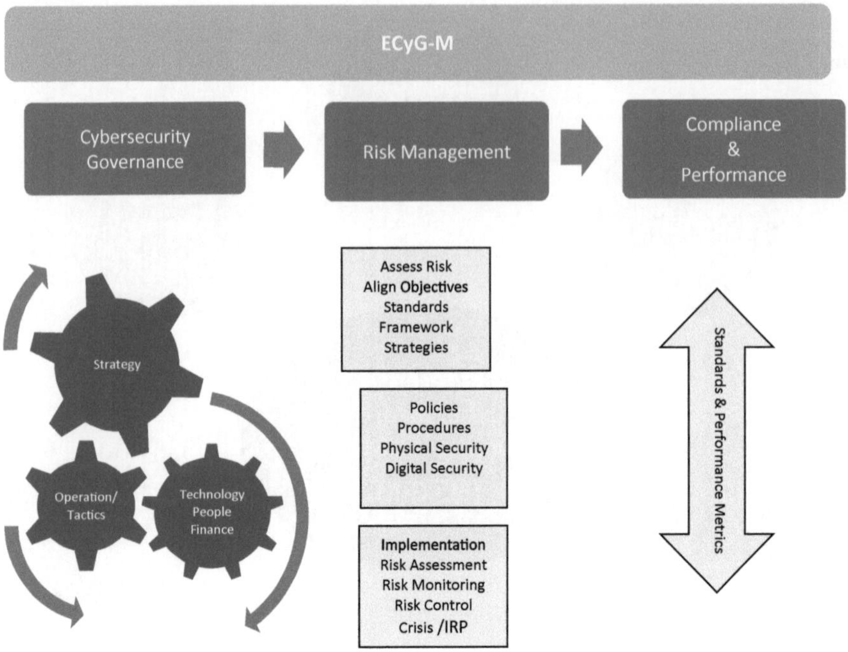

Fig. 10.5 Strategic ECYG-M

reduce risk through explicit rules and practical implementation programs by aligning the organization's business objectives with a cyber risk strategy (Collier et al., 2013). Risk management encompasses all aspects of cyber activity, including strategic planning and day-to-day operations. Consequently, its design enables firms to identify and mitigate the most critical risks in the company's key networks, data, and systems. Building a risk-based strategy still necessitates a maturity-based approach as its foundation (McKinsey and Company, 2019), thus making both models complementary. With a risk-based strategy, management prioritizes, identifies, and addresses gaps and vulnerabilities that represent significant risks to the company, rather than focusing solely on maturity.

The ECyG-M framework combines hierarchical structures, rational goal-setting, and a five-line accountability model to establish a chain of authority, responsibility, and accountability. It also incorporates maturity frameworks, risk-based approaches, a learning organization, and Hofstede's cultural dimension models for cybersecurity risk control strategies (Fig. 10.3). By embedding these models and principles into the ECyG-M, we emphasize the significance of their constructs and connections to cybersecurity governance, as previously discussed. The ECyG-M serves as a reference model, promoting inclusivity and facilitating transparent communication. Cybersecurity governance strategies, policies, objectives, regulations, standards, guidelines, risks, threats, mitigation procedures, and metrics are all interconnected. The comprehensive perspective of the E-CyG outlines the essential components of the strategic and tactical processes necessary for demonstrating responsibility, due diligence, performance, and accountability. The following illustrates the cyber strategy development process:

For cybersecurity, goals and objectives should be realistic and align with the organization's risk tolerance and financial situation. Some companies may develop their cybersecurity plans independently. However, if they lack top-notch security experts in-house, they should seek professional guidance to avoid significant losses resulting from serious cybersecurity mistakes. When a company lacks in-house expertise, it should consider hiring external cybersecurity experts to help establish a robust governance framework. This is crucial for the Board of Directors and leadership to receive clear guidance, perform due diligence to assess cybersecurity risks in target companies, meet regulatory and compliance requirements, integrate security into new technologies during transitions, and evaluate damage, enhance defenses, and rebuild trust after a significant security incident. Therefore, when internal resources are limited, compliance is complicated, or quick, high-quality governance implementation is required, it is advantageous to enlist the help of outside cybersecurity specialists. They contribute knowledge, effectiveness, and legitimacy to a company's cybersecurity plan.

10.5.1 Constructs and Components

The primary goals and objectives of the inherent value chain of the ECyG-M are to create value by protecting the company's digital assets and information, ensuring their confidentiality, integrity, and availability, and reducing the risk of cyberattacks that could lead to financial loss, reputational harm, and legal liability. The following subsections outline the necessary steps and actions required to achieve these goals, as detailed in Table 10.4. We focus our discussions on how these constructs and components are organized within the ECyG-M framework and how they translate into operational actions within the broader ERM context.

10.5.1.1 Strategic Alignment

Organizations can cultivate a robust security stance that safeguards assets while enhancing overall performance and competitiveness by aligning their cybersecurity policies with their organizational objectives. This alignment fosters stakeholder trust, enhances customer satisfaction, and propels business growth. When policies align with organizational goals, they ensure that business priorities protect essential digital assets, thus reinforcing a risk-based approach to cybersecurity.

Security measures designed with business operations in mind minimize disruptions and enhance productivity, fostering operational efficiency. Therefore, during strategy development, stakeholders—including shareholders, the Board of Directors, senior management, and representatives from various departments—should be

Table 10.4 Developing the cybersecurity governance strategy

Steps	Actions
Strategic alignment: Establish cybersecurity goals and objectives that align with the business model.	The goals and objectives align with the security objectives and broader business plans.
Risk profile and culture	Risk culture and risk tolerance are communicated to all staff.
Assess cybersecurity posture	Describe the relationship between the organization and critical infrastructure. Cybersecurity is vital for effective protection.
Risk assessment documentation	The assessment and evaluation results are documented in the risk register. Therefore, the company must routinely review and update its risk register to reflect emerging risks and their corresponding mitigating measures.
Governance model architecture—Building the cybersecurity frameworks	Customize the model and/or adopt cybersecurity standards to strengthen organizational resilience. Describe the decision-making process, oversight, and the roles involved.
Evaluate technology and control options	Conduct a cost-benefit analysis of options for preventing cyber threats by aligning governance and technology needs.
Policies and procedures	Develop and establish policy documents and procedures to guarantee effective governance and compliance.
Oversight, report, review, and evaluate	It is essential to outline the nature and frequency of internal reporting and communication for monitoring, review, and evaluation. Establish performance metrics for assessment.
Education and change	Outline performance management and leadership responsibilities, emphasize the company's risk culture, and ensure governance aligns with operational and business principles.

involved to ensure that diverse perspectives and needs are considered, thus protecting the business (Ayuso et al., 2014).

Aligning an organization's cybersecurity governance with its Enterprise Risk Management (ERM) program creates holistic visibility and a unified approach to risk, ensuring that security efforts support business objectives while minimizing threats. This alignment ensures that cybersecurity initiatives are not solely IT oriented, reactive, or compartmentalized, but rather strategic, cost-effective, and driven by value and business needs. This strategy enhances organizational resilience, regulatory compliance, and risk management maturity.

10.5.1.2 Risk Tolerance and Culture

The level of cyber risk that a company is willing to accept to achieve its goals is known as its risk tolerance. Prioritizing security investments strategically depends on identifying which risks require mitigation, allocating resources to ensure that cybersecurity spending aligns with business objectives, balancing acceptable risk with industry requirements, and establishing incident response readiness, which defines how to react to breaches. A mismatch between risk tolerance and security procedures can lead to ineffective defenses or unnecessary restrictions on company activities.

The way stakeholders, employees, and leadership perceive and respond to cybersecurity is influenced by an organization's culture. A strong security culture reduces human error, prioritizes and nurtures cybersecurity among the Board of Directors and executives, facilitates better collaboration and communication among stakeholders by overcoming a silo mentality, and encourages proactive environments that promote ongoing learning and development, enabling employees to adapt more effectively to threats. Slow incident response, insider risks, and compliance gaps all stem from a weak security culture.

10.5.1.3 Corporate Cybersecurity Posture

A corporate cybersecurity posture refers to an organization's overall ability to defend against cyberattacks, manage risks, and respond to incidents. It is assessed through a structured approach that considers people, processes, and technologies. This process involves threat modeling, assessing existing controls, and scoping the cyber threat landscape to achieve a comprehensive understanding of the organization's cybersecurity maturity and capabilities. It also includes identifying and prioritizing the networks, business systems, and data that are essential to business operations. The goal is to pinpoint the threats and vulnerabilities associated with these digital assets. A clear cybersecurity posture is both a business necessity and an IT concern. It directly impacts market reputation, financial health, compliance, and risk governance. In the current threat environment, organizations that proactively evaluate and improve their posture gain a strategic edge.

10.5.1.4 Risk Assessment Documentation

A change record or risk register is required to document what was altered and why, ensuring compliance. Reports to leadership must also be provided, and old versions must be preserved for compliance or audit purposes. Compliance records must additionally be maintained for updated policies and procedures, including approval logs, risk assessments, treatment plans, and training records to show staff awareness programs. Other auditing evidence includes access logs that indicate who accessed sensitive data, incident reports detailing how breaches were managed, and patch management records demonstrating vulnerability mitigation.

Table 10.5 Risk register elements

Risk ID	An individual code uniquely identifying each risk (e.g., CR-1).
Risk description	A thorough explanation of the danger (e.g., downtime due to ransomware attack, credential theft due to phishing attempts).
Risk category	This refers to the kind of danger, such as ransomware, phishing, insider threats, or third-party risks.
Risk owner	The person or team responsible for risk management.
Probability or likelihood	The probability that the hazard will materialize (e.g., low, medium, or high).
Impact (severity)	The possible adverse effects (financial, operational, regulatory, or reputational) that could arise if the risk materializes.
Risk level	A risk matrix determines the risk score by multiplying "likelihood" by "impact."
Existing controls	Security measures currently exist to lower risk, such as firewalls, IDPS, SIEM, and MFA.
Mitigation strategies	Programs or risk-reduction techniques to strengthen risk awareness or protection (e.g., sophisticated technology, breach simulations, IR training).
Residual risk	The residual risk, or the level of risk that remains after controls are implemented, cannot be eliminated but must be accepted.
Status	The actual risk state, such as whether it is exposed, managed, or tolerated.
Mitigation timeline	When mitigation efforts must be completed.
Action plan	Using MFA access control, endpoint detection and response (EDR/XDR), and awareness training are examples of actions that can reduce risk.
Review date	The date the risk will be examined.

A Cybersecurity Risk Register is a systematic record that identifies, assesses, tracks, and manages cybersecurity risks within an organization. It serves as a central repository for documenting risks, their severity, mitigation strategies, and ownership. The benefits of a Cybersecurity Risk Register include a centralized risk tracking mechanism that provides visibility and a holistic view of all cybersecurity risks present in the organization. It captures essential information about each risk, enabling the tracking and prioritization of risks based on severity for informed decision-making. The risk register is necessary for compliance with NIST CSF, ISO 27001, GDPR, and HIPAA. A well-structured risk register typically consists of the following elements (Table 10.5):

10.5.1.5 Governance Model Architecture

The overarching ERM process provides direction for adopting a relevant framework that aligns the cybersecurity strategy with business objectives. This section compares well-known frameworks and standards, discusses their relevance to various industries, and offers practical guidance on integrating them into an effective enterprise cybersecurity governance strategy. We start by analyzing current standards and frameworks, including industry-specific ones, to enhance information technology security and improve threat mitigation strategies for cybersecurity resilience. Thus, the available approaches to building the model include adopting an appropriate framework that is organically customized, drawing from relevant standards (i.e., NIST, ISO, COBIT), or combining to both guide and direct the organization's strategic and tactical cybersecurity governance function.

Numerous governance frameworks and best practices, including NIST SP800–53, COBIT 2019, ISO 27001, 27,002, and other established standards, are available for organizations to develop their cybersecurity governance framework. The design and implementation of a cybersecurity governance framework rely on operational standards for guidance. These standards offer insights into recommended frameworks, principles, structures, policies, procedures, and controls for implementing security measures within the ERM operational framework (Oh & Ho, 2022).

NIST CSF: The National Institute of Standards and Technology (NIST CSF) has established a comprehensive list of privacy and security rules for federal information systems. The 2024 edition, Revision 5, includes improved supply chain risk management and privacy controls. It also offers an analytical framework for evaluating an organization's maturity in its cybersecurity function. This assessment provides valuable insights into the optimal stage for implementing the company's cybersecurity strategy.

ISO 38500: ISO 38500 (2024)[4] proposes a strategy for implementing an enterprise digital management framework by outlining processes and tools that organizations can use to establish IT governance. Many of these processes and tools are relevant and provide references for designing cybersecurity governance frameworks.

ISO/IEC 27001: It is an international standard that outlines the requirements for an Information Security Management System (ISMS). It is widely acknowledged, certified, and relevant across various industries, such as technology, government, healthcare, telecommunications, and finance. This standard highlights the significance of continuous improvement and effective risk management.

COBIT 2019: COBIT 2019 is a comprehensive framework applicable to companies of all sizes, including government, non-profit, and for-profit entities. It provides a structure for managing and governing enterprise IT that aligns IT objectives with business goals. This business framework for enterprise IT governance employs a common language to communicate goals, objectives, and anticipated results to all stakeholders involved (Oh & Ho, 2022). Additionally, it provides a useful framework for companies to strike a balance between commercial value and risk management.

The framework provides a set of methods for managing IT risks within an organization, ensuring proper operation and emphasizing value creation through effective

[4] ISO/IEC 38500: 2024 Information technology—Governance of IT for the organization. The document describes the roles and responsibilities of the Board of Directors, executive management, and IT specialists, who are among the stakeholders participating in IT governance. It emphasizes the crucial role of controlling IT risks and ensuring that investments in IT add value for the company.

IT governance, while also enabling flexibility in engaging with other frameworks. As a result, it can be easily integrated with various industry standards and best practices in enterprise risk management, service delivery, new project development, and performance reviews for monitoring and risk control.

The model documentation should also outline the organizational structure, linkages, reporting lines, and associated responsibilities. It is essential to clearly define the board-approved structure and management procedures that facilitate oversight and delegation of decision-making authority, including veto, reporting, and escalation rights. This involves detailing the various types of Board of Directors and management committees and describing the structures of these committees.

10.5.1.6 Technology Control and Evaluation Options

Cybersecurity technology and control evaluation options during the governance framework design process include the procedures, techniques, and resources that businesses use to assess and implement security measures aimed at protecting their digital assets (NIST, 2022, 2023). The availability of cybersecurity resources varies by industry and organizational size; generally, larger companies are better equipped to tackle cybersecurity challenges (Smith & Pate-Cornell, 2018). NIST (2022, 2023) supports the evaluation of cybersecurity controls by offering a wide range of customizable measures to protect organizational processes, assets, personnel, and other elements from various threats. The "Implementation" and "Functional" methods represent two categories of cybersecurity controls (ISO/IEC 27001, 2022; NIST, 2022, 2023), which refer to two distinct approaches for applying and assessing security controls.

Implementation Method

This method focuses on the technical installation, setup, and management of security measures. The goal of deployment techniques, tools, and processes (e.g., setting up firewalls, encryption, and MFA) is to achieve a specific outcome, such as proper installation and configuration, rather than serving a general purpose.

- Technical Controls: Safeguards utilizing technology, including intrusion detection systems, firewalls, encryption, and authentication.
- Administrative Controls: They consist of policies, procedures, and guidelines that specify security practices (such as security awareness training).
- Physical Controls: Physical safeguards encompass surveillance cameras, security personnel, and biometric entry systems.

Functional Method

The functional method is objective based and focuses on the purpose and outcome of security controls rather than the means of their implementation. It defines what a control is intended to do (e.g., mitigate, prevent, monitor, detect, respond) and aligns with NIST CSF, ISO 27001, COBIT, or CIS Controls.

- Preventive Control: Preventive controls aim to prevent security issues through technologies like access permissions and firewalls.
- Detective Controls: They utilize video surveillance or SIEM systems to identify incidents as they occur or after they have happened.
- Corrective Controls: Utilize technologies such as backup systems and intrusion prevention systems to mitigate the impact of incidents.
- Deterrent Controls: Utilize security staff and warning signs to deter threats.
- Compensating Controls: Compensating controls are employed when primary controls are either not feasible or impractical.

Since the implementation method focuses on the technical execution of tools and configurations, and the functional method on security outcomes, such as goals, strategies, and risk mitigation, a robust cybersecurity program should balance both, defining functional requirements first and then selecting the best implementation methods. Other tools for evaluating technology include conducting penetration tests, measuring control maturity against industry frameworks, directing and assessing information technology (IT) and operational technology (OT) systems, and identifying system vulnerabilities (ISO/IEC 27001, 2022; NIST, 2022).

10.5.1.7 Policies and Procedures

Policies lay the foundation for cybersecurity governance, acting as written regulations that shape an organization's security posture, risk management, and compliance efforts. Their strategic importance spans various areas, including creating transparent governance and accountability, requiring proactive risk management, minimizing legal risk, ensuring compliance, building stakeholder confidence, and enhancing operational efficiency through clear directions and procedures.

Robust cybersecurity policies and procedures give businesses a competitive advantage by attracting partners and clients who prioritize data security. Aligning these policies with legal standards ensures regulatory compliance, prevents penalties, and fosters trust among stakeholders. The firm develops comprehensive cybersecurity policies and processes that cover all aspects of the organization's cybersecurity framework. Policies should be user friendly and flexible, promoting compliance without hindering operations. It is also crucial to document and distribute these policies and procedures to all relevant parties, clearly outlining the functional duties and responsibilities for the operational management of cybersecurity processes within the company.

10.5.1.8 Oversight, Report, Review, and Evaluate

Oversight, reporting, review, and assessment are critical components of cybersecurity governance that ensure effective risk management, regulatory compliance, and ongoing improvement. This step involves defining the nature and frequency of internal reporting and communication for monitoring, review, and evaluation, as well as setting performance metrics for assessment. These components are integrated into a robust cybersecurity governance framework to guarantee compliance, resilience, and alignment with corporate objectives. Failing to consider any of these elements increases the risk of violations, penalties, and damage to one's reputation.

Oversight ensures that leadership comprehends the threat landscape and its associated dangers, enabling them to allocate resources effectively. The Board of Directors, risk committee, and CISO are accountable for cybersecurity oversight and hold subordinates and relevant stakeholders responsible for security outcomes. Reporting on cybersecurity developments enhances transparency and supports informed decision-making. Regular reviews are crucial for validating effectiveness, promoting continuous improvement, and informing policy adaptation.

Cybersecurity governance policies establish an organization's security posture, outline its compliance requirements, and define its risk management strategies. Regular evaluation of these policies ensures that they remain relevant, effective, and aligned with corporate objectives and emerging threats.

10.5.1.9 Education, Corporate Culture, and Talent

The organization's overall ability to manage cyber risk is improving through a culture of risk awareness, education, training, and organizational change. It's essential to cultivate an environment where everyone recognizes cybersecurity as a crucial part of their job. To enhance staff understanding and compliance, the firm must consistently communicate the importance of cybersecurity and provide training. Management should inform employees about the benefits the company gains from effective cyber risk management. The design and processes of the operational model may be iterative, evolving through education and experience, with components of the model adjusted during or after implementation and in response to changes in the business and regulatory landscapes.

10.6 Implementation

Implementing an enterprise cybersecurity governance process involves several steps to ensure that cybersecurity risks are identified, managed, and monitored effectively, aligning with business objectives. This process and its components help to address the five challenges highlighted by Swinton and Hedges (2019). Figure 10.6 illustrates the broad and significant steps in the implementation process.

The implementation process consists of six discrete steps and the actions and significance of these steps are detailed as follows:

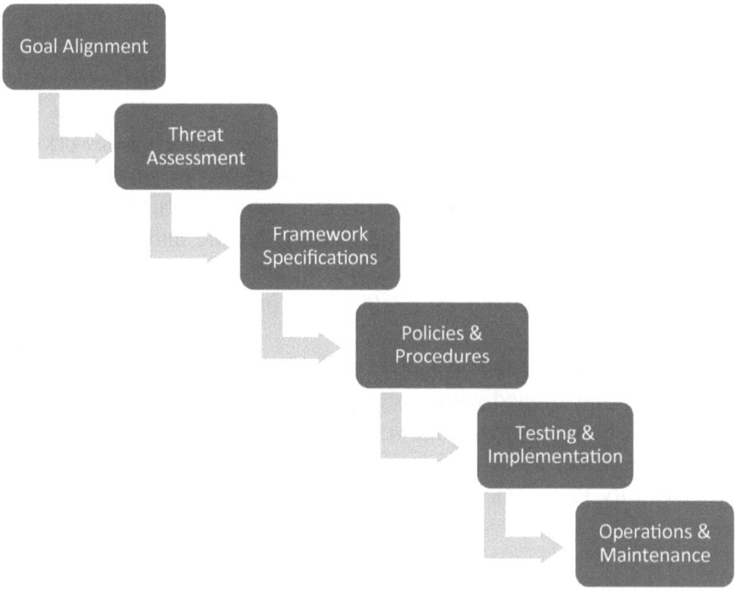

Fig. 10.6 Implementation process

- Goal alignment is crucial because cybersecurity policies and measures are closely related to the organization's overall business objectives, risk tolerance, and regulatory requirements. Goal alignment ensures that cybersecurity governance is strategic, risk based, and business driven. It enhances corporate purpose and cooperation between business executives and cybersecurity personnel, promoting proactive oversight, resource allocation, and a security posture that safeguards corporate value.
- Threat assessment is crucial for identifying, evaluating, and prioritizing potential threats to an organization's digital assets. It ensures that security measures are based on risks, informed by risks, and aligned with business objectives. It transforms intangible hazards into actionable information, ensuring that measures are proactive, prioritized, and relevant to the business without compromising the protection of critical assets or squandering resources.
- The framework specification provides an organized and standardized approach to addressing cybersecurity risks. It ensures uniformity, compliance with regulations, and alignment with industry best practices. The foundation of cybersecurity governance is described as a framework that converts theoretical policies into practical, measurable, and auditable procedures. Aligning corporate strategy with technical security ensures that defenses are systematic, compliant, and adaptable enough to respond to evolving threats.
- Policies and procedures serve as the operational backbone of cybersecurity governance, transforming strategic goals into enforceable guidelines and actionable

practices. They implement cybersecurity governance, turning concepts into practical, measurable, and enforced activities. Without these, governance remains theoretical, leaving businesses exposed to unmanaged risks, inconsistent controls, and compliance gaps.
- Implementation operationalizes cybersecurity governance frameworks, not just documentation. While testing confirms that protections are sufficient, framework implementation ensures that cybersecurity governance is structured and adheres to best practices. They convert policies into robust, flexible, and measurable security postures. The value of the structured approaches for managing cyber risks, as proposed by NIST CSF and ISO 27001, can only be realized through proper implementation and thorough testing.
- Operations and maintenance (O&M) ensure that security controls remain relevant, efficient, and aligned with evolving business requirements and risks. Even the most well-implemented frameworks deteriorate over time without ongoing O&M, placing enterprises at risk. Framework O&M serves as the foundation of cybersecurity governance, making sure that security does not stagnate after implementation.

10.7 Governance Compliance and Performance Evaluation

Various key performance indicators (KPIs) are available for organizations to track and assess their security posture. NIST states that organizations might establish benchmarks or goals against which compliance and performance can be evaluated using measurements and metrics. The core cybersecurity outcomes of the framework—identify, protect, detect, respond, and recover—help manage cybersecurity risk. In addition to measuring effectiveness, compliance, and performance evaluation, it allows the firm to identify weaknesses in its cybersecurity posture and allocate resources accordingly.

10.7.1 Policy and Regulatory Compliance

To reduce risks, align security with corporate objectives, and foster stakeholder trust, effective cybersecurity governance relies on clearly defined policies and stringent adherence to regulatory compliance. High compliance rates lower the risks of cyberattacks, legal issues, and regulatory violations by reducing ambiguity, enhancing oversight, and enforcing security measures. It delineates roles and enforces accountability, establishes baselines for controls, promotes the adoption of best practices, and drives continuous improvement. Therefore, it is essential to assess how well policies, systems, procedures, and laws satisfy compliance standards.

Table 10.6 Key performance metrics

KPIs	Objectives
Policy exception rate	The number of security policy deviations.
Regulatory compliance score	Evaluates compliance with frameworks and regulations.
Frequency of security incidents	Monitor incident frequency to determine the long-term efficacy of security measures.
Remediation rate for audit findings	The proportion of compliance deficiencies filed.
Mean time to respond (MTTR)	Measure the typical time needed to contain and clean up an event. Lowering MTTR reduces possible harm.
Awareness levels	Evaluate using tests and simulations to determine the effectiveness of training initiatives.
Mean time to detect (MTTD)	A shorter MTTD indicates faster detection capabilities, as it calculates the average time it typically takes to find a security incident.
Vulnerability management	The rate at which vulnerabilities are identified, mitigated, and resolved. A higher rate indicates proactive vulnerability management.

10.7.2 Measuring Performance

Performance evaluation underpins effective cybersecurity governance, as it ensures that cybersecurity controls are assessed for their effectiveness by verifying that policies, procedures, and personnel activities align with business goals and risk tolerance. Therefore, it is crucial for evaluating resilience and guiding ongoing development. Organizations can identify gaps, optimize resources, and demonstrate accountability by systematically assessing their performance.

The best practices for effective performance reviews include establishing clear key performance indicators (KPIs) and aligning these measures with corporate objectives. It is also necessary to use the NIST CSF, CIS Controls, or ISO 27001 standards as a guide for structured assessments. Regular performance reviews and reporting enable the Board of Directors and executives to adjust their strategy in response to threat information and audit findings, as well as translate technical measurements into business risk terms. Table 10.6 presents the discussions on selected KPIs to assess performance.

10.7.3 Key Risk Indicators

Measurable metrics, known as key risk indicators (KRIs), are used to identify and assess potential threats to a company's cybersecurity posture. They help organizations proactively uncover vulnerabilities, monitor threats, and implement corrective actions before a breach occurs. Besides facilitating risk monitoring, key risk indicators (KRIs) are essential for evaluating the effectiveness of cybersecurity programs. By tracking key results indicators (KRIs) over time, organizations can measure their performance, pinpoint areas for improvement, and refine their security measures. KRIs can evaluate security measures such as Mean Time to Respond (MTTR) to assess response efficacy, Patch Management to quantify unpatched significant vulnerabilities, and Mean Time to Detect (MTTD) to gauge the effectiveness of security monitoring tools like SIEM or EDR.

10.7.4 Continuous Improvement

Cybersecurity is a dynamic field, and continuous improvement is essential due to the ever-evolving threat landscape, and static defenses quickly become obsolete. This environment compels organizations to adopt strategies that enable them to proactively enhance their security systems and quickly adapt to emerging challenges. Continuous improvement initiatives ensure that cybersecurity governance does not stagnate but rather adapts, strengthens, and aligns with new risks and business requirements.

Continuous improvement promotes proactive risk management by conducting regular audits, penetration testing, and threat intelligence assessments to identify vulnerabilities. It ensures that policies and controls remain relevant as cyber threats evolve, strengthens compliance and reduces legal risks through regular updates, maximizes security ROI by identifying underperforming tools and reinvesting budgets, and fosters a culture of cyber resilience through regular staff training and risk awareness education.

10.8 Governance Challenges Going Forward

As cyber threats become increasingly sophisticated and regulatory landscapes evolve, companies face growing governance challenges. Cybersecurity governance encounters various obstacles that require attention and solutions. By addressing these issues, businesses can enhance their cybersecurity posture and ensure resilience in a constantly changing threat environment. The key cybersecurity governance challenges that organizations must confront in the future, along with mitigation strategies, are outlined below.

- Companies face substantial challenges from fast-changing cyber threats, including AI-powered attacks, quantum computing hazards, and state-sponsored hacking, which surpass standard protections. The growing use of mobile devices for business purposes leads to an expanded attack surface. To safeguard their organizations, businesses must keep pace with rapid technological advancements, including the rise of cloud computing and the Internet of Things (IoT) devices.

Therefore, protecting these devices from various risks is becoming more crucial and challenging. Mitigation strategies would include utilizing AI-powered security technologies (e.g., behavioral analytics), implementing a Zero-Trust Architecture (ZTA), implementing strict access controls to mitigate the impact of breaches, and continually monitoring threat intelligence.

- Securing endpoints, such as laptops, cell phones, and tablets, will become increasingly complex as remote work becomes more prevalent, thereby compounding cloud and hybrid work risks, which can lead to data leaks and unmanaged attack surfaces. The solutions would be to use Cloud Security Posture Management (CSPM) technologies and Secure Access Service Edge (SASE) for remote workforce protection.
- The lack of technical knowledge at all levels of the firm suggests an inadequate appreciation of the threats and measures designed for the infrastructure. However, ongoing awareness training and education can help address this issue.
- Businesses must be proactive in response to emerging dangers, such as those utilizing artificial intelligence or targeting supply networks. They should implement strategies like continuous monitoring and zero-trust architectures.
- Organizations face challenges in effectively defending against cyber threats due to a significant shortage of qualified cybersecurity specialists. This global shortage of skilled professionals requires businesses to develop strategies for attracting and retaining talent, such as offering opportunities for in-house training, professional development, and fostering a positive work environment.
- Due to limited resources, businesses must prioritize projects that offer the most significant risk reduction. Firms need to manage budget constraints to secure adequate funding, and cybersecurity measures should be evaluated to determine their effectiveness and advantages (i.e., return on investment, or ROI).
- Protecting the privacy of people's data is becoming more important as data collection and analysis become more widespread. Organizations face severe financial and reputational damage due to the rising frequency of data breaches and unauthorized access to sensitive information. Businesses that handle personal data must take proactive measures to ensure compliance with relevant legislation (e.g., GDPR, HIPAA) and prevent data breaches. The key strategies for effectively protecting data privacy include collecting only necessary data and specifying its use, restricting and securing data access, ensuring that third-party partners protect data, mitigating human error through training, de-identifying data to protect user identities, and continuously verifying the effectiveness of privacy controls.
- Another challenge arises when navigating complex regulations, such as the GDPR, for compliance purposes. Businesses must ensure that their security measures are effective and comply with the law. Complying with numerous cybersecurity laws and guidelines can be both challenging and costly. Mitigating strategies include establishing Governance, Risk, and Compliance (GRC) platforms for centralized tracking, conducting regular compliance gap assessments, and seeking or hiring the services of skilled compliance officers.

A multi-layered security strategy encompassing effective governance, technological advancements, staff training, and adherence to legal and industry best practices may help mitigate these issues. Cybersecurity governance in the future will require flexibility, automation, and integration with corporate objectives. In an increasingly hostile digital environment, businesses that proactively address these issues can mitigate risk, ensure compliance, and maintain stakeholder trust.

10.9 Conclusion

In cybersecurity, both individual components (e.g., hardware, software, rules, staff) and the governance procedures that ensure their appropriate integration and functioning are crucial. Enterprise governance processes within the ERM (i.e., IT/CyG, TM/CyG, HR/CyG, FIN/CyG, ECyG-M) are essential for creating a comprehensive governance framework that aligns strategies, policies, procedures, and technologies to function cohesively without gaps or weaknesses in the security value chain. While strong individual security enablers and their components are essential, governance acts as the binder that connects them into a unified, resilient security ecosystem. Without effective governance, even the most advanced security tools can fail due to misconfigurations, poor integration, or human error. Hence, a well-organized governance process is vital to maintaining cybersecurity effectiveness throughout the entire value chain.

A dynamic, adaptive, and value-creating cybersecurity governance framework ensures that security keeps pace with evolving threats, fosters business innovation, and delivers a measurable return on investment (ROI). Organizations can leverage real-time intelligence, risk-based decision-making, and business alignment to transform cybersecurity from a compliance burden into a strategic advantage. Furthermore, modern businesses require a comprehensive cybersecurity governance strategy integrated into a cohesive enterprise risk management framework. The collaboration between cybersecurity initiatives and ERM ensures that security management is proactive and well planned, making it a crucial element of digital transformation. Organizations that merge these areas build public trust, develop resilient infrastructure, reduce operational risks, ensure regulatory compliance, gain a competitive edge, add value, and foster faster and more secure innovation.

References

Anderson, J. (1972). Information security in a multi-user computer environment. *Advances in Computers, 12*, 1–36.

Anderson, R. (2022). *A guide to building dependable distributed systems* (3rd ed.). Wiley.

Ayuso, S., Rodríguez, M. A., García-Castro, R., & Ariño, M. A. (2014). Maximizing stakeholders' interests: An empirical analysis of the stakeholder approach to corporate governance. *Business & Society, 53*(3), 414–439. https://doi.org/10.1177/0007650311433122

Collier, Z., Linkov, I., & Lambert, J. (2013). Four domains of cybersecurity: A risk-based systems approach to cyber decisions. *Environment Systems and Decisions, 4*(33), 469–470.

Deloitte. (2013). *Developing an Effective Governance Operating Model: A Guide for Financial Services Boards and Management Teams.* Retrieved from February 11, 2025, from https://www2.deloitte.com/content/dam/Deloitte/global/Documents/Financial-Services/dttl-fsi-US-FSI-Developinganeffectivegovernance-031913.pdf

Herrmann, D., & Pridöhl, H. (2020). Basic concepts and models of cybersecurity. In M. Christen, B. Gordijn, & M. Loi (Eds.), *The ethics of cybersecurity*. https://link.springer.com/chapter/10.1007/978-3-030-29053-5_2

Hillson, D. (1997). Towards a risk maturity model. *International Journal of Project and Business Risk Management, 1*(Spring), 35–45.

Hoffmann, R., Napiorkowski, J., Protasowicki, T., & Stanik, J. (2020). Risk-based approach in scope of cybersecurity threats and requirements. *Procedia Manufacturing, 44*, 655–662.

Hofstede, G. (1980). *Culture's consequences: International differences in work-related values.* Sage.

Hofstede, G., Hofstede, G. J., & Minkov, M. (2010). *Cultures and organizations: Software of the mind* (3rd ed.). McGraw-Hill.

ISO/IEC 27001. (2022). *Information security, cybersecurity and privacy protection—Information security management systems — Requirements.* International Organisation for Standardisation.

Lerbinger, O. (1997). *The crisis manager: Facing risk and responsibility.* Mahwah, Lawrence, N., Erlbaum Associates.

Li, Y., Schoenfeld, A. H., diSessa, A. A., Graesser, A. C., Benson, L. C., English, L. D., & Duschl, R. A. (2019). On thinking and STEM education. *Journal for STEM Education Research, 2*(1), 1–13.

McKinsey & Company. (2019). *The Risk-based Approach to Cybersecurity.* McKinsey. https://www.mckinsey.com/business-functions/risk/our-insights/the-risk-based-approach-to-cybersecurity

Mihm, J., Loch, C., Wilkinson, D., & Huberman, B. (2010). Hierarchical structure and search in complex organizations. *Management Science, 56*(5), 831–848. https://www.researchgate.net/publication/220534200_Hierarchical_Structure_and_Search_in_Complex_Organizations

Mitchell, S. (2007). GRC360: A framework to help organizations drive principled performance. *International Journal of Disclosure and Governance, 4*(4), 279–296.

NIST, National Institute of Standards and Technology. (2022). *Assessing security and privacy controls in information systems and organizations.* Special Publication 800–53A Revision 5. https://nvlpubs.nist.gov/nistpubs/SpecialPublications/NIST.SP.800-53Ar5.pdf

NIST, National Institute of Standards and Technology. (2023). *Guide to Operational Technology (OT), Security, SP 800-82r3.* https://nvlpubs.nist.gov/nistpubs/SpecialPublications/NIST.SP.800-82r3.pdf

Nolan, C., Lawyer, G., & Dodd, R. (2019). Cybersecurity: Today's most pressing governance issue. *Journal of Cyber Policy, 4*(3), 425–441.

Oh, K., & Ho, B. (2022). *Cybersecurity risk management: An Enterprise risk management approach.* Nova Science Publishers.

Onumo A., Cullen A. & Awan, I. (2017). Empirical study of cultural dimensions and cybersecurity development. Presented at: FiCloud 2017: *The 5th International Conference on Future Internet of Things and Cloud*. 21–23 Aug 2017, Prague, Czech Republic.

Quarantelli, E. L. (1988). Disaster crisis management: A summary of research findings. *Journal of Management Studies, 25*(4), 373–385.

Rivkin, J., & Siggelkow, N. (2003). Balancing search and stability: Interdependencies among elements of organizational design. *Management Science, 49*(3), 290–311.

Simon H. A. (1962). The architecture of complexity. *Proc Am Philos Soc 106*, 467–482.

Smith, M., & Pate-Cornell, M. (2018). Cyber risk analysis for a smart grid: How smart is smart enough? A multiarmed bandit approach to cyber security investment. *IEEE Transactions on Engineering Management, 65*(3), 434–447.

Swinton, S., and Hedges, S. (2019). *Cybersecurity governance, Part 1: 5 Fundamental Challenges.* Carnegie Mellon University, Software Engineering Institute's Insights (blog). Accessed September 27, 2024. https://insights.sei.cmu.edu/blog/cybersecurity-governance-part-1-5-fundamental-challenges/

Taylor, F. (1911). *The principles of scientific management.* Harper and Brothers.

MIX
Papier aus verantwortungsvollen Quellen
Paper from responsible sources
FSC® C105338

If you have any concerns about our products,
you can contact us on
ProductSafety@springernature.com

In case Publisher is established outside the EU,
the EU authorized representative is:
Springer Nature Customer Service Center GmbH
Europaplatz 3, 69115 Heidelberg, Germany

Printed by Libri Plureos GmbH
in Hamburg, Germany